J0059569

Copyright © 2018 by Marie D'Abreo.
All rights reserved.
No part of this book may be reproduced
in any form without written permission
from the publisher.

ISBN 978-0-9915285-7-8
Printed and bound in the USA

Library of Congress Catalog
2018914497

Far Out Press
San Francisco, CA

BOOK TWO

BEAUTIFUL

Living with the Frenemy

by Marie D'Abreo

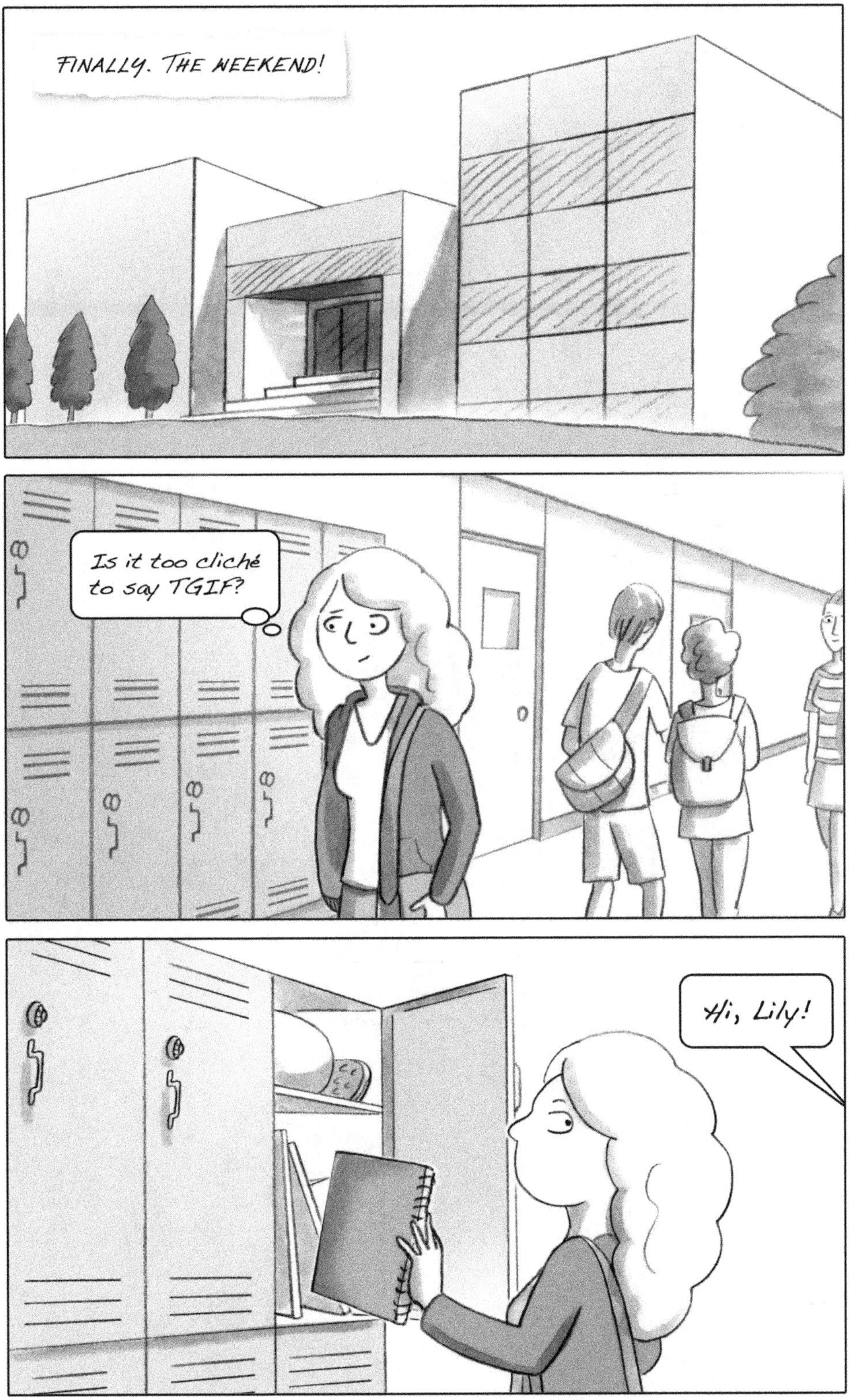
FINALLY. THE WEEKEND!
Is it too cliché to say TGIF?
Hi, Lily!

Hey, Ariel.

Now she's trying to be friendly?

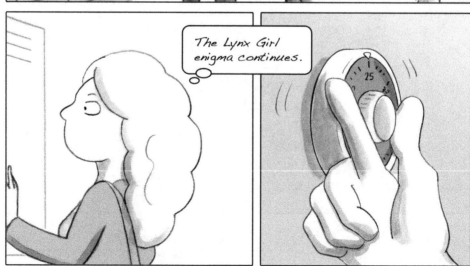

The Lynx Girl enigma continues.

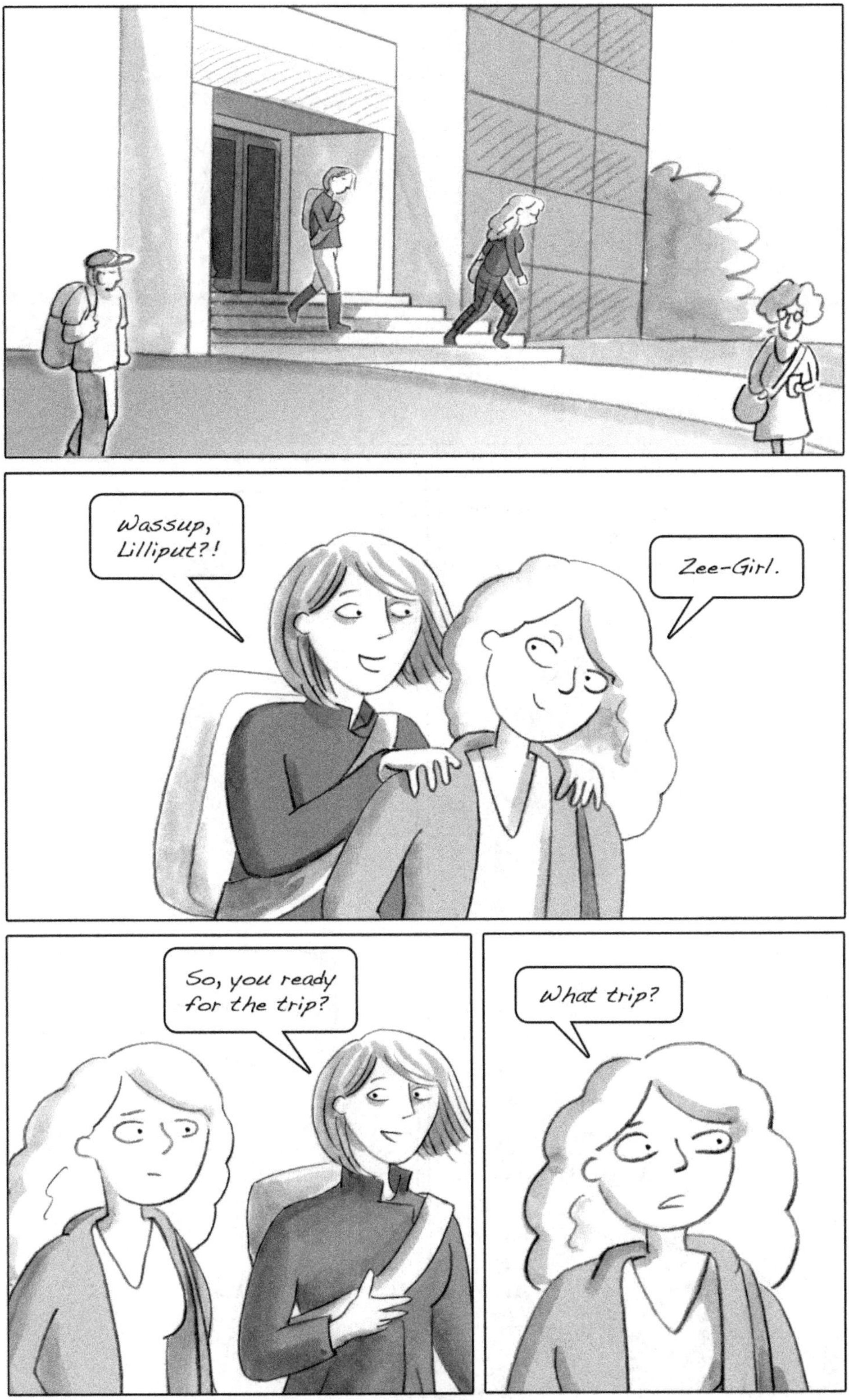
Wassup, Lilliput?!
Zee-Girl.
So, you ready for the trip?
What trip?

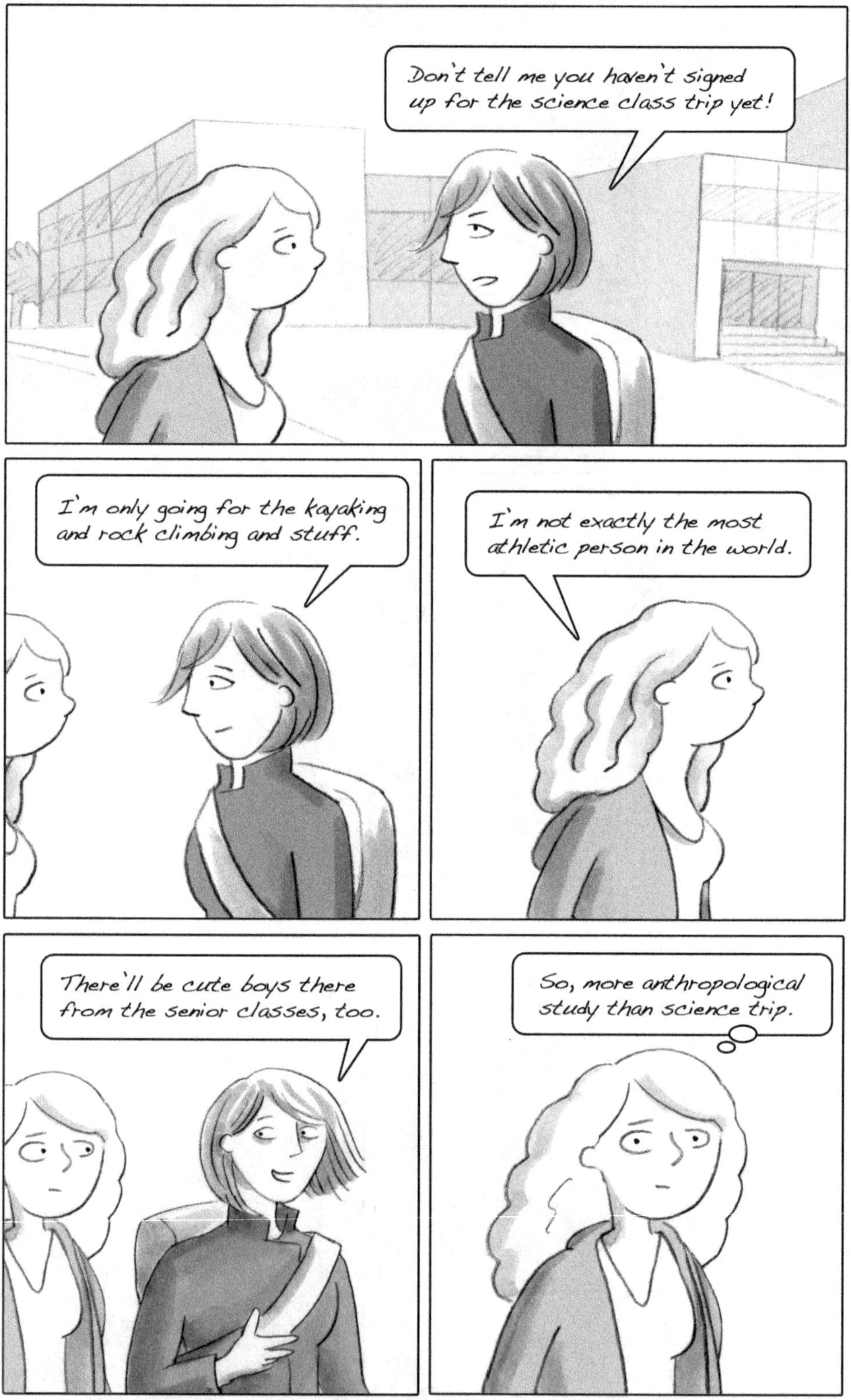
Don't tell me you haven't signed up for the science class trip yet!
I'm only going for the kayaking and rock climbing and stuff.
I'm not exactly the most athletic person in the world.
There'll be cute boys there from the senior classes, too.
So, more anthropological study than science trip.

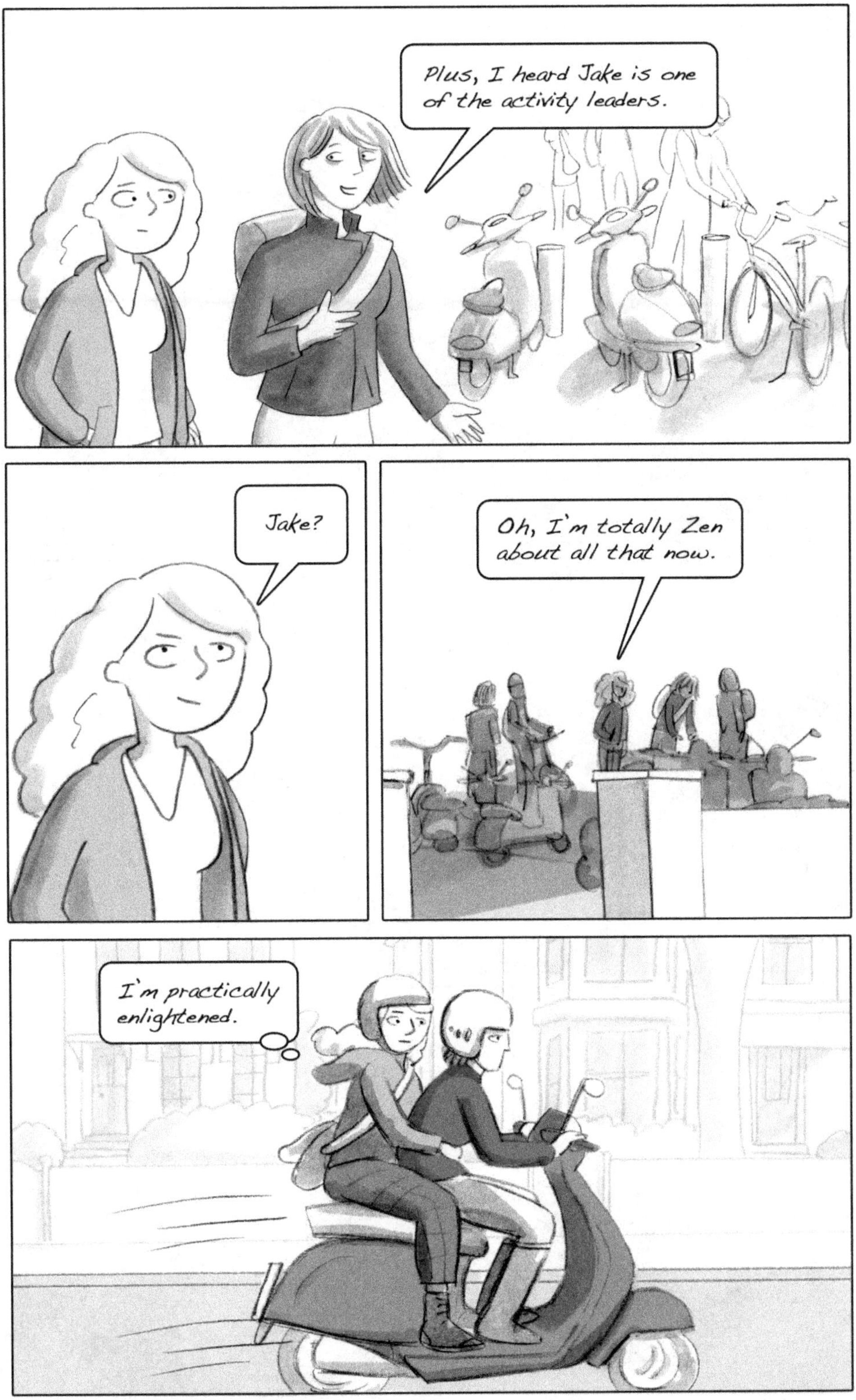

Plus, I heard Jake is one of the activity leaders.
Jake?
Oh, I'm totally Zen about all that now.
I'm practically enlightened.

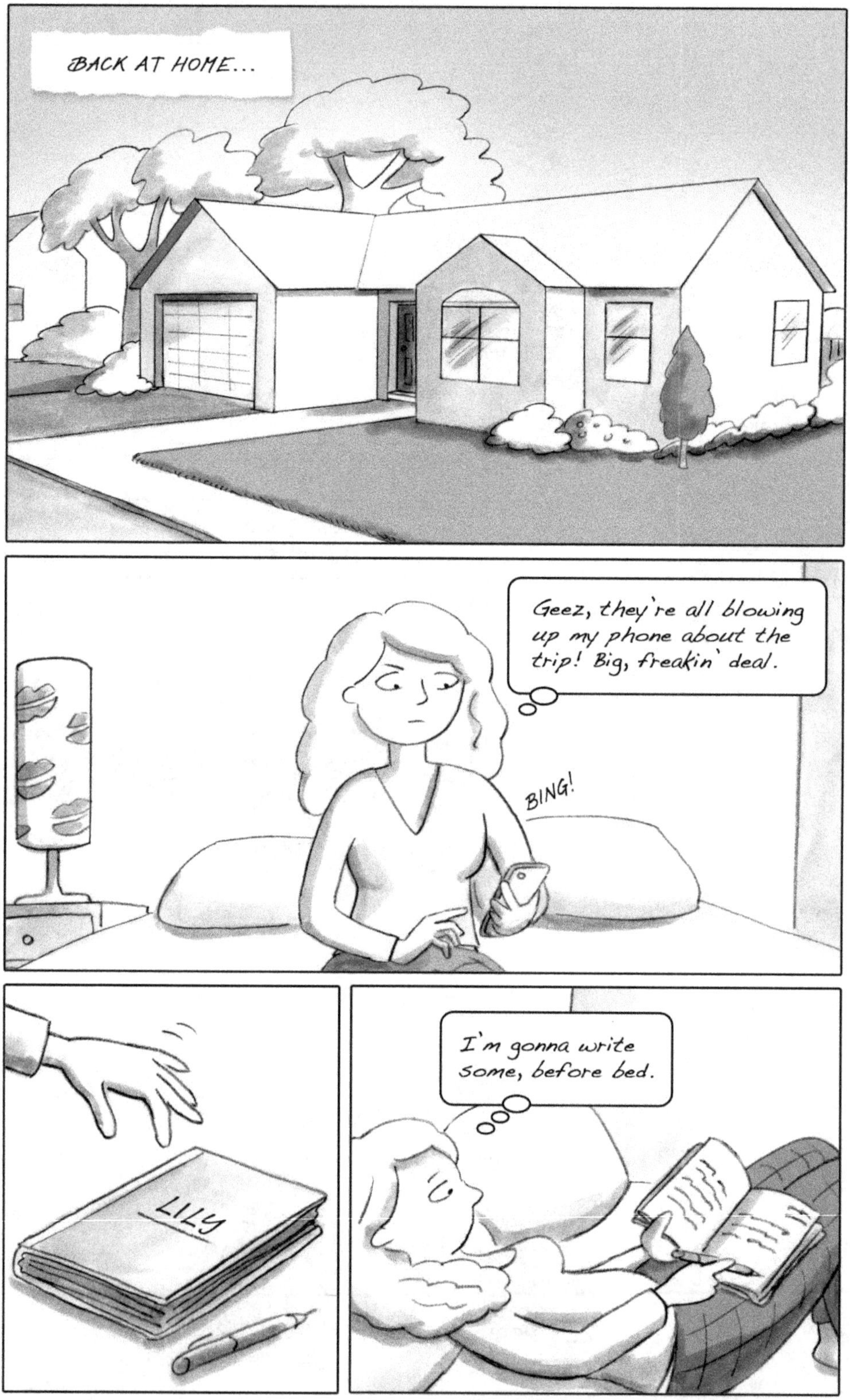
BACK AT HOME...
Geez, they're all blowing up my phone about the trip! Big, freakin' deal.
BING!
LILY
I'm gonna write some, before bed.

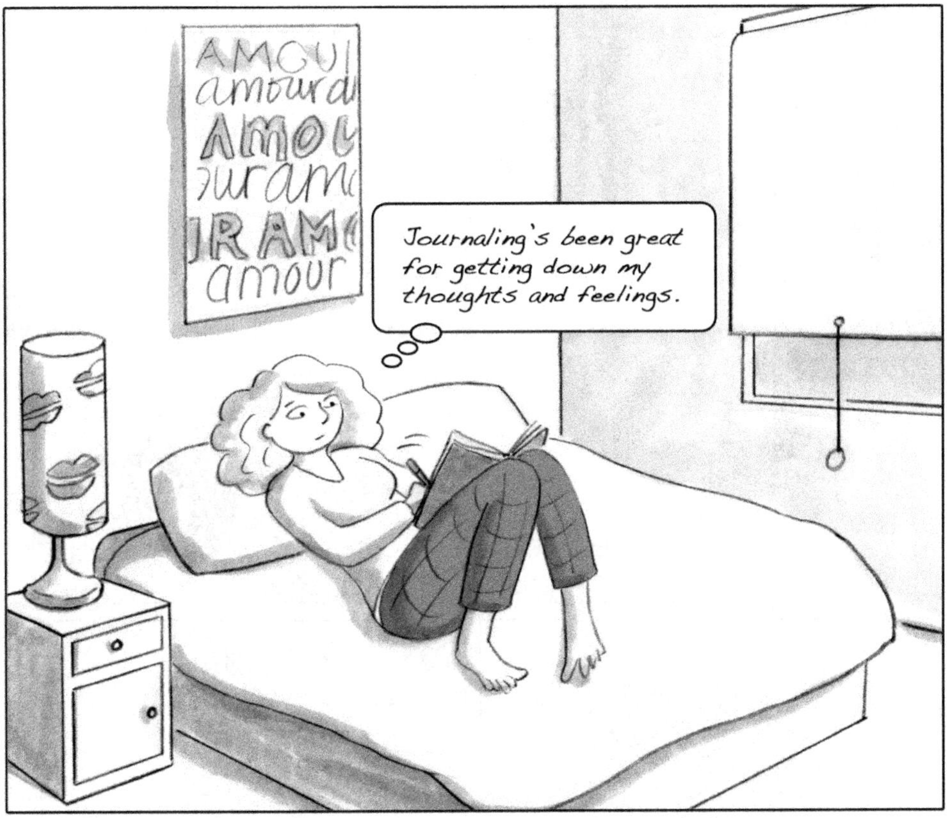
AMOUR
amour
Journaling's been great for getting down my thoughts and feelings.

FRIDAY

As we speak, Zeta and friends are going bananas group texting about this science trip. Turns out Zee's boyfriend, Tag, can't go cuz he caught the flu and that leaves a spot open for me – who completely forgot about the whole thing anyway! I mean, seriously. Camping at our age? Now if it was a hotel on a beach in Mexico or Hawaii, I'd be all over that. But mosquitoes, bed bugs and wiping your nether regions with a leaf? You gotta be kidding me.

Hold on, incoming text message. Sender unknown.

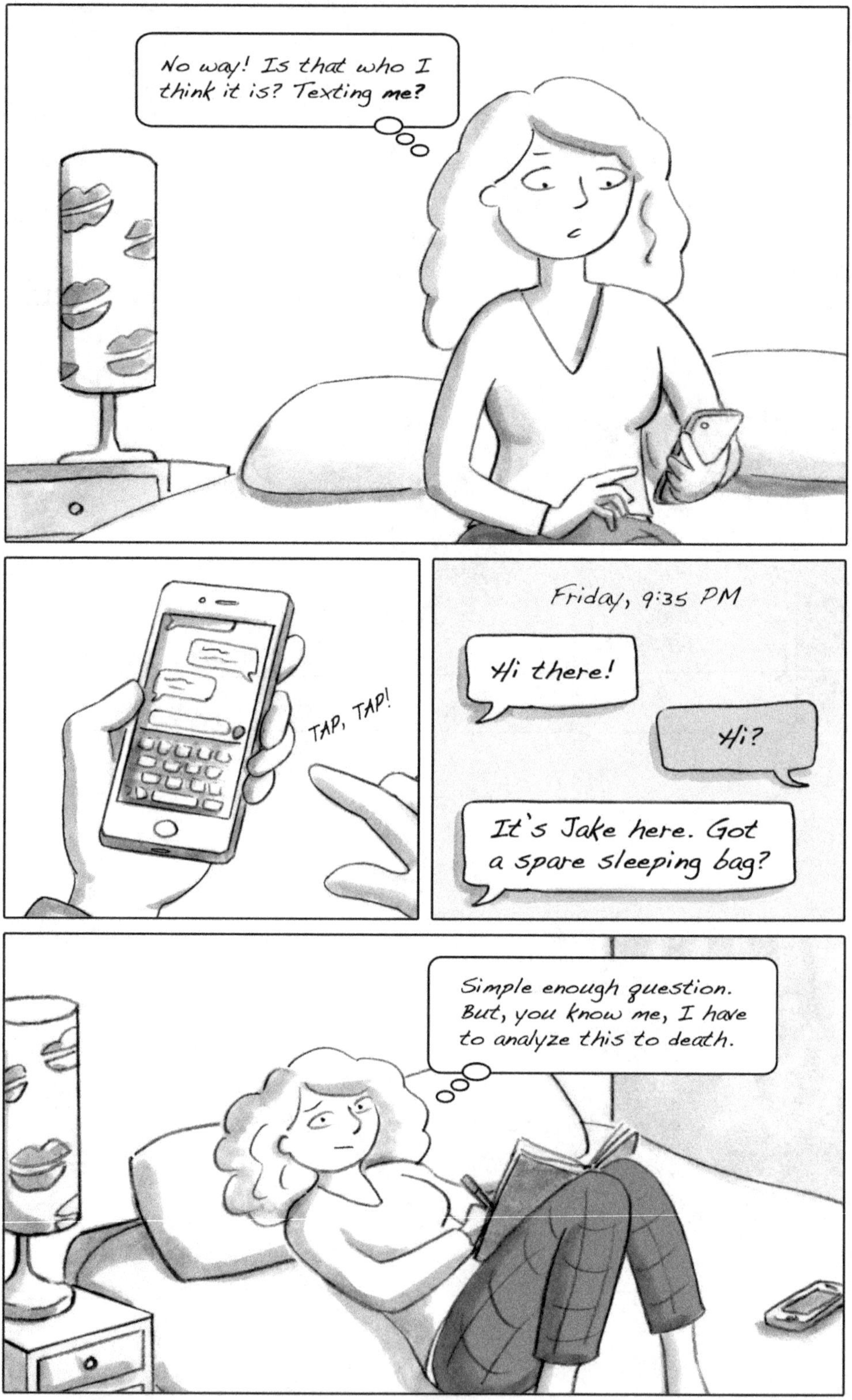
No way! Is that who I think it is? Texting **me?**
TAP, TAP!
Friday, 9:35 PM
Hi there!
Hi?
It's Jake here. Got a spare sleeping bag?
Simple enough question. But, you know me, I have to analyze this to death.

I can't take it! Jake just texted me – and only me –
to ask if I've got a spare sleeping bag. Never mind that I
MIGHT ACTUALLY HAVE ONE (thereby pretty much
guaranteeing we'll need to meet up).

Why is he asking ME of all people?

1) Has already asked everyone else who's going
2) Is a total cheapskate who can't afford his own stuff
3) Is making up an excuse to contact me (my preferred choice)
4) All of the above

Who cares?! I exist to him! I am in his phone! Now I just gotta
decide if I wanna do this reality show/endurance test that is
camping with a bunch of near-strangers in log cabins. 'Survivor',
anyone? Why has mankind gone to all the trouble of advancing
out of cave dwellings and fending off saber-toothed tigers only to
go back and live in the dirt? Makes no sense to me.

But, love will make you do strange things. I'm gonna find that
extra sleeping bag if it kills me. Or at least 'til I'm sleepy.

We leave at dawn! (Actually, Monday, noon-ish.)

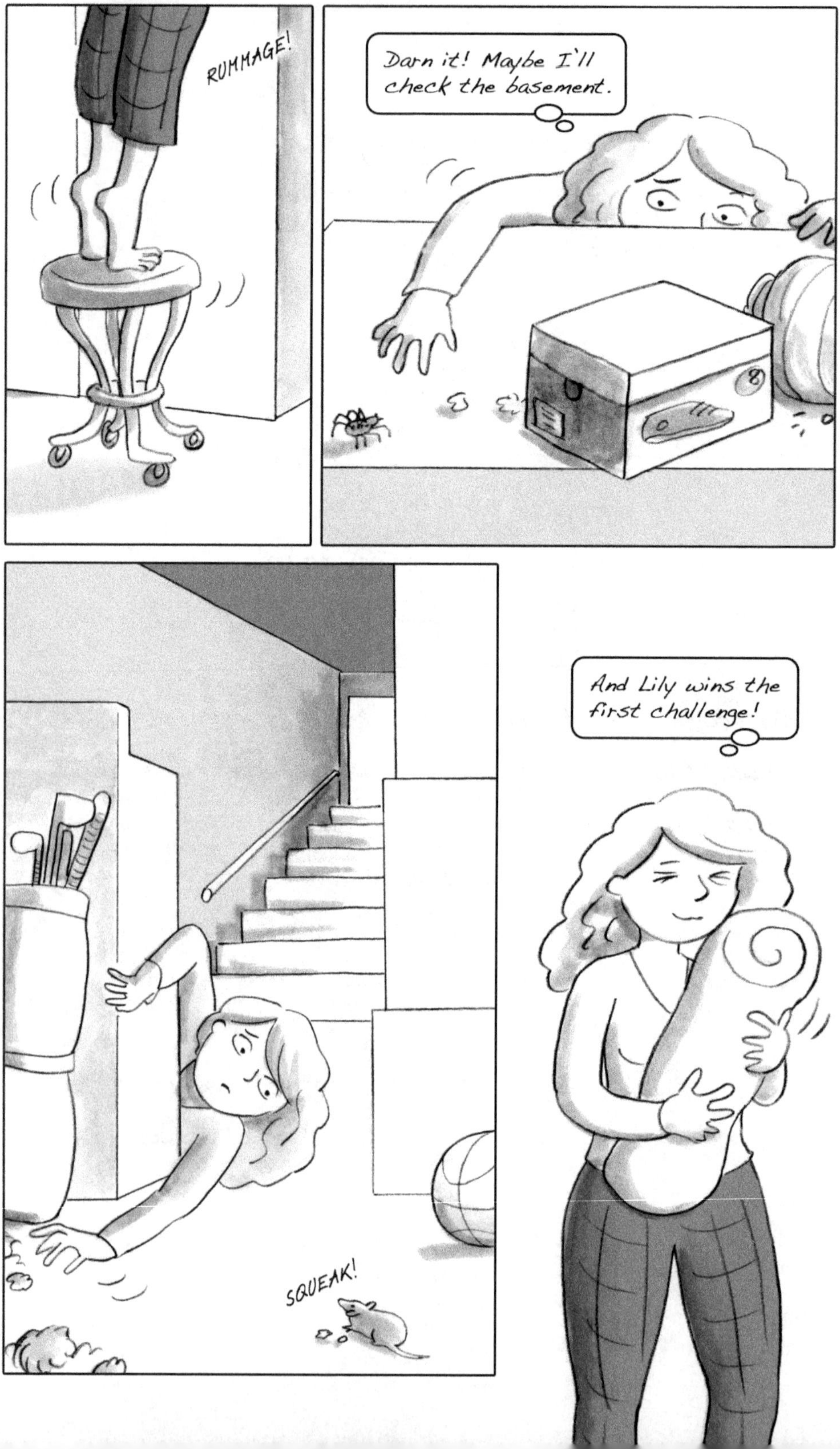
RUMMAGE!
Darn it! Maybe I'll check the basement.
SQUEAK!
And Lily wins the first challenge!

Man makes plans
and God laughs.

YIDDISH PROVERB

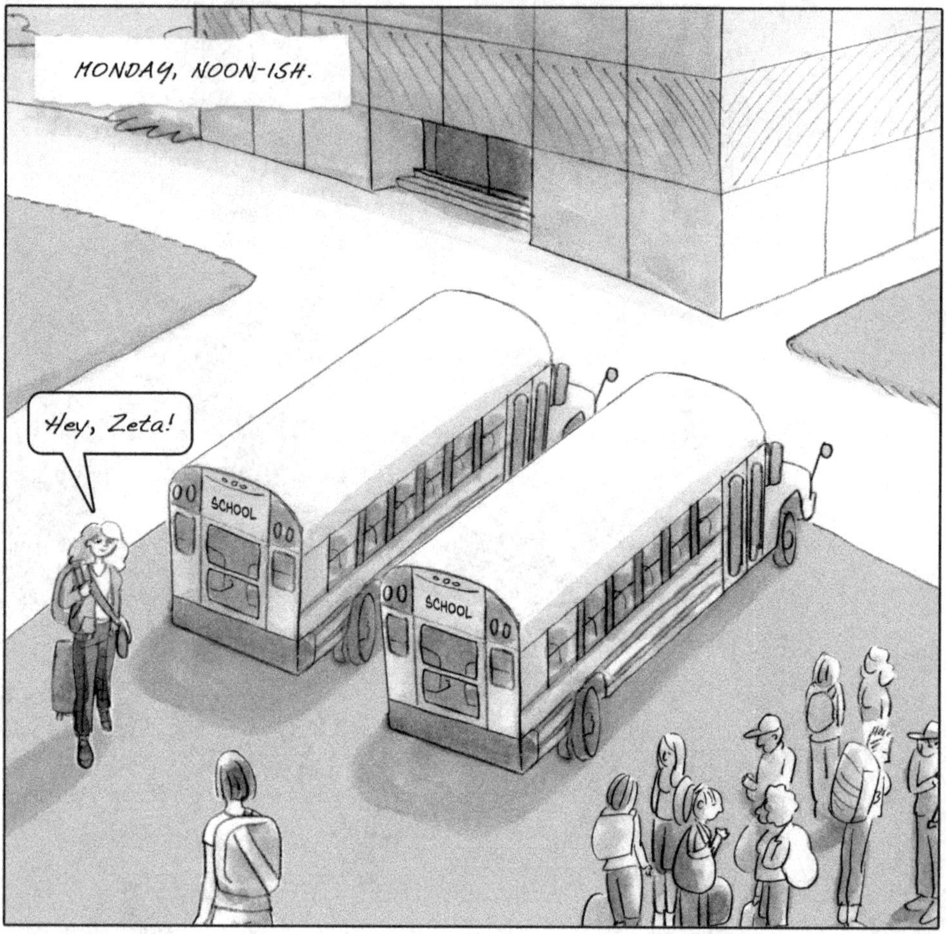
MONDAY, NOON-ISH.
Hey, Zeta!
SCHOOL
SCHOOL

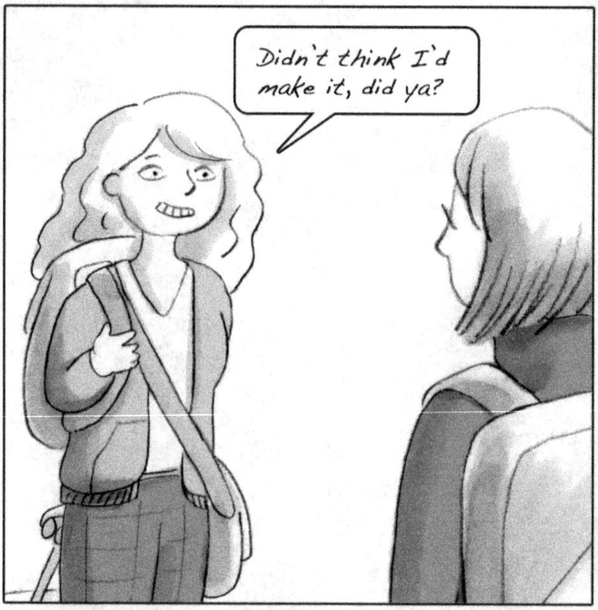
Didn't think I'd make it, did ya?

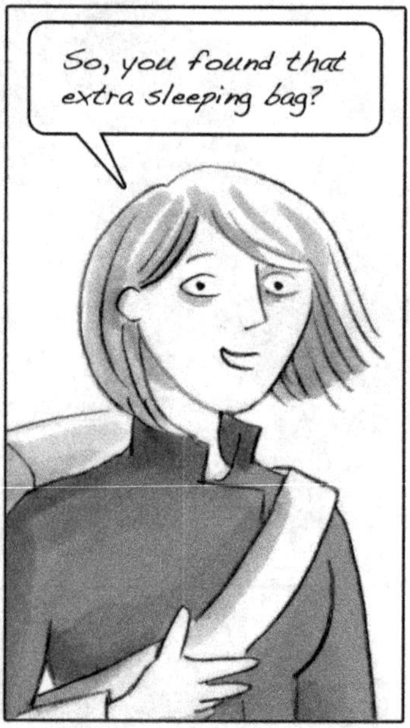
So, you found that extra sleeping bag?

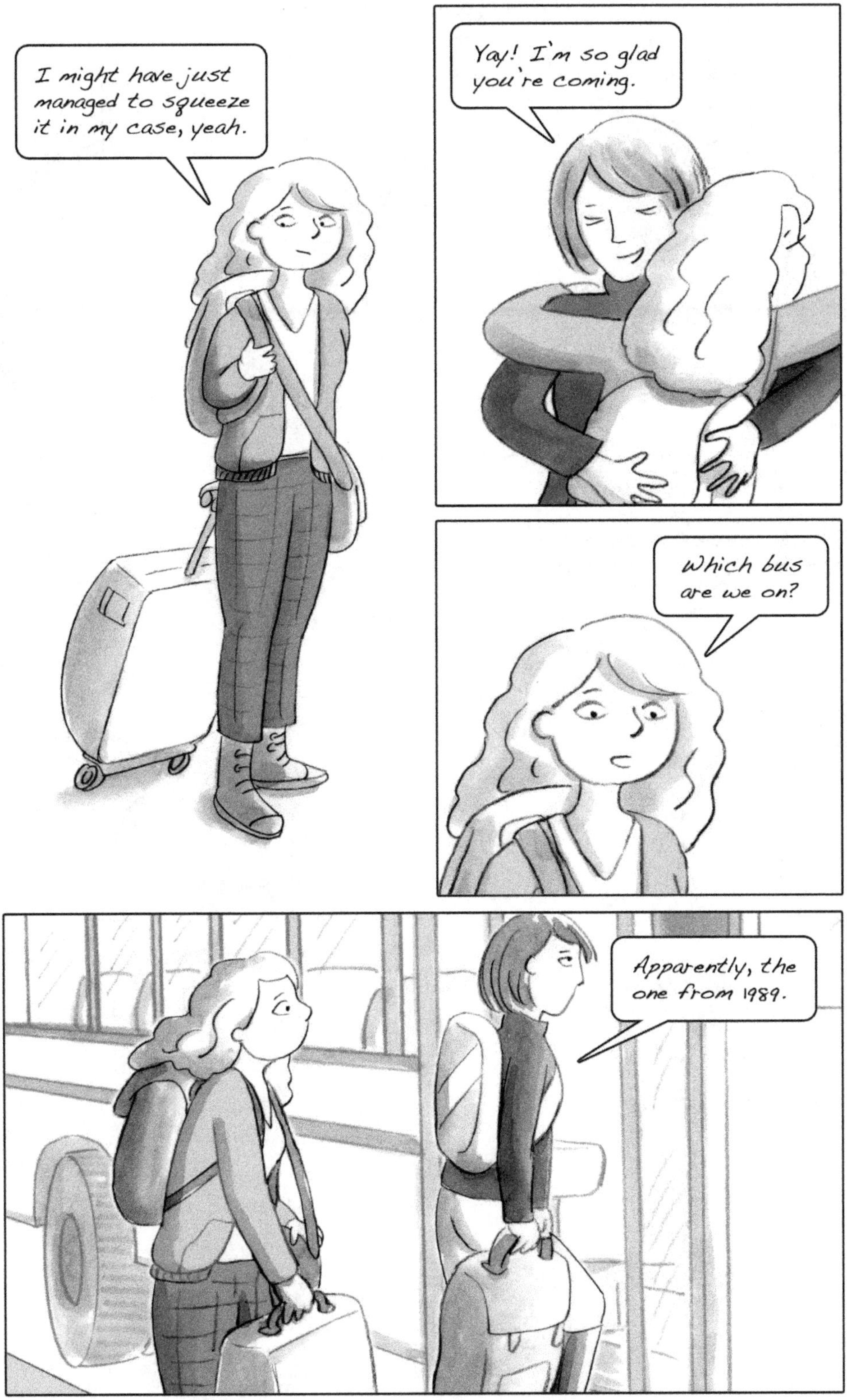
I might have just managed to squeeze it in my case, yeah.
Yay! I'm so glad you're coming.
Which bus are we on?
Apparently, the one from 1989.

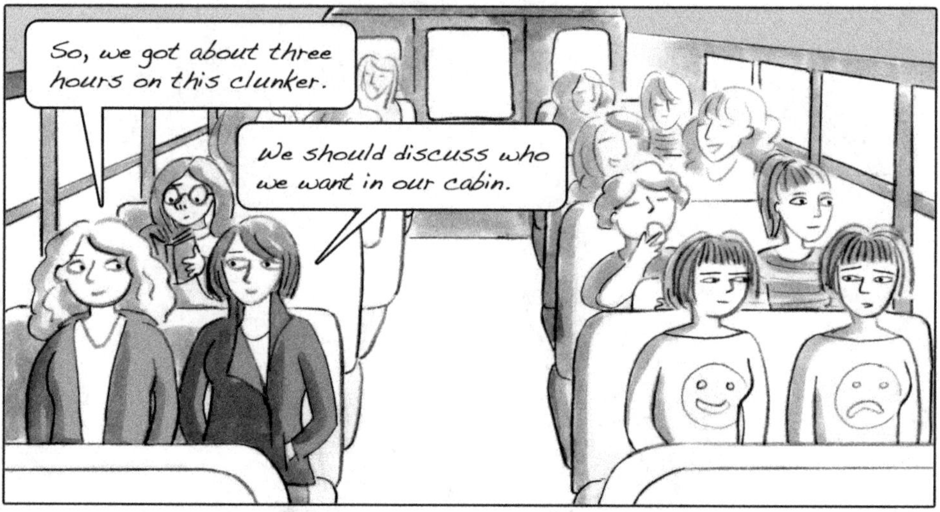
So, we got about three hours on this clunker.
We should discuss who we want in our cabin.

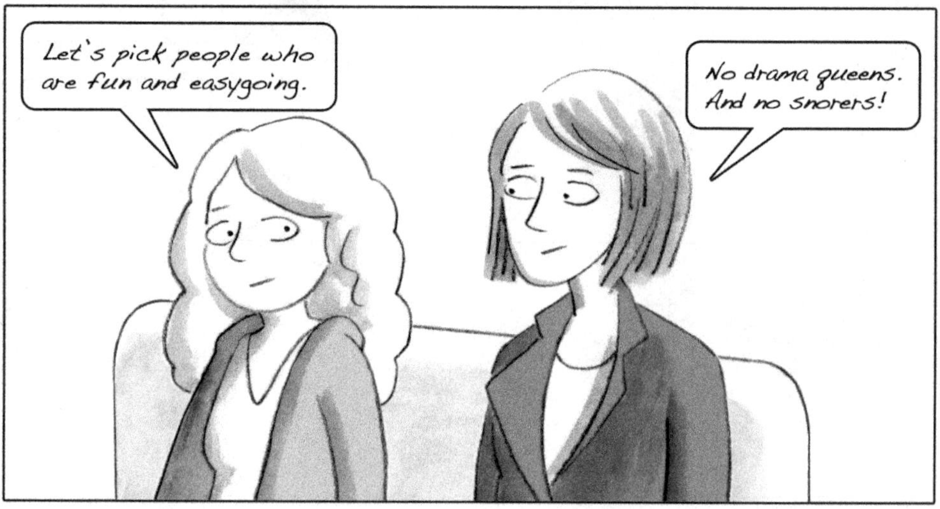
Let's pick people who are fun and easygoing.
No drama queens. And no snorers!

THE TWINS

Sue and Lou would be perfect. Quiet as mice. A tad boring, perhaps. But the loudest noise you'll hear is the video game sound effects coming through their headphones.

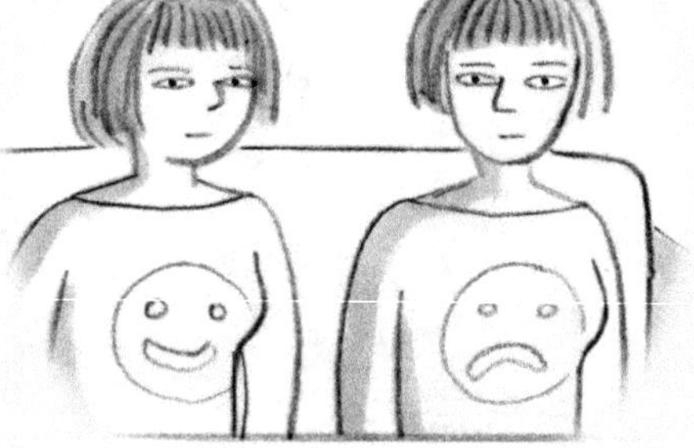

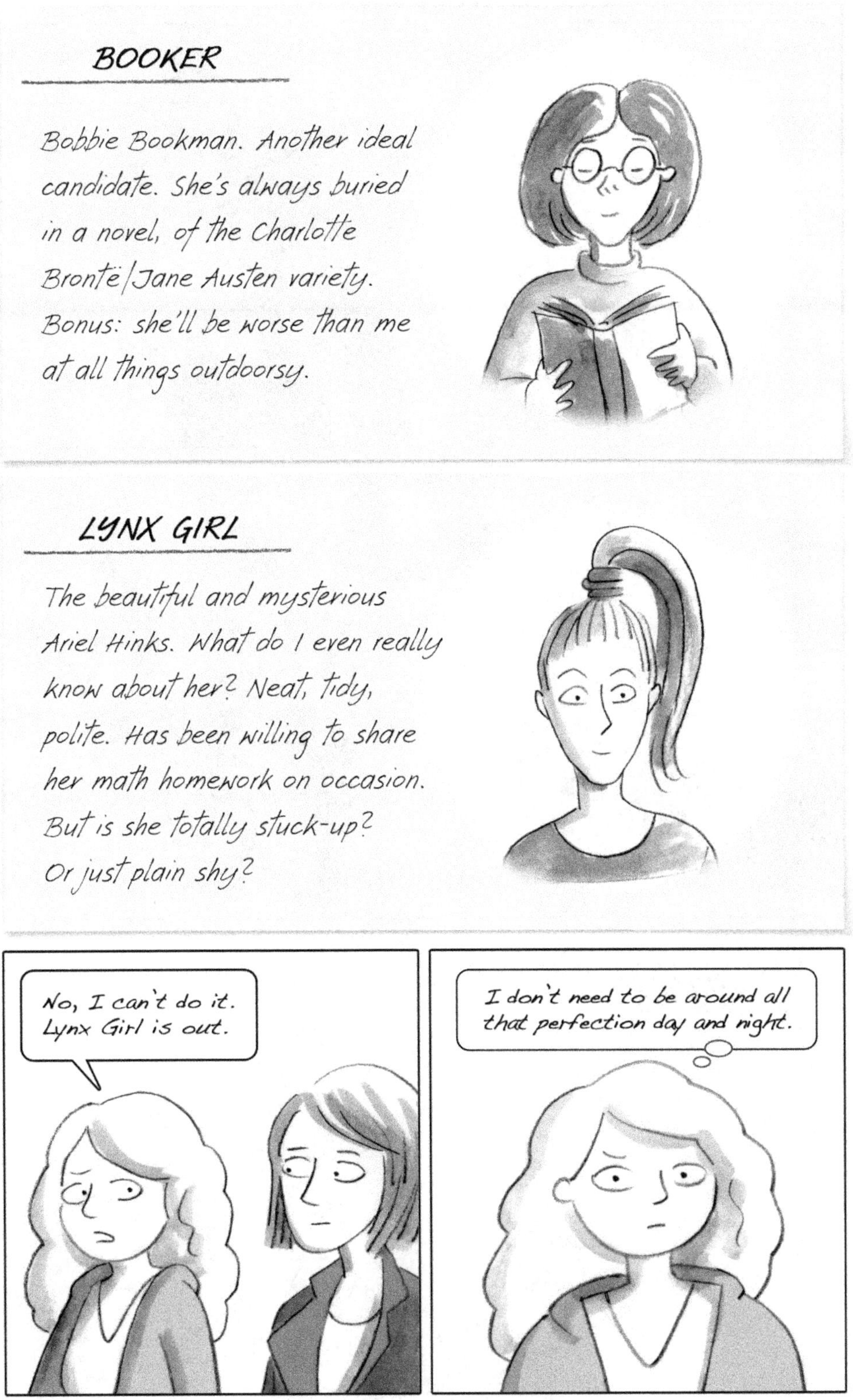
BOOKER
Bobbie Bookman. Another ideal candidate. She's always buried in a novel, of the Charlotte Brontë/Jane Austen variety. Bonus: she'll be worse than me at all things outdoorsy.
LYNX GIRL
The beautiful and mysterious Ariel Hinks. What do I even really know about her? Neat, tidy, polite. Has been willing to share her math homework on occasion. But is she totally stuck-up? Or just plain shy?
No, I can't do it. Lynx Girl is out.
I don't need to be around all that perfection day and night.

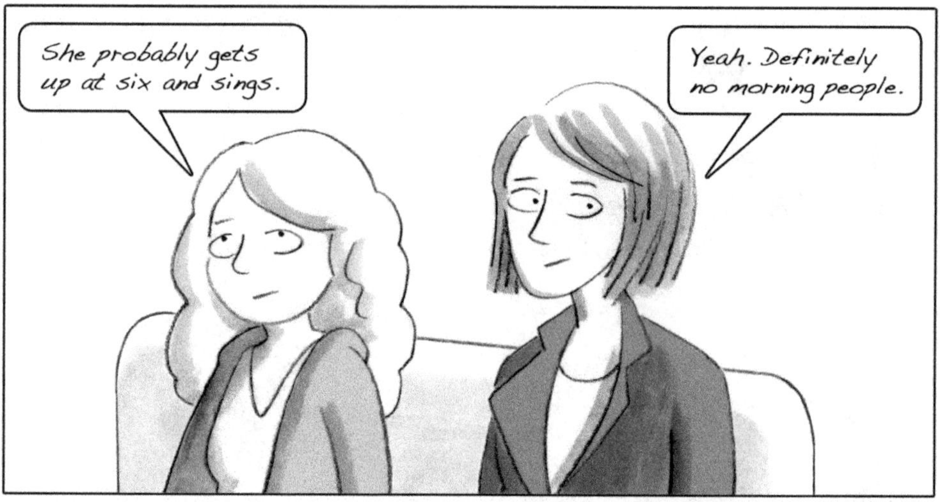
She probably gets up at six and sings.
Yeah. Definitely no morning people.

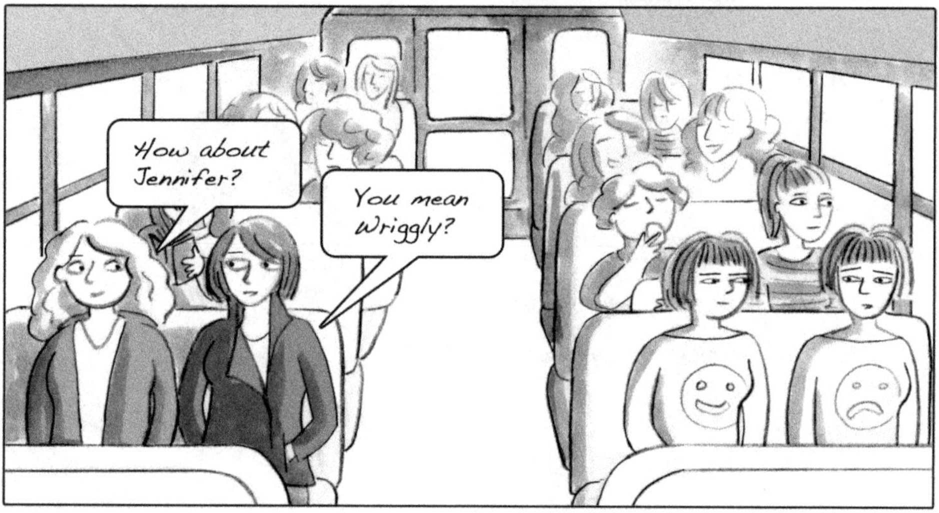
How about Jennifer?
You mean Wriggly?

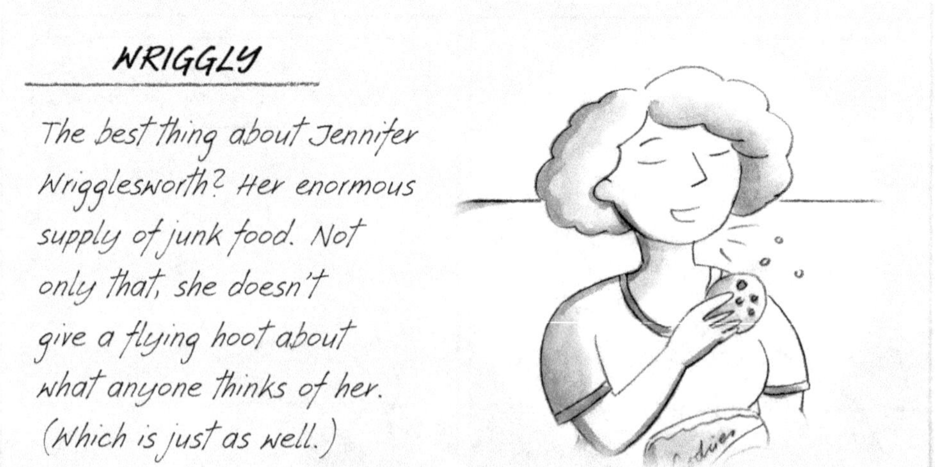
WRIGGLY
The best thing about Jennifer Wrigglesworth? Her enormous supply of junk food. Not only that, she doesn't give a flying hoot about what anyone thinks of her. (Which is just as well.)

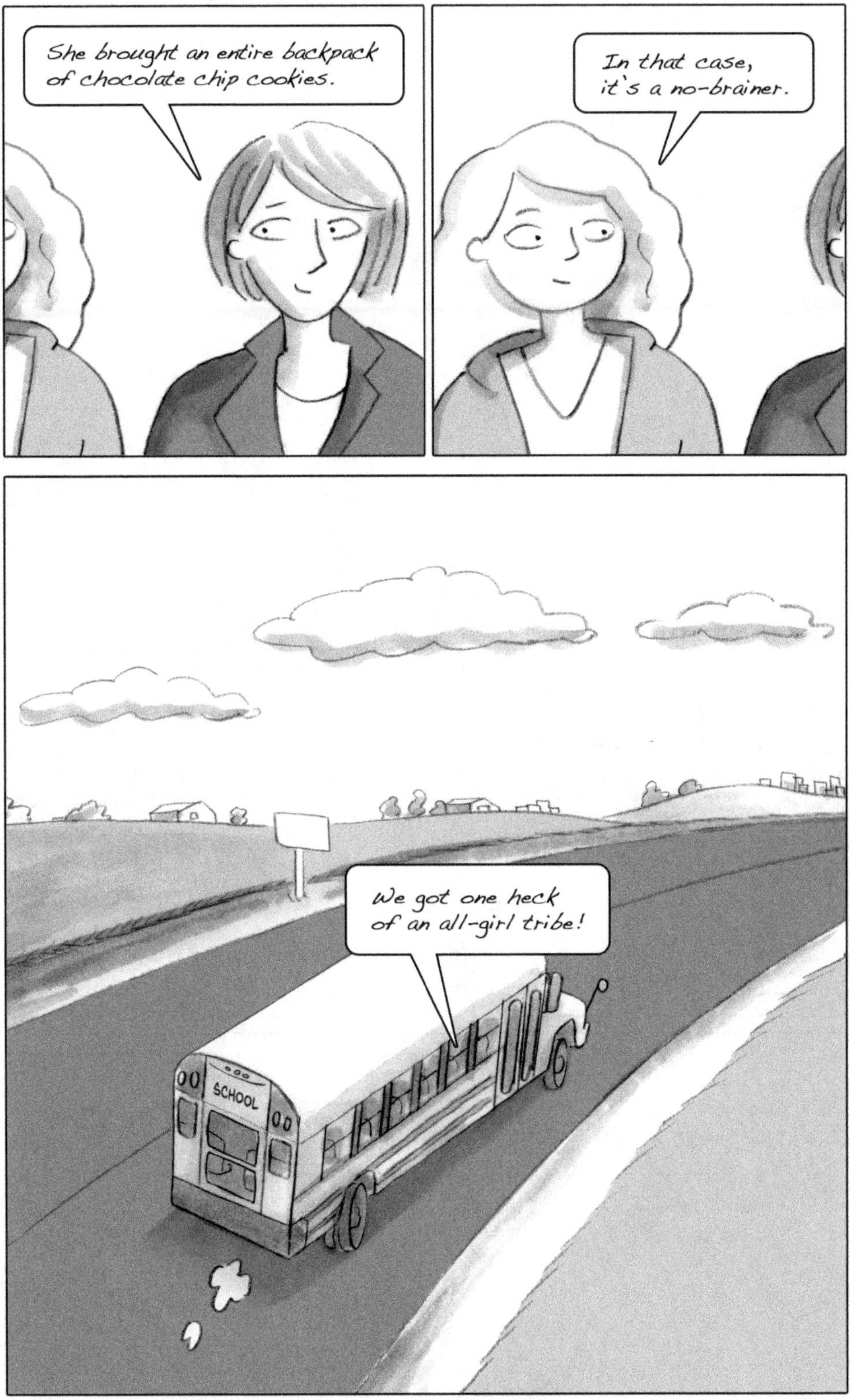
She brought an entire backpack of chocolate chip cookies.
In that case, it's a no-brainer.
We got one heck of an all-girl tribe!
SCHOOL

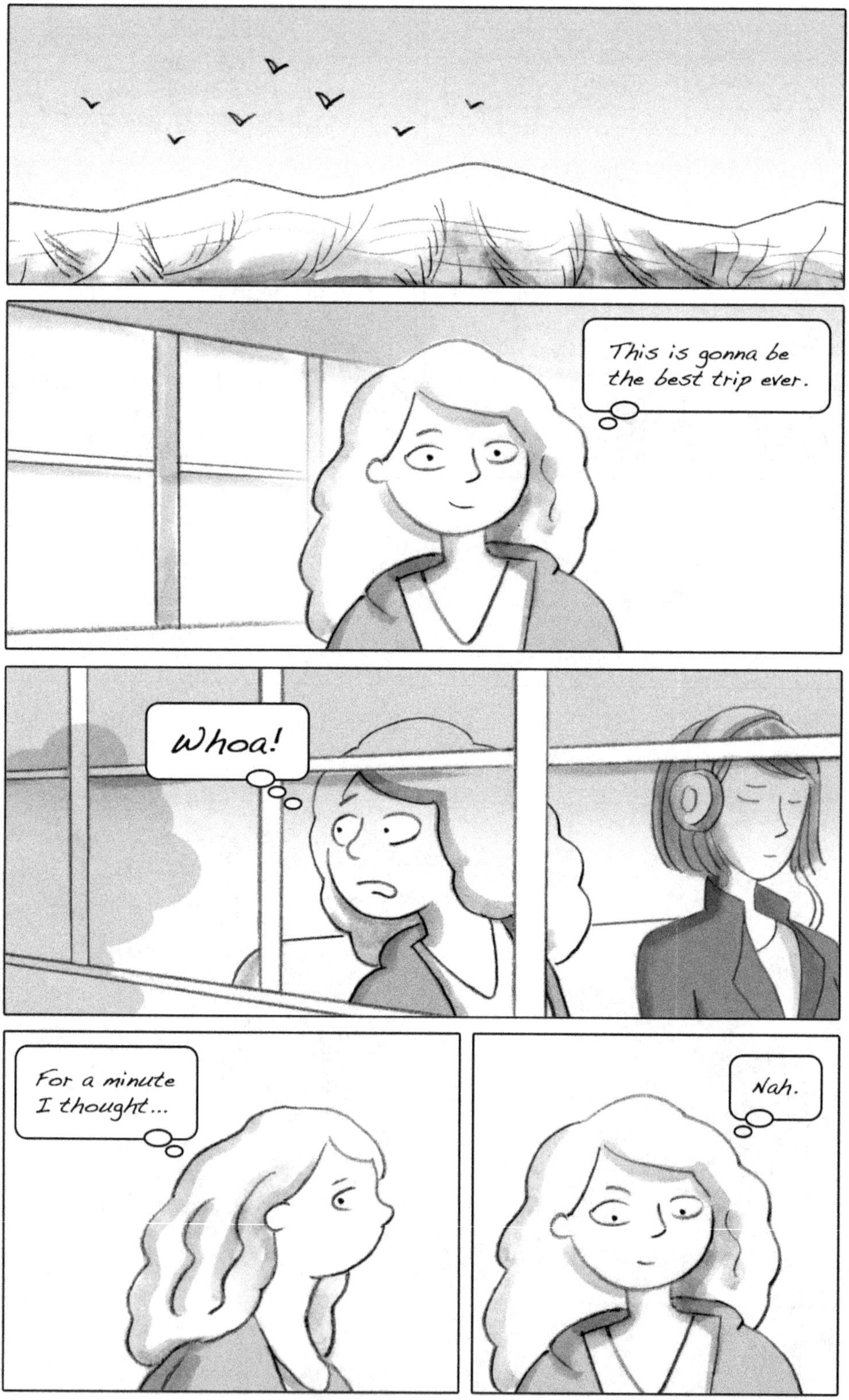
This is gonna be the best trip ever.
Whoa!
For a minute I thought...
Nah.

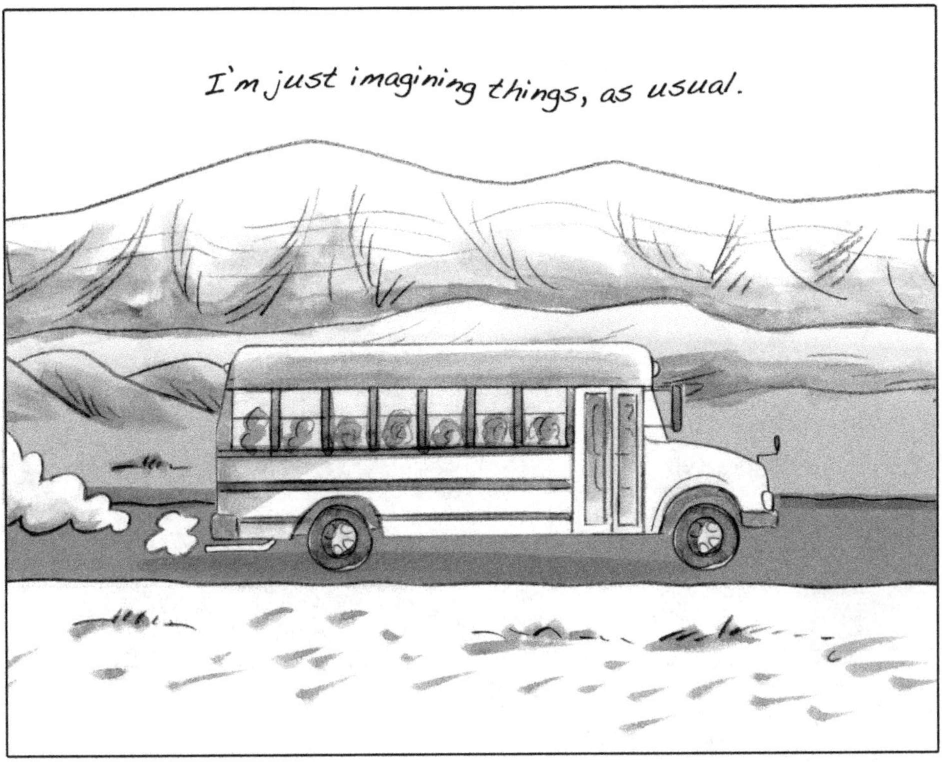
I'm just imagining things, as usual.

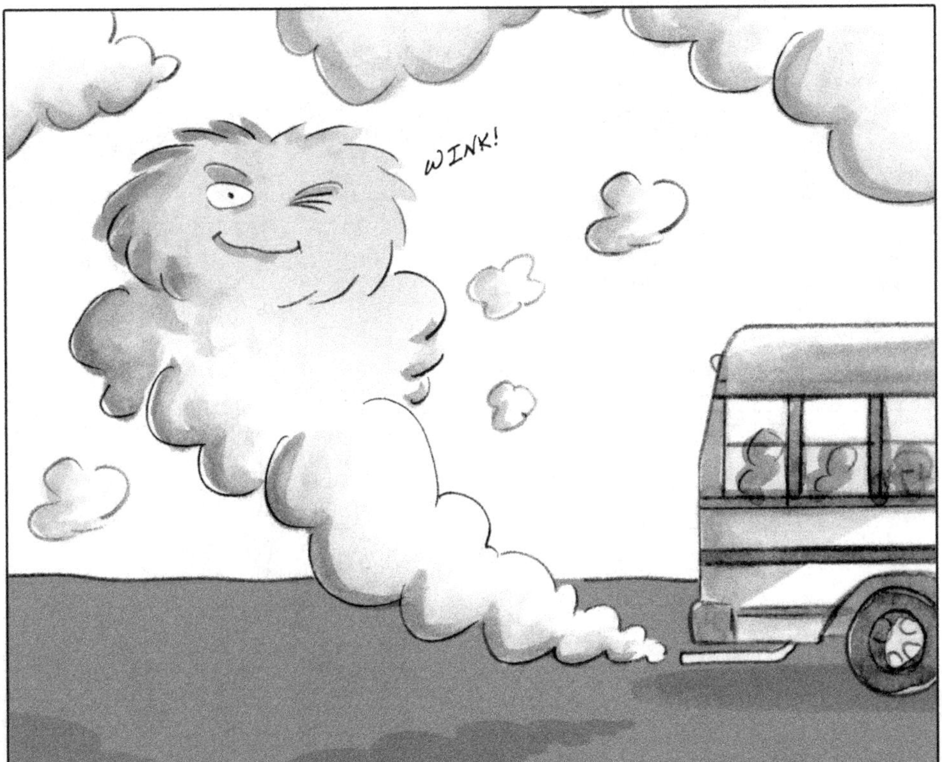
WINK!

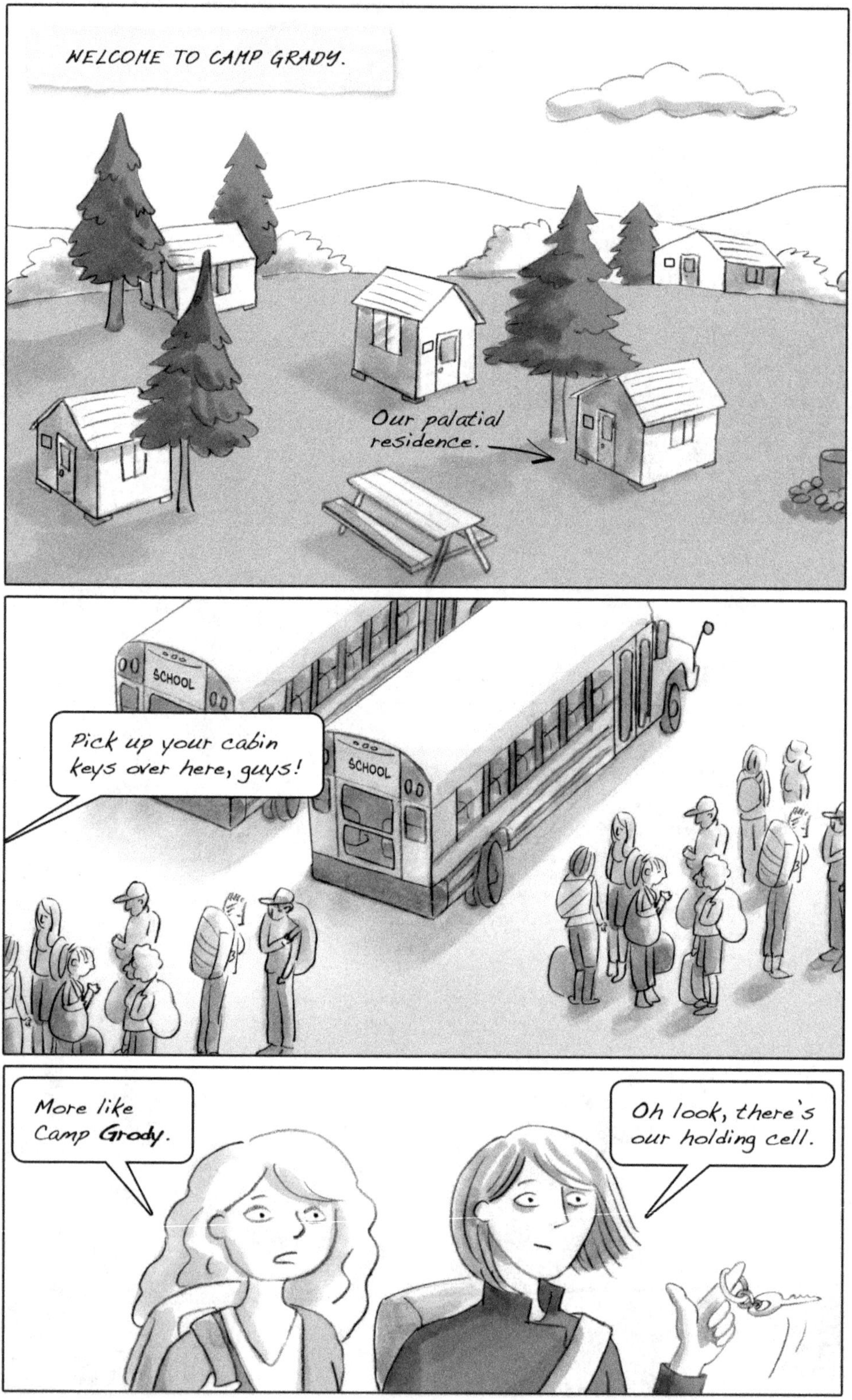
WELCOME TO CAMP GRADY.
Our palatial residence.
SCHOOL
SCHOOL
Pick up your cabin keys over here, guys!
More like Camp **Grody**.
Oh look, there's our holding cell.

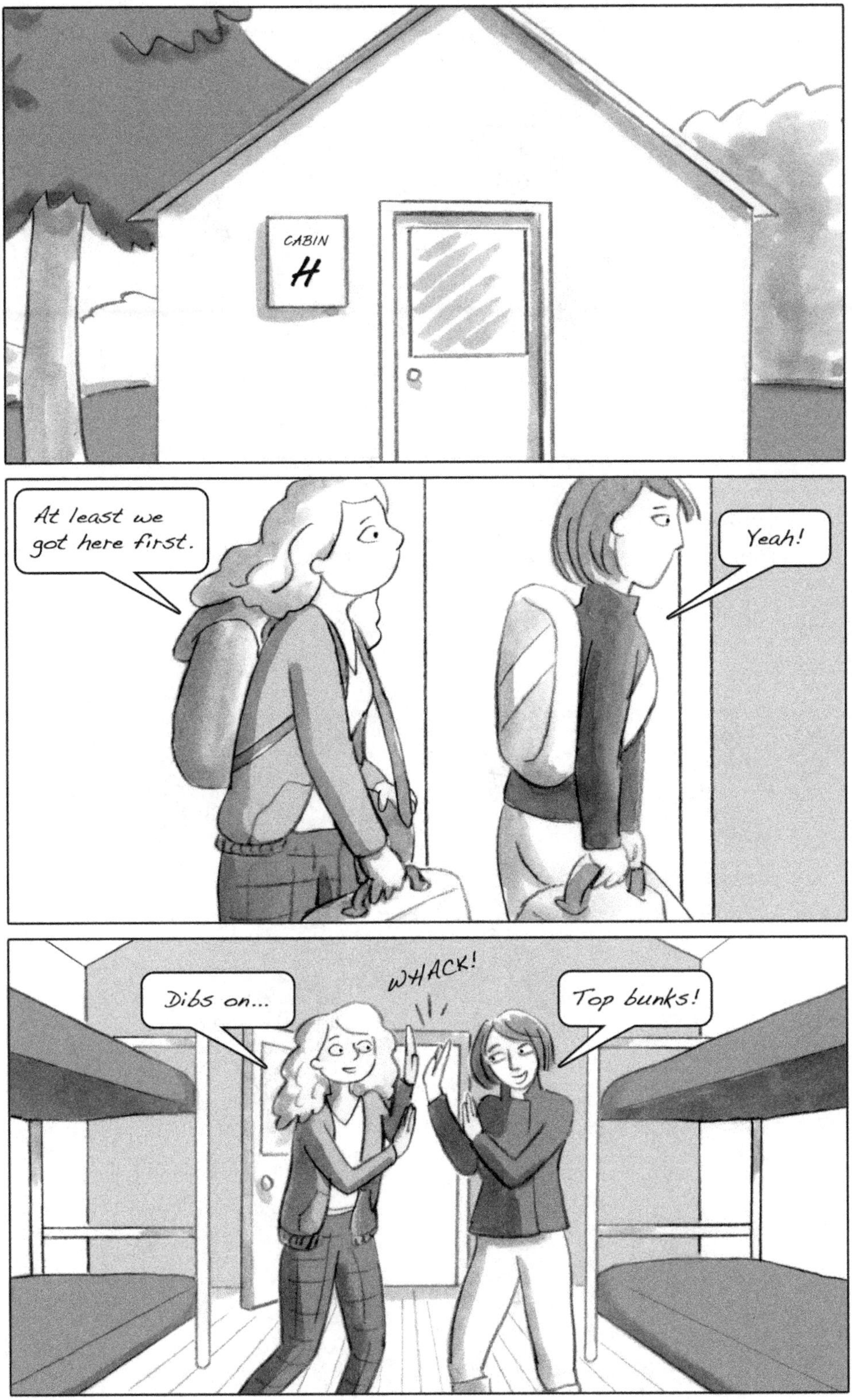
CABIN
H
At least we got here first.
Yeah!
Dibs on...
WHACK!
Top bunks!

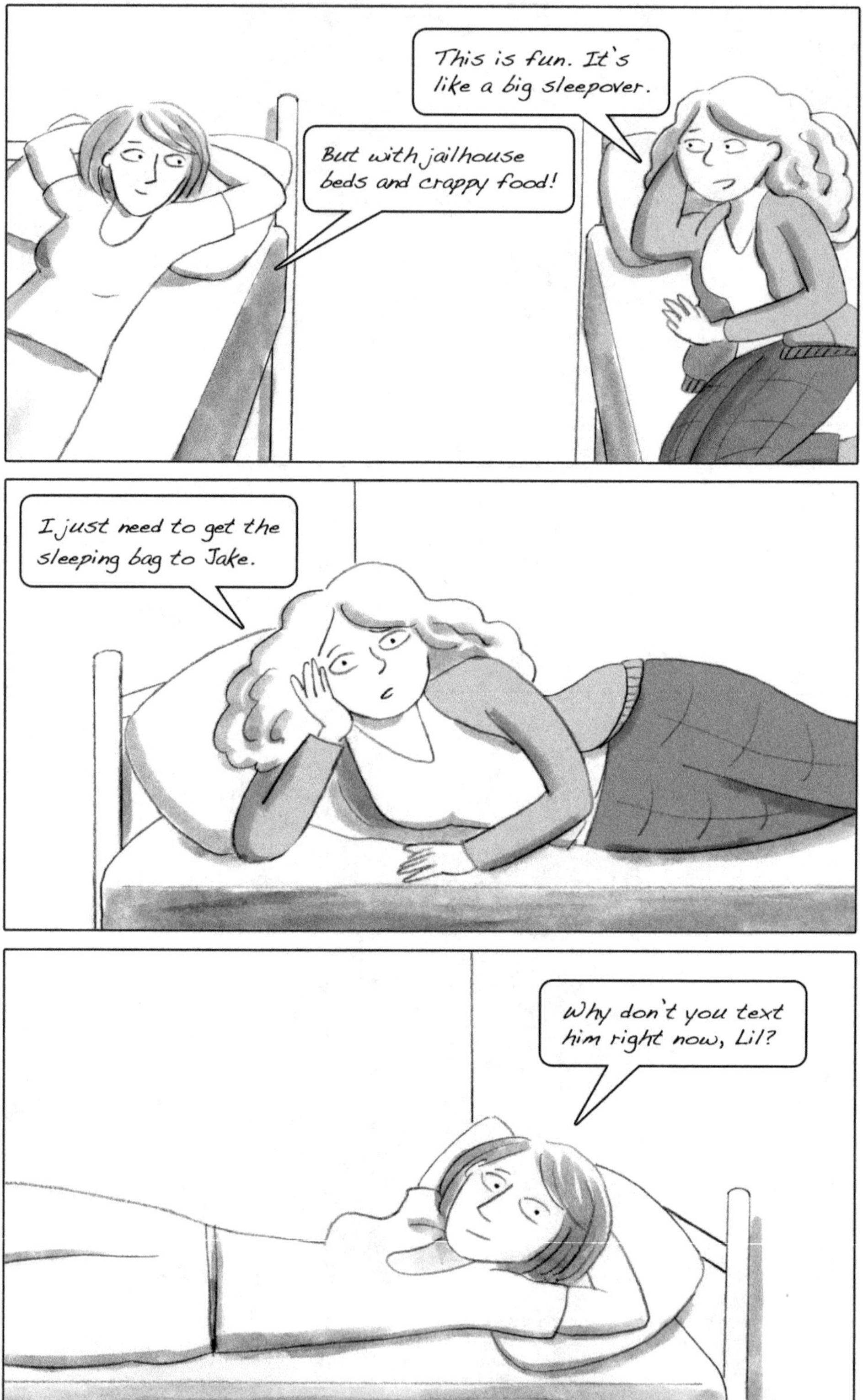

This is fun. It's like a big sleepover.
But with jailhouse beds and crappy food!
I just need to get the sleeping bag to Jake.
Why don't you text him right now, Lil?

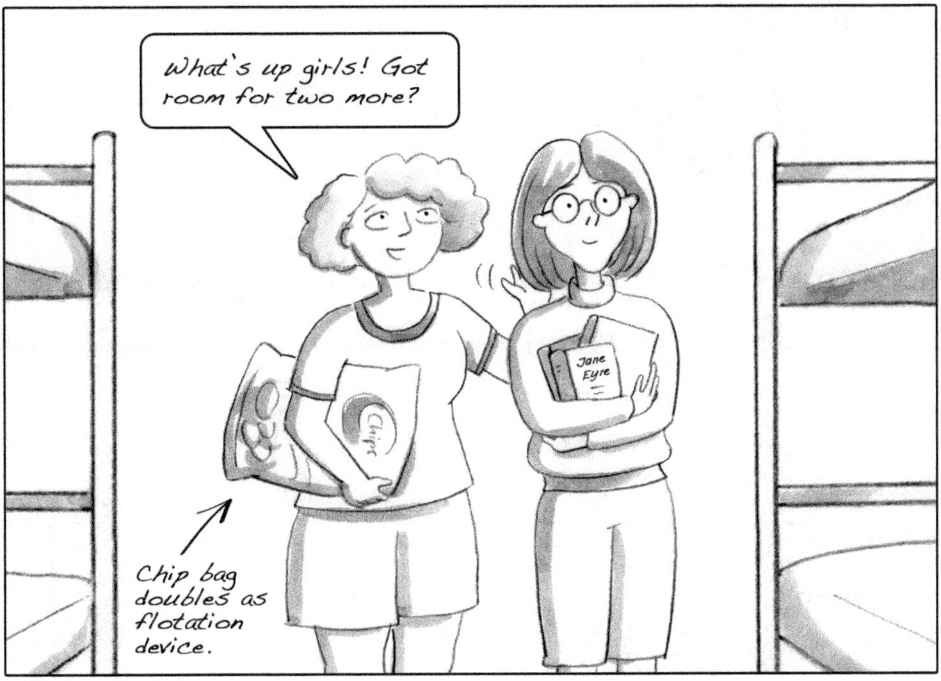
What's up girls! Got room for two more?
Jane Eyre
Chips
Chip bag doubles as flotation device.

The girls we asked to share with showed up and said they don't mind being on the bottom bunks. Booker looks like she meant to sign up for the English trip and Wriggly has brought us the BIGGEST bag of sour cream potato chips known to man. I think we're all gonna get along great.

Apparently, The Twins brought a tent, which is good cuz we only have four beds. More power to 'em for roughing it. I'll take our spartan but weatherproof Prisoner Cell Block H any day – thanks very much!

Should I text Jake? Just like that? Must sound totally cool and casual. Or perhaps even professional? Geez, how about I learn to relax? Ah, but how...

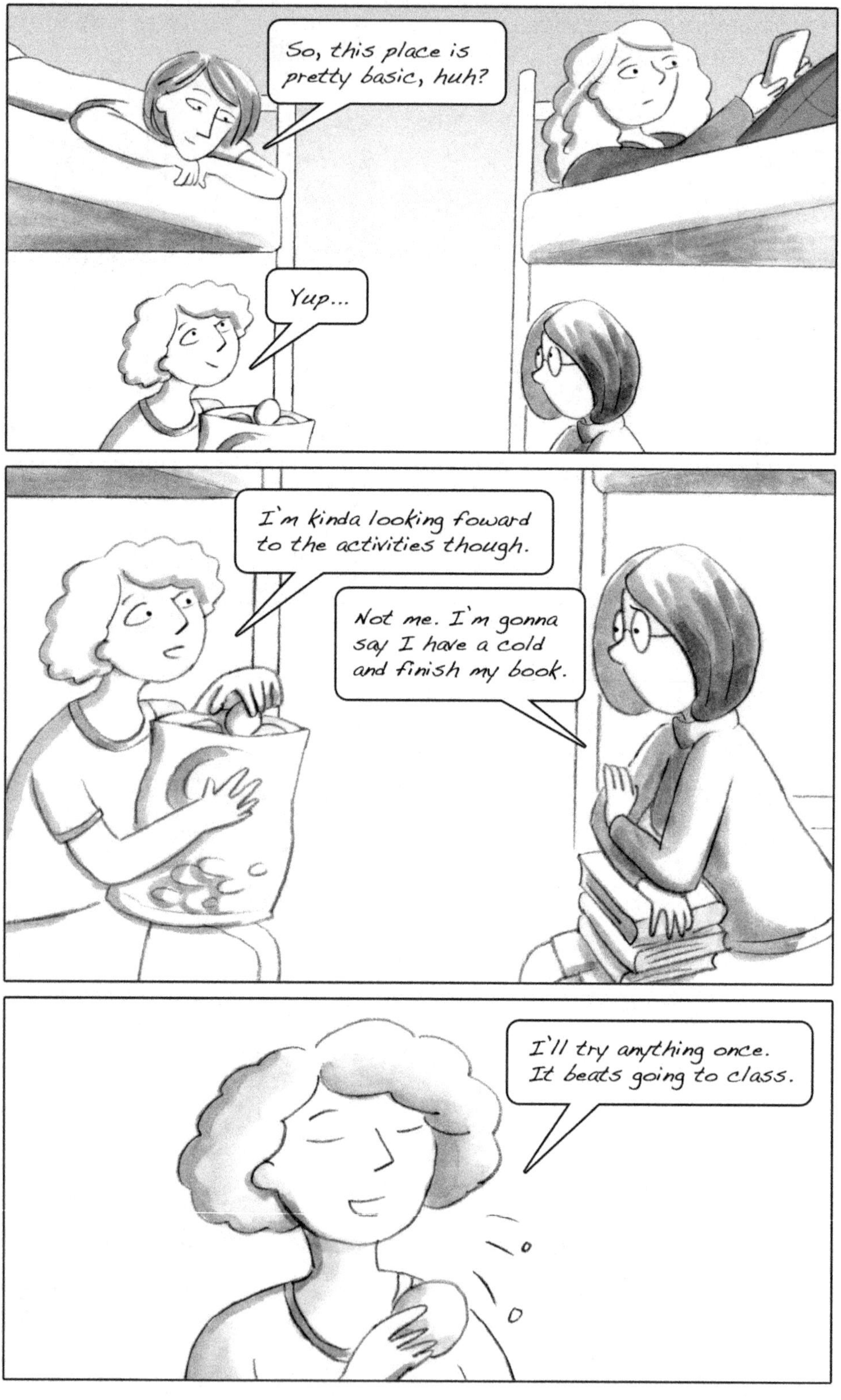
So, this place is pretty basic, huh?
Yup...
I'm kinda looking foward to the activities though.
Not me. I'm gonna say I have a cold and finish my book.
I'll try anything once. It beats going to class.

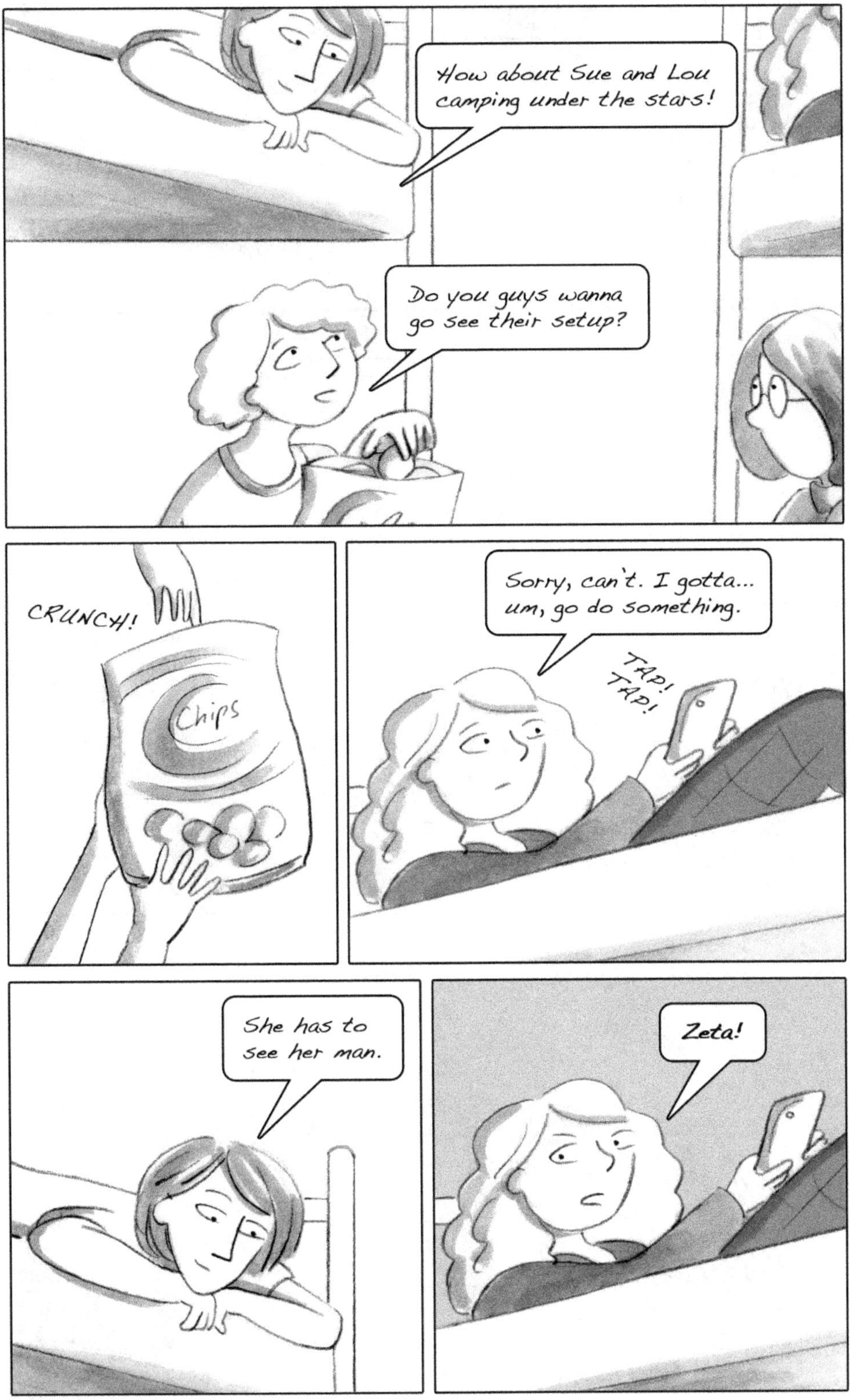
How about Sue and Lou camping under the stars!
Do you guys wanna go see their setup?
CRUNCH!
Chips
Sorry, can't. I gotta... um, go do something.
TAP! TAP!
She has to see her man.
Zeta!

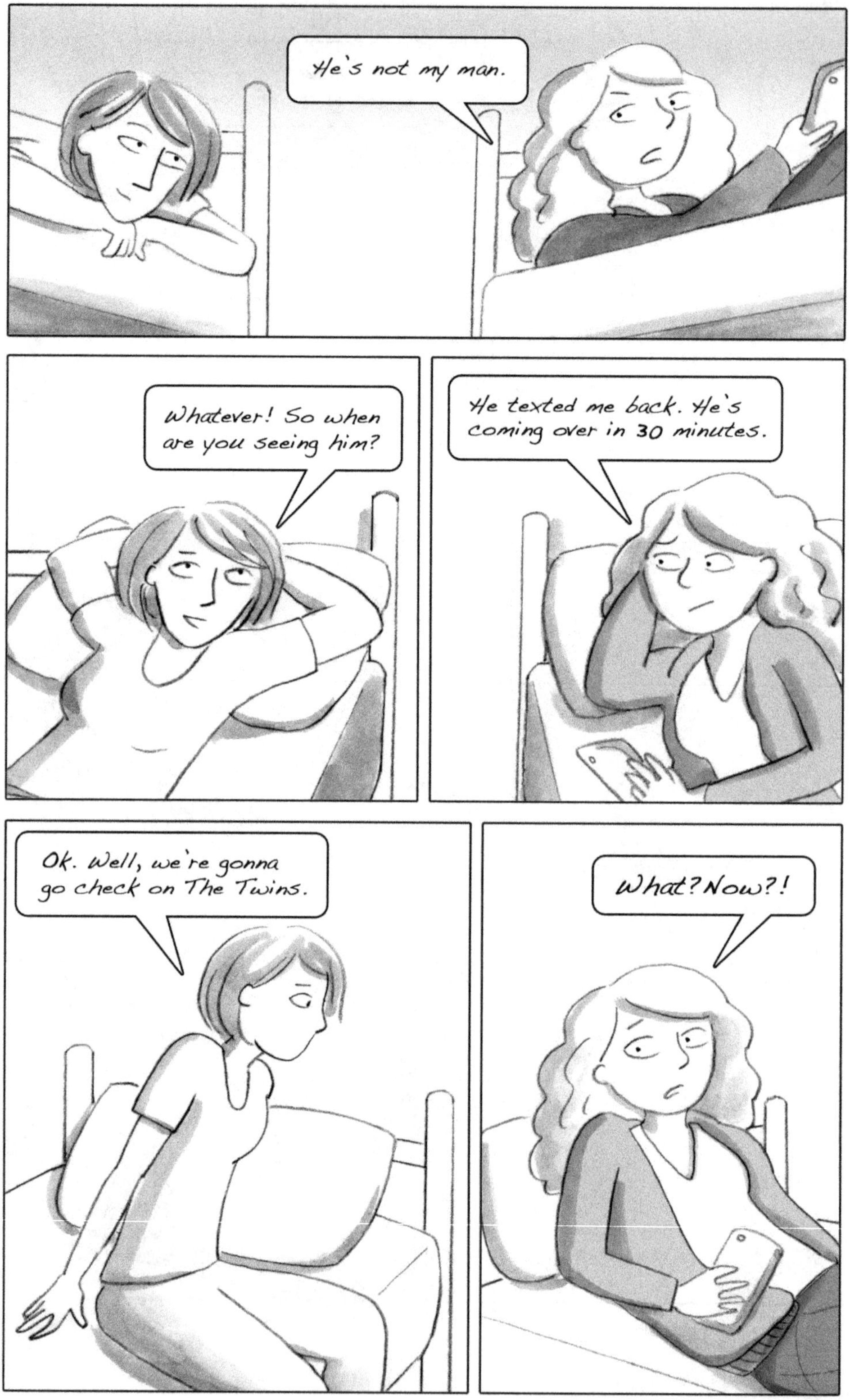
He's not my man.
Whatever! So when are you seeing him?
He texted me back. He's coming over in 30 minutes.
Ok. Well, we're gonna go check on The Twins.
What? Now?!

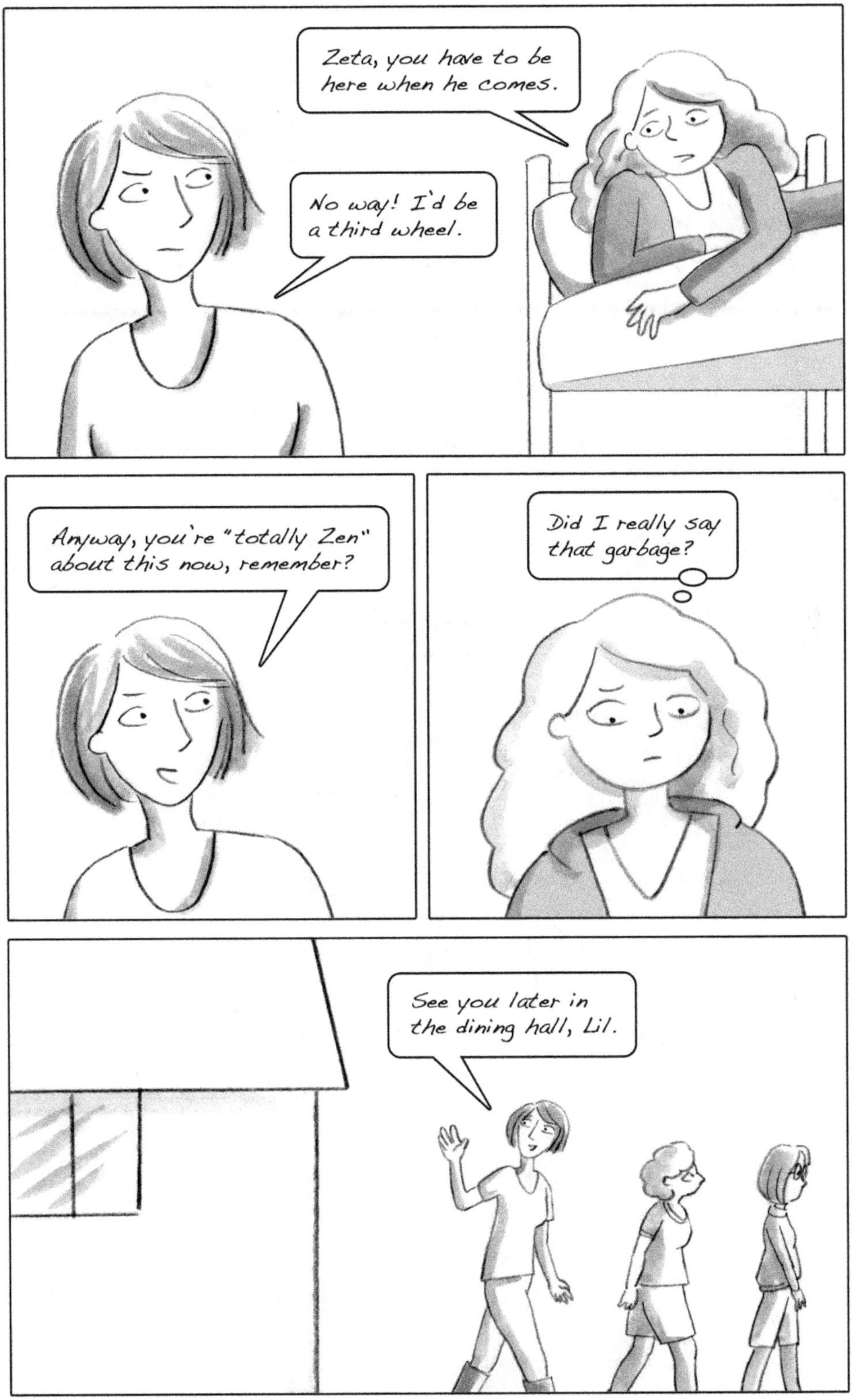
Zeta, you have to be here when he comes.
No way! I'd be a third wheel.
Anyway, you're "totally Zen" about this now, remember?
Did I really say that garbage?
See you later in the dining hall, Lil.

No big deal, Lily, you've got this. You're only handing over a sleeping bag. To a PERSON. This person's name is Jake. This doesn't have to become a big dramafest. It's simple: the more you can be yourself, the better. (Your REAL SELF, of course.) You can choose how you feel, right? Change your thoughts, change your world!? (Something like that.)

OMG. This is sounding like a motivational speaker pitch. I need to chill out, that's all. I've heard guided meditation is a thing.

Bloop!
Ahhh, yes...
Breathe in...
Breathe out.
You are relaxed...
And peaceful.
(Soothing chimes)

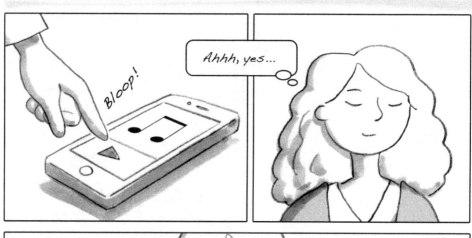

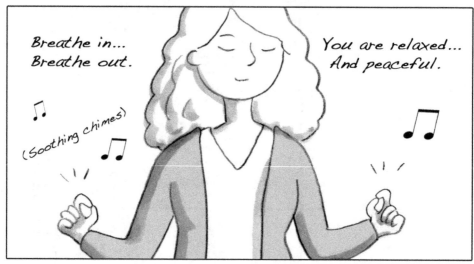

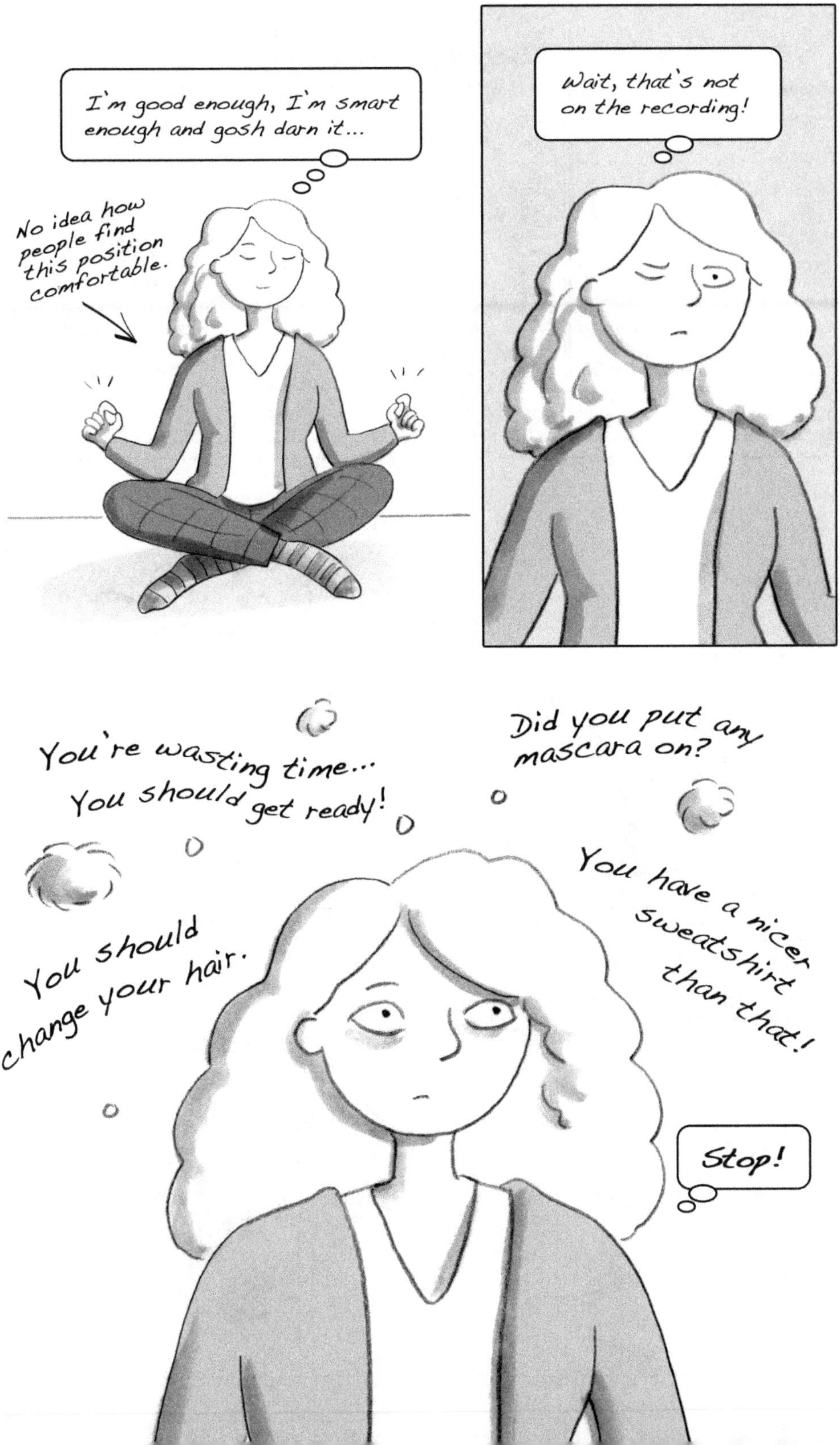
I'm good enough, I'm smart enough and gosh darn it...
No idea how people find this position comfortable.
Wait, that's not on the recording!
You're wasting time... You should get ready!
Did you put any mascara on?
You should change your hair.
You have a nicer sweatshirt than that!
Stop!

This is just the monkey mind...

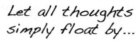

Let all thoughts simply float by...

Tune into the blissful music.

(Tibetan bells)

Sense into the radiant beauty of your inner being.

Oh, now I'm in the zone. Nothing could disturb this...

BZZZT!

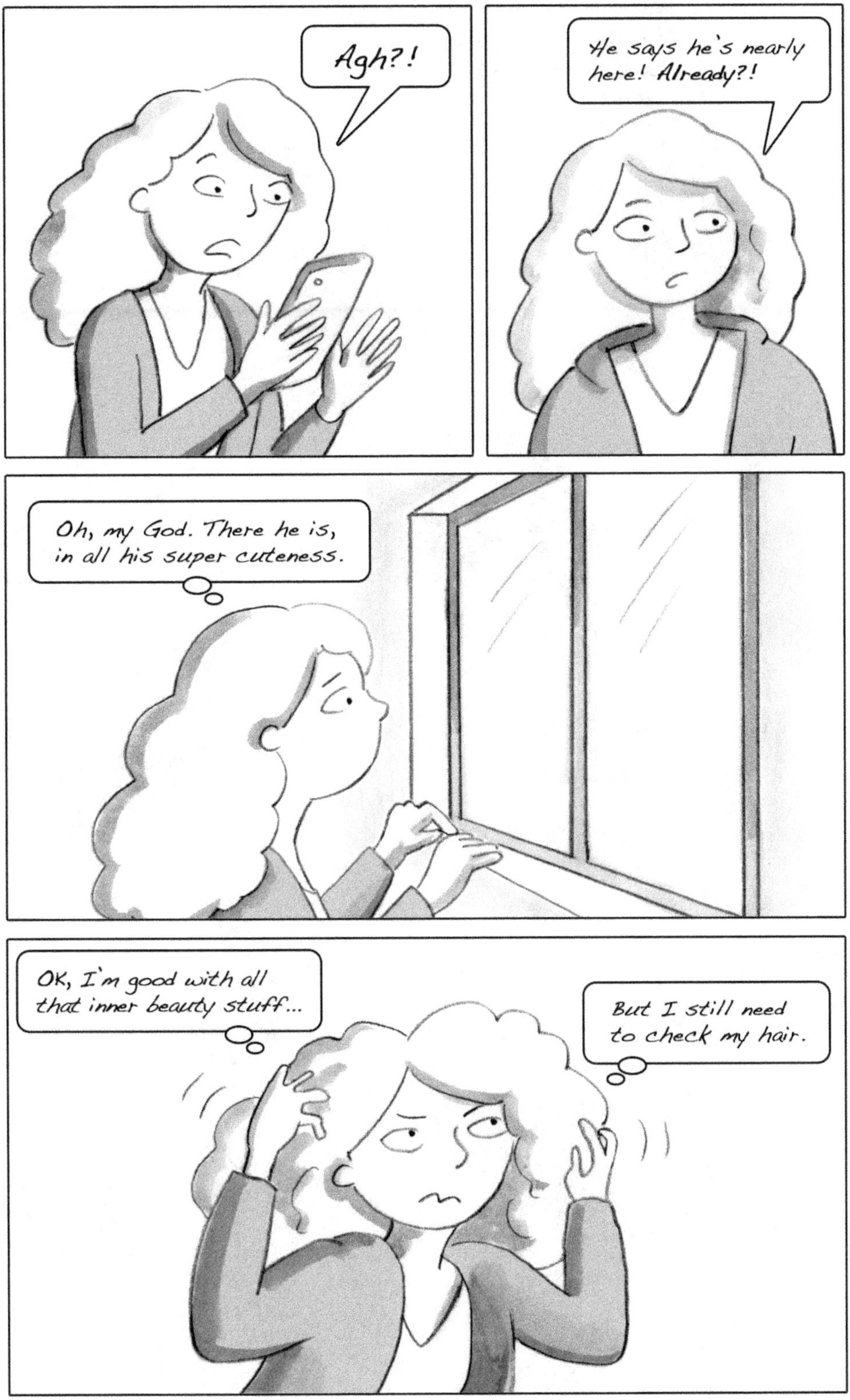
Agh?!
He says he's nearly here! Already?!
Oh, my God. There he is, in all his super cuteness.
OK, I'm good with all that inner beauty stuff...
But I still need to check my hair.

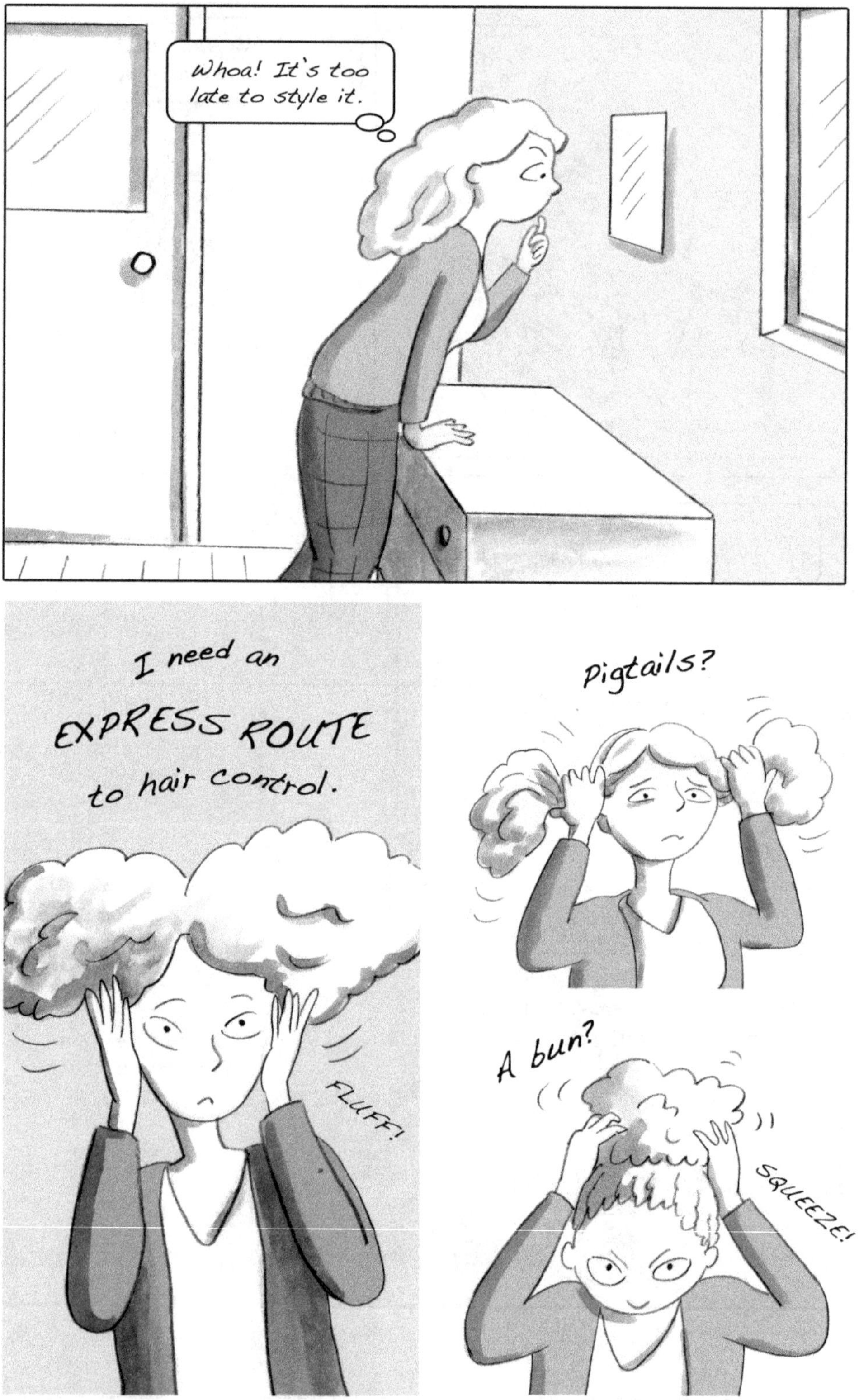
Whoa! It's too late to style it.
I need an EXPRESS ROUTE to hair control.
FLUFF!
Pigtails?
A bun?
SQUEEZE!

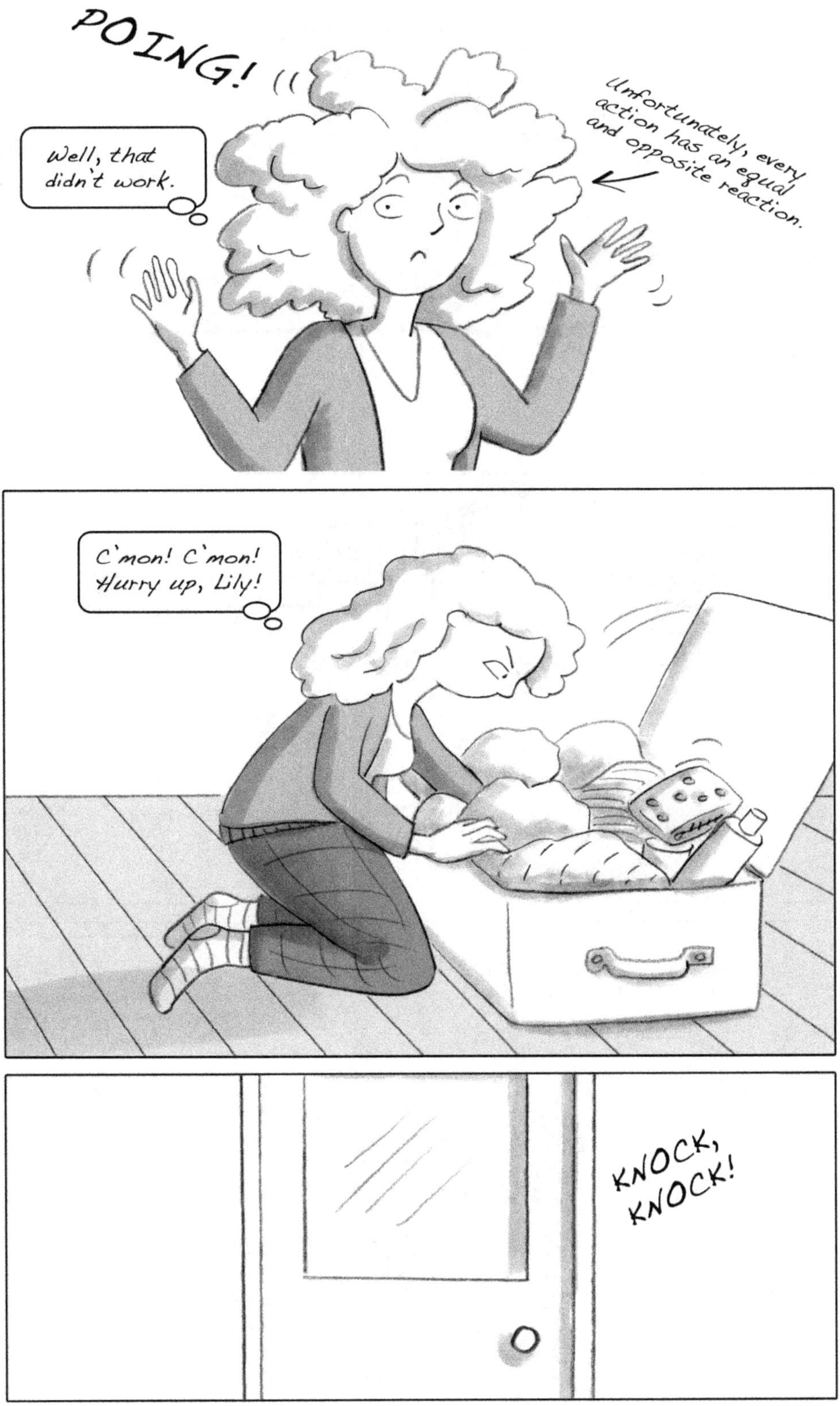
POING!
Well, that didn't work.
Unfortunately, every action has an equal and opposite reaction.
C'mon! C'mon! Hurry up, Lily!
KNOCK, KNOCK!

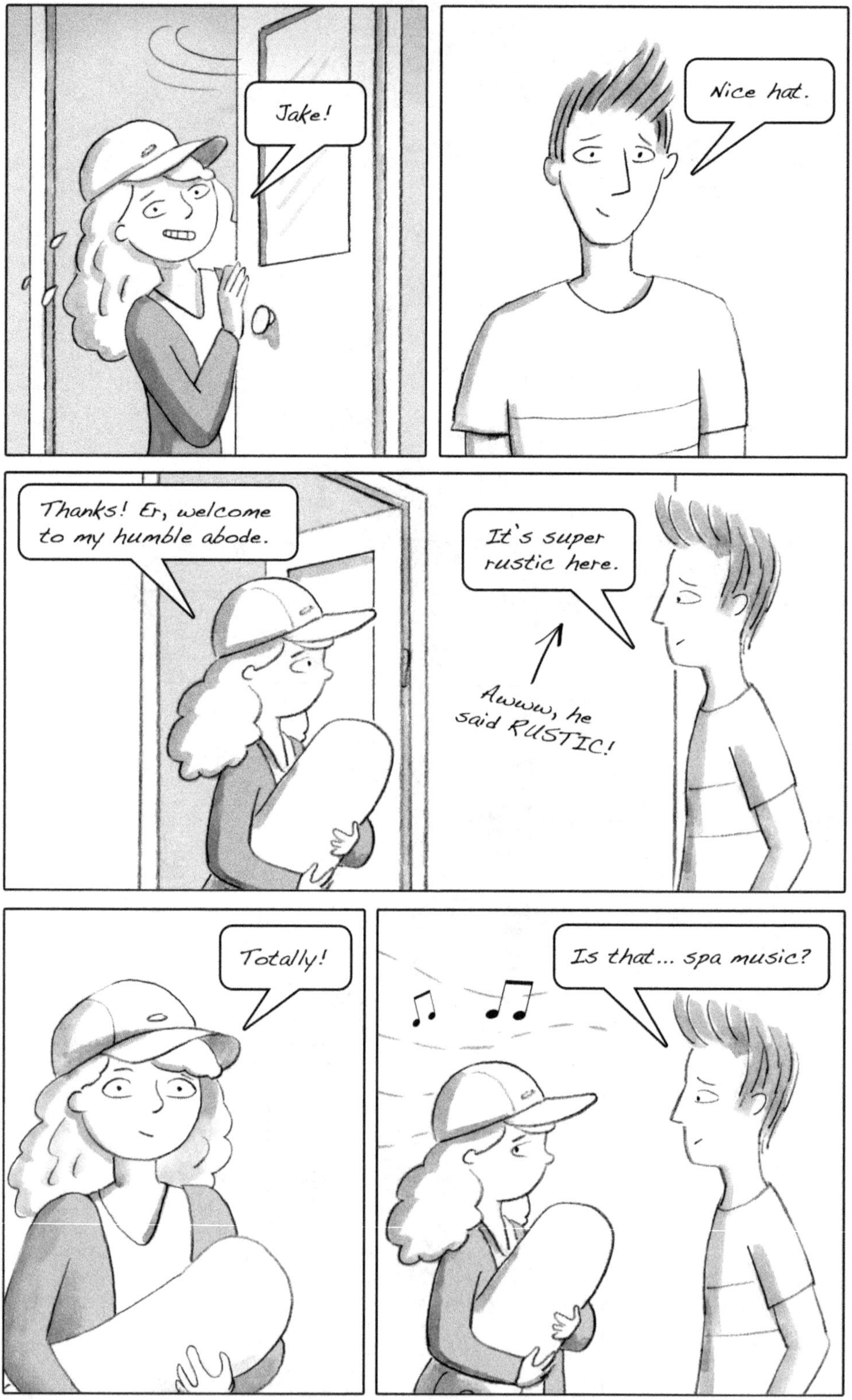
Jake!
Nice hat.
Thanks! Er, welcome to my humble abode.
It's super rustic here.
Awww, he said RUSTIC!
Totally!
Is that... spa music?

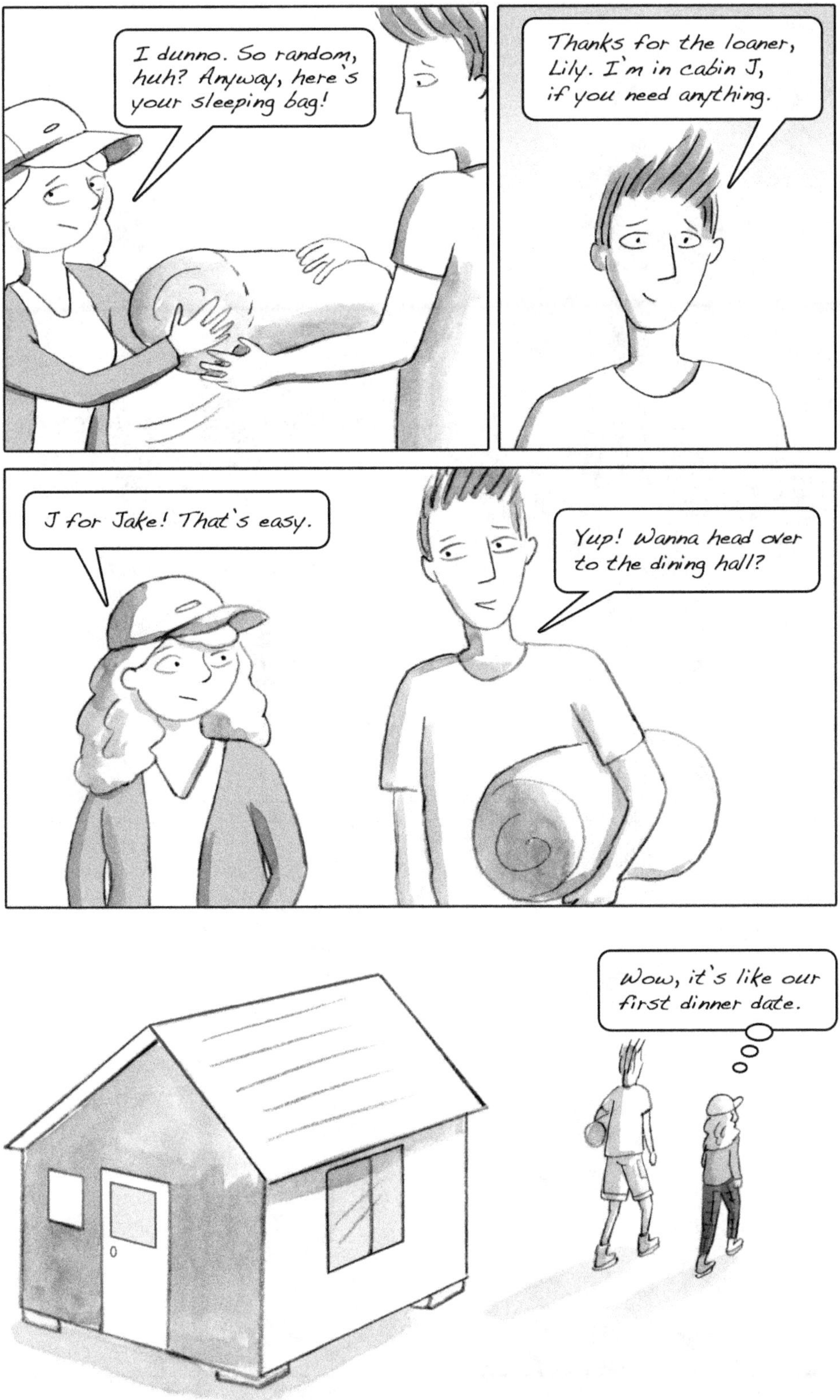
I dunno. So random, huh? Anyway, here's your sleeping bag!
Thanks for the loaner, Lily. I'm in cabin J, if you need anything.
J for Jake! That's easy.
Yup! Wanna head over to the dining hall?
Wow, it's like our first dinner date.

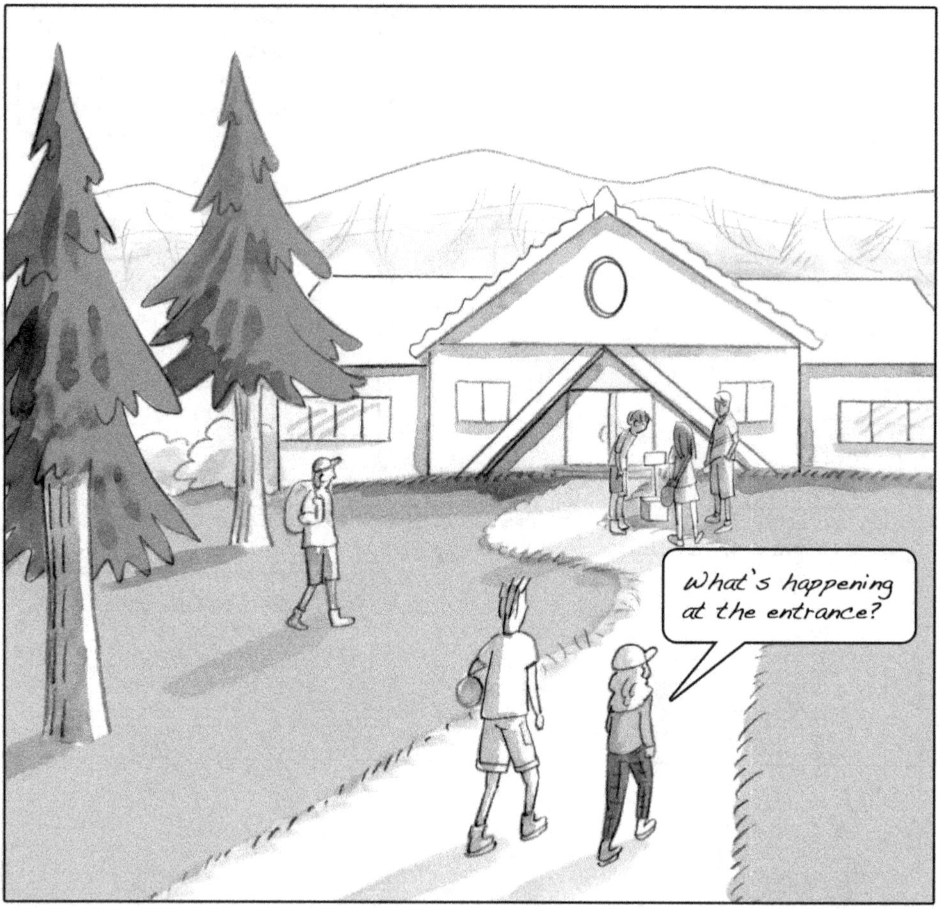
What's happening
at the entrance?

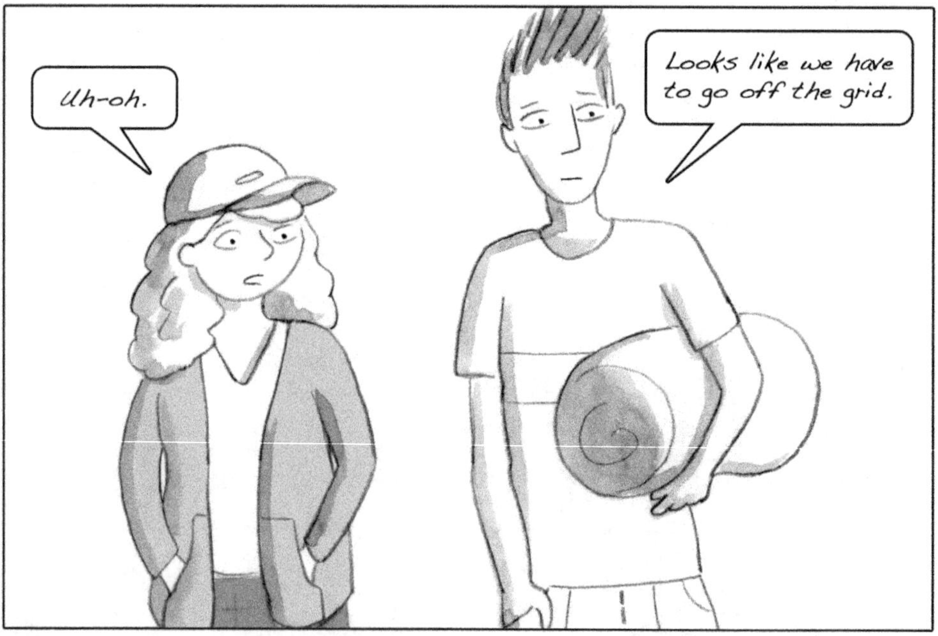
Uh-oh.
Looks like we have
to go off the grid.

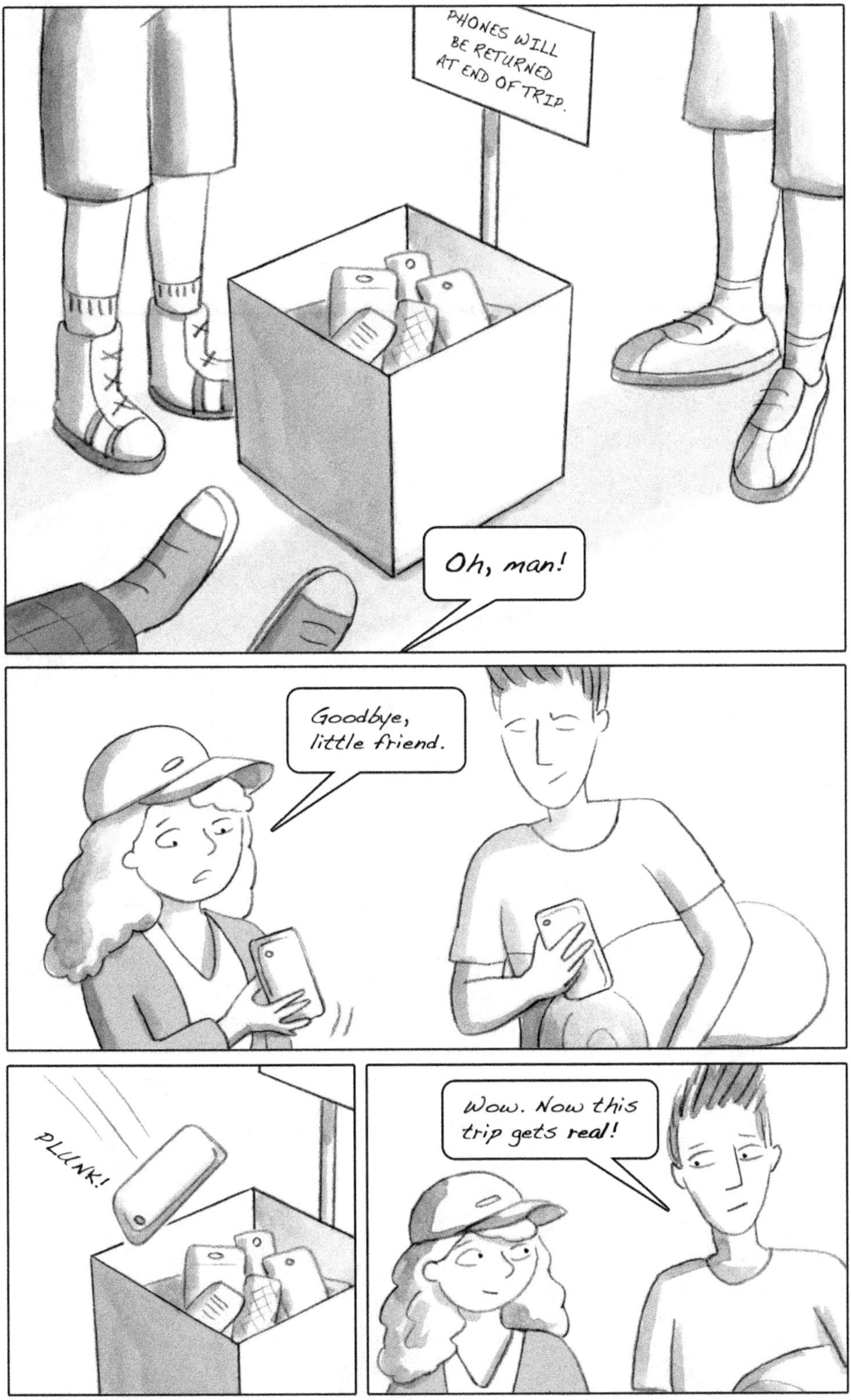
PHONES WILL BE RETURNED AT END OF TRIP.
Oh, man!
Goodbye, little friend.
PLUNK!
Wow. Now this trip gets **real**!

MONDAY p.m.

You're not gonna believe this, dear diary. I met up with Jake today and it was AWESOME!!! He was so nice. And except for a minor hair snafu – deftly taken care of with a ball cap – I felt pretty relaxed. Maybe it was the Buddhist controlled breathing, Gregorian chants, Hindu chakra wind chimes or the yogic twisting of my legs into a pretzel... who knows? But in the end, I had this feeling that it's OK to... just be me. It was easy to be with him. (Isn't that how you know it's "meant to be"?)

Oh, and so much for The Twins braving the elements. They didn't even come to the dinner hall because they barbequed their own food, drank sparkling water and watched the sunset from their lawn chairs. Ahem! I believe that's called GLAMPING? Not camping?

I have a really good feeling about this.
It's all going to work out with Jake and me.

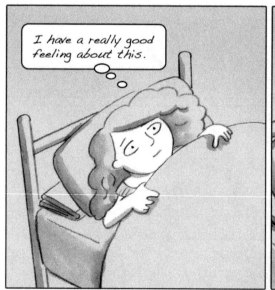

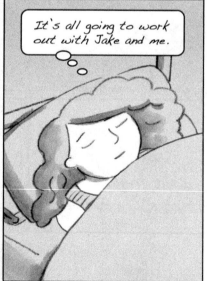

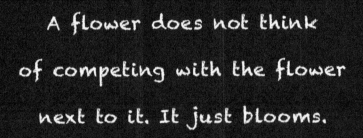

A flower does not think

of competing with the flower

next to it. It just blooms.

ZEN SHIN

TUESDAY

I barely slept thanks to Wriggly's snoring! No wonder The Twins look fresh as daisies: I just strolled by their glamping setup...

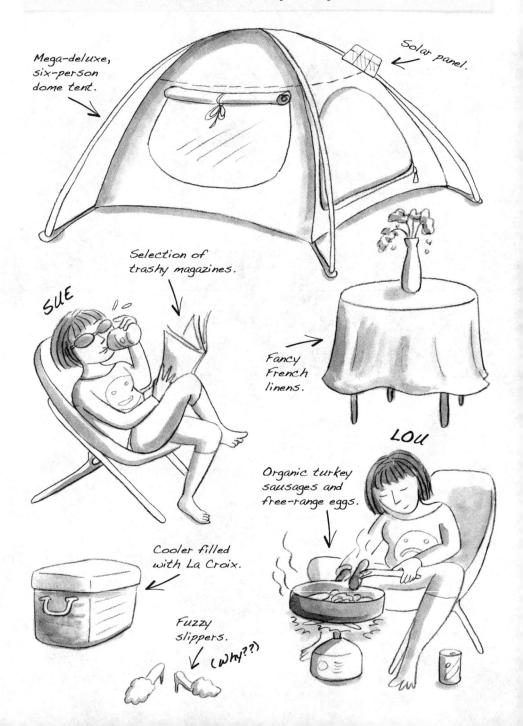

Mega-deluxe, six-person dome tent.

Solar panel.

Selection of trashy magazines.

SUE

Fancy French linens.

LOU

Organic turkey sausages and free-range eggs.

Cooler filled with La Croix.

Fuzzy slippers.

(why??)

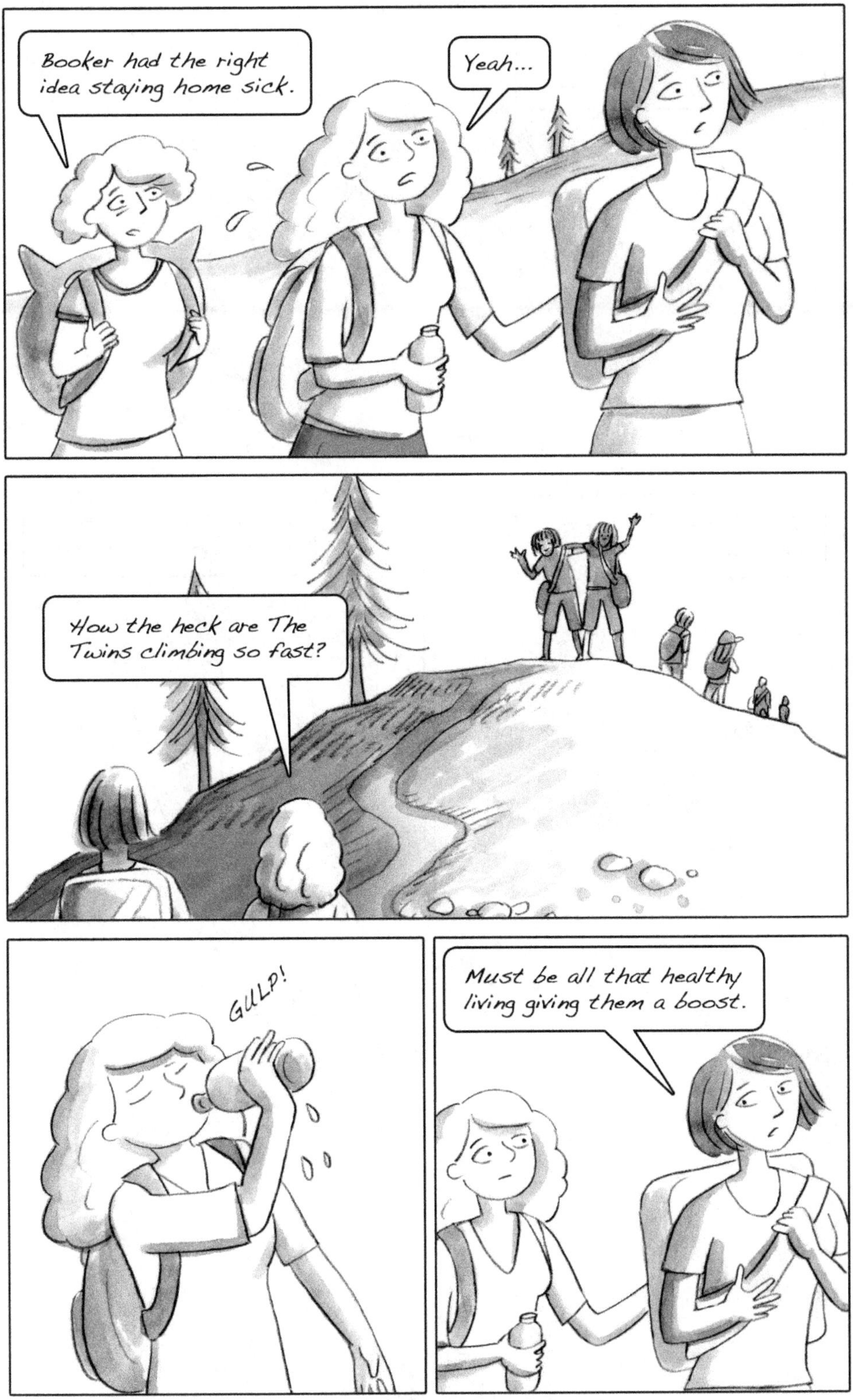
Booker had the right idea staying home sick.
Yeah...
How the heck are The Twins climbing so fast?
GULP!
Must be all that healthy living giving them a boost.

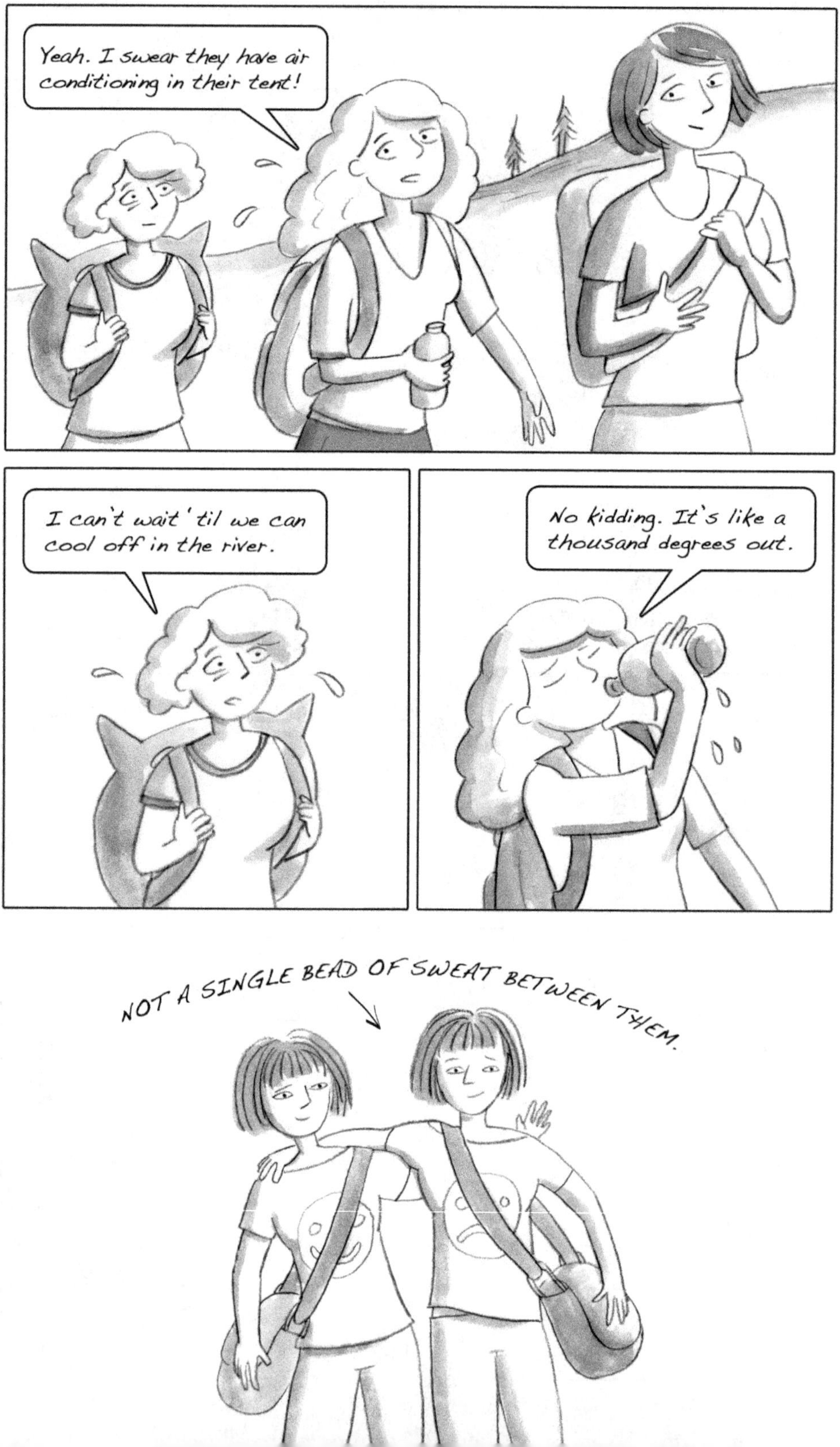
Yeah. I swear they have air conditioning in their tent!
I can't wait 'til we can cool off in the river.
No kidding. It's like a thousand degrees out.
NOT A SINGLE BEAD OF SWEAT BETWEEN THEM.

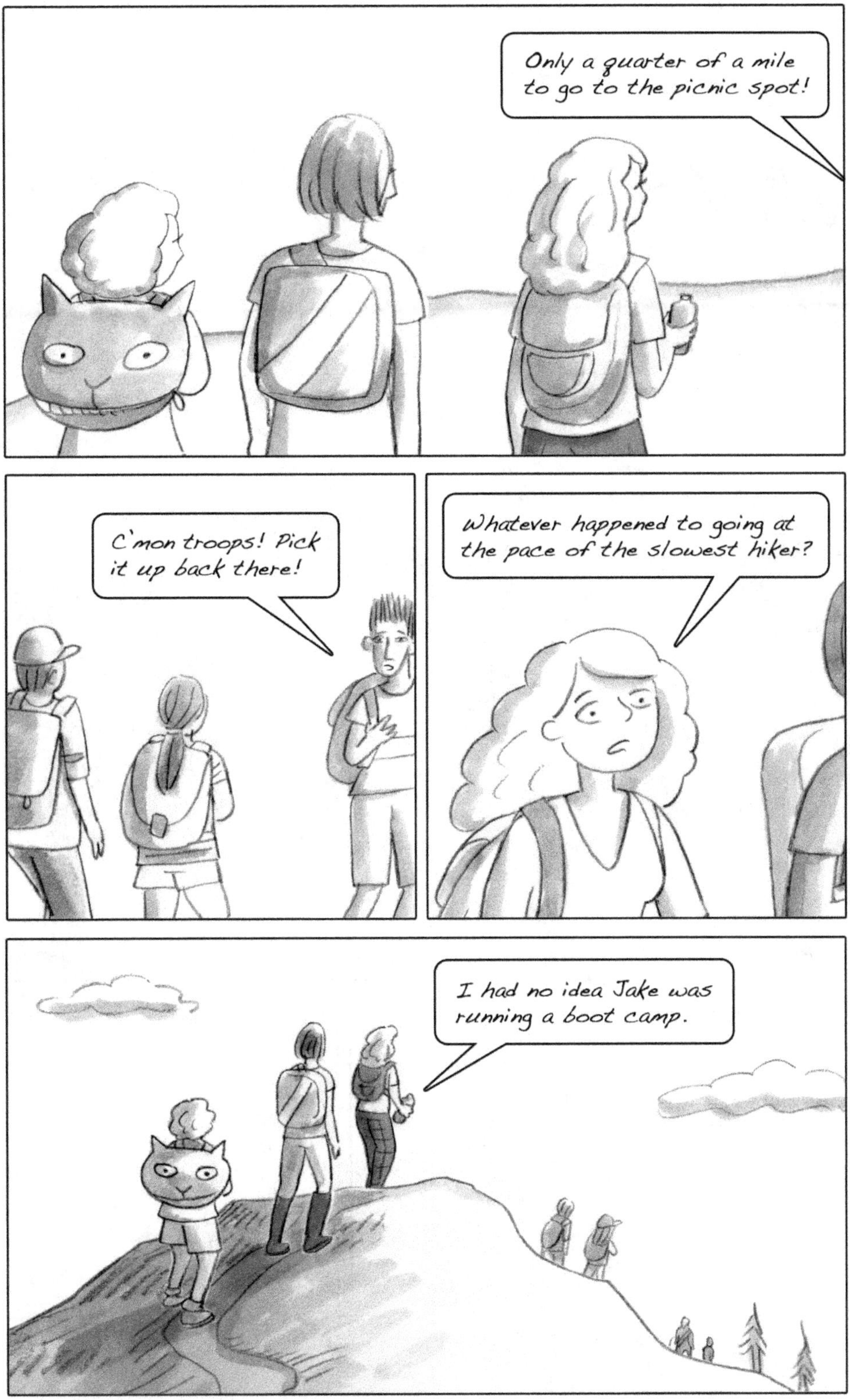
Only a quarter of a mile to go to the picnic spot!
C'mon troops! Pick it up back there!
Whatever happened to going at the pace of the slowest hiker?
I had no idea Jake was running a boot camp.

Let's chill out here for lunch.

Remember to collect three river samples for your fieldwork.

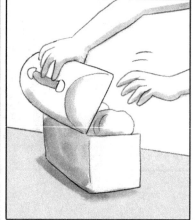

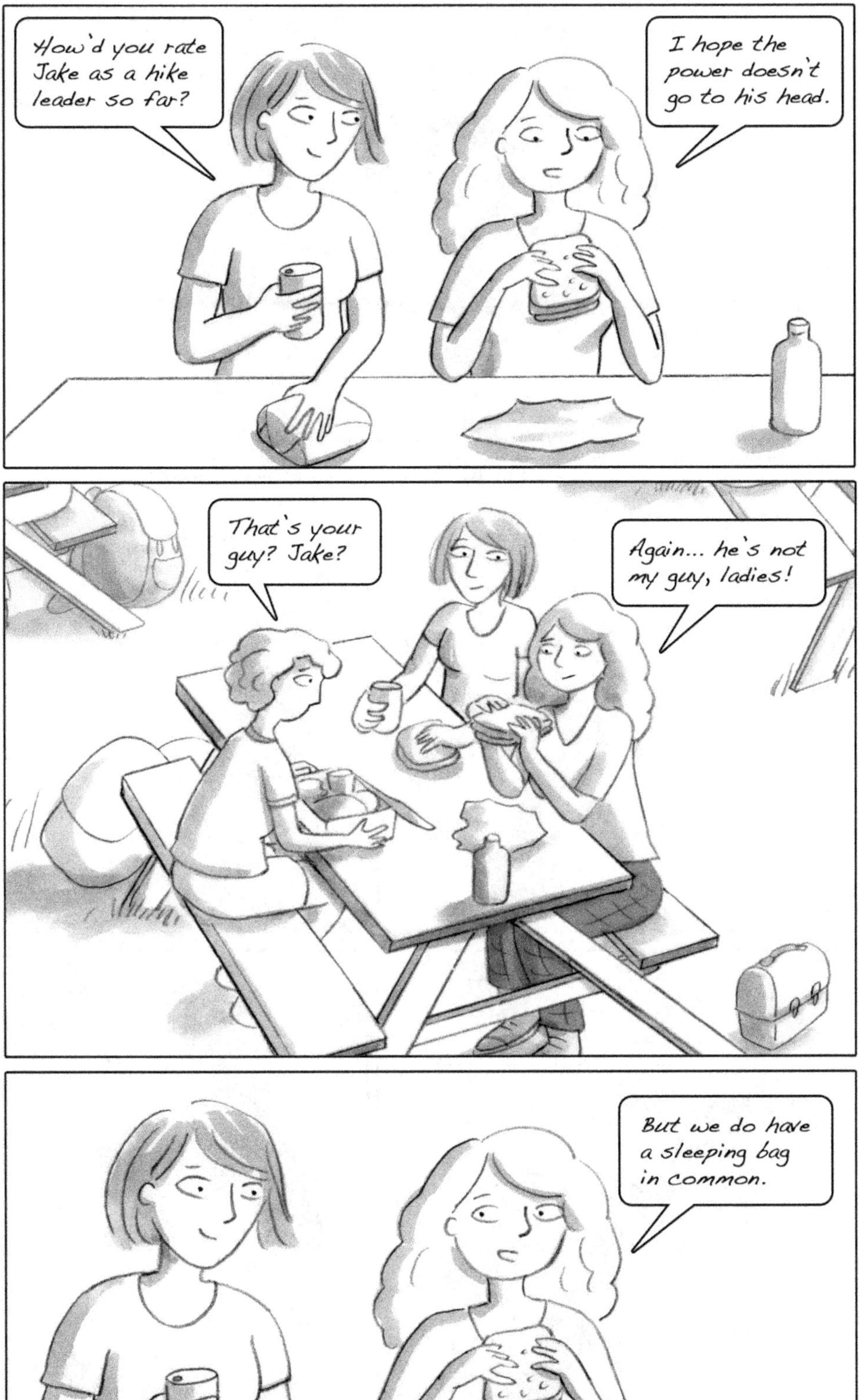
How'd you rate Jake as a hike leader so far?
I hope the power doesn't go to his head.
That's your guy? Jake?
Again... he's not my guy, ladies!
But we do have a sleeping bag in common.

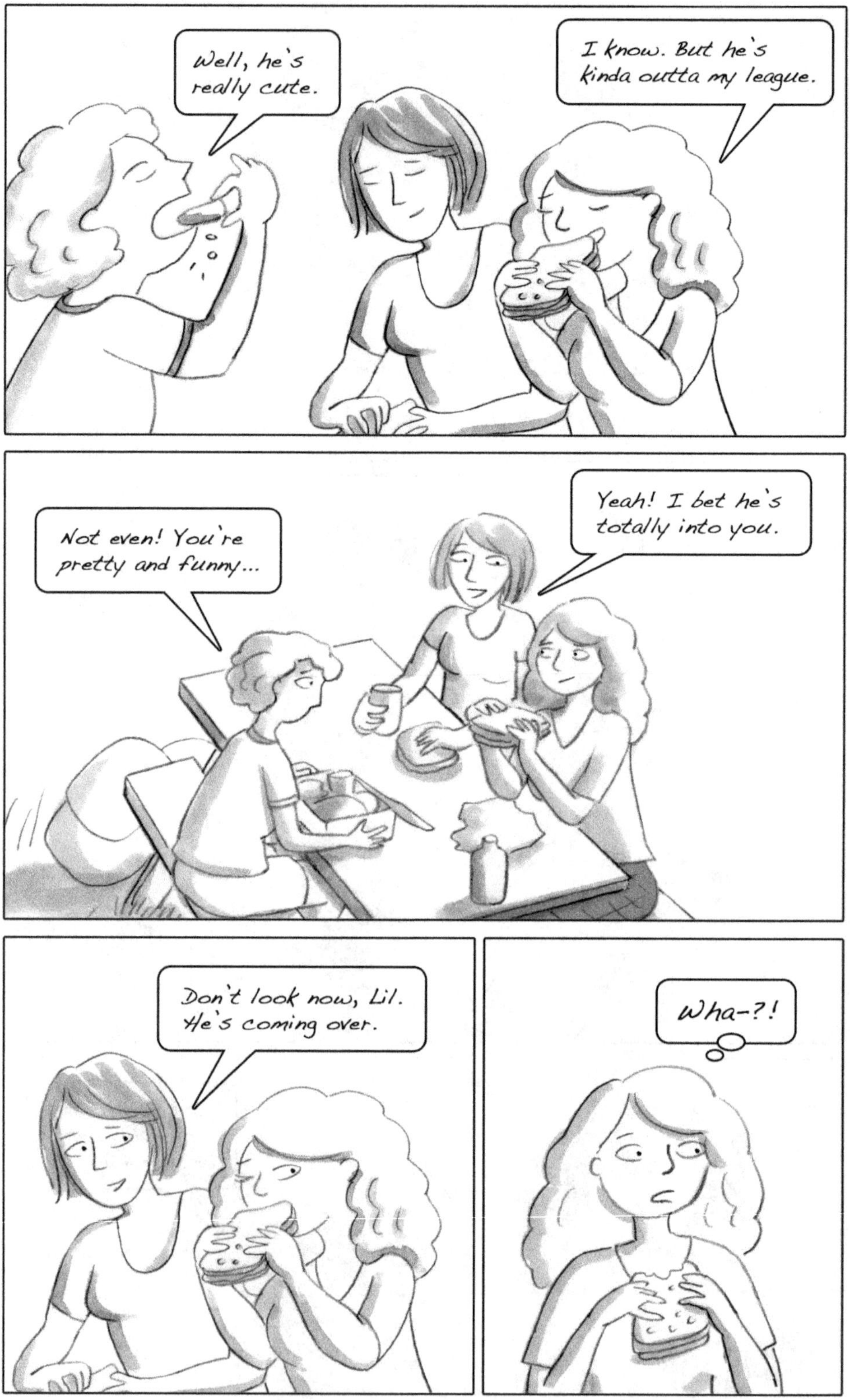
Well, he's really cute.
I know. But he's kinda outta my league.
Not even! You're pretty and funny...
Yeah! I bet he's totally into you.
Don't look now, Lil. He's coming over.
Wha-?!

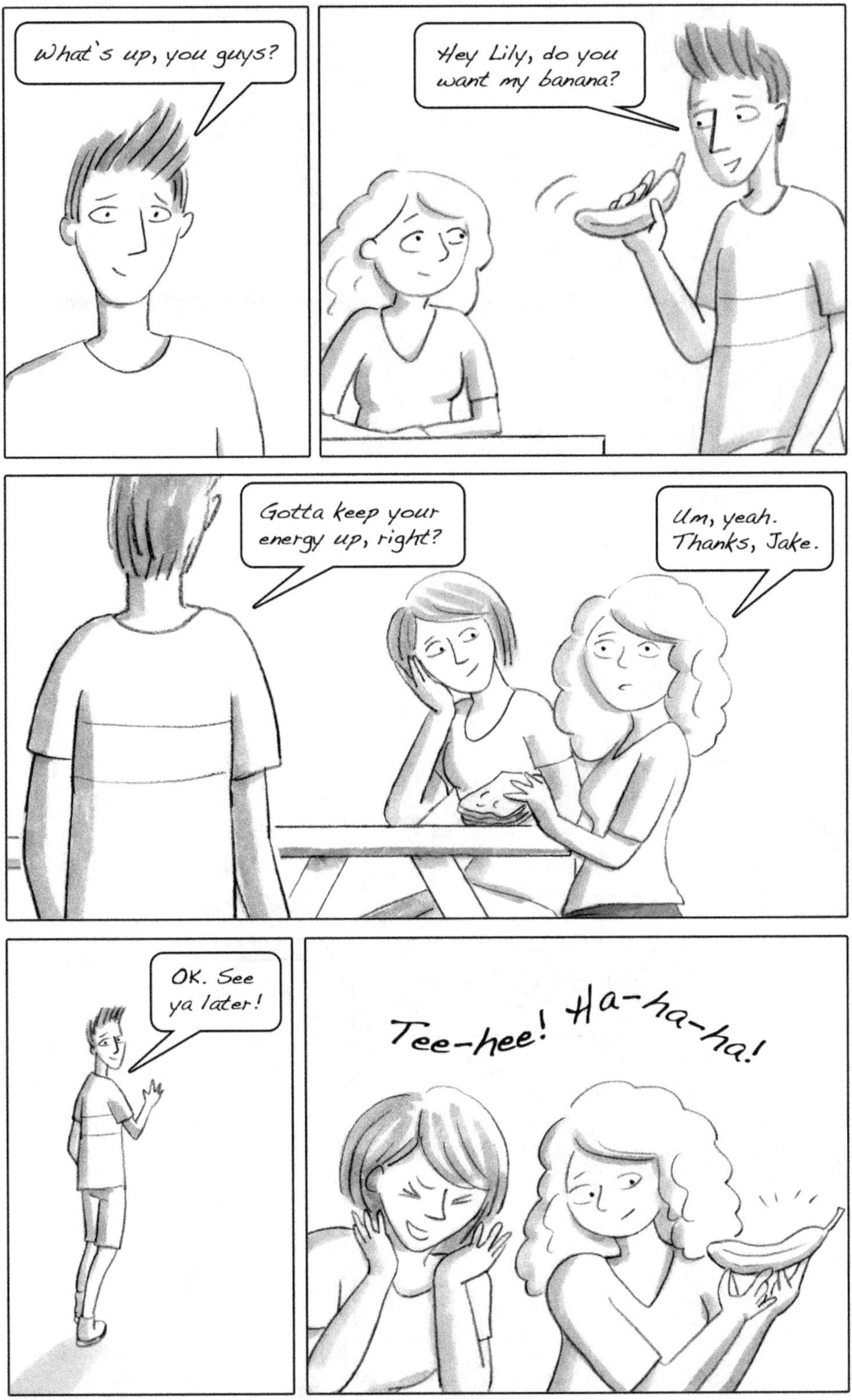
What's up, you guys?
Hey Lily, do you want my banana?
Gotta keep your energy up, right?
Um, yeah. Thanks, Jake.
OK. See ya later!
Tee-hee! Ha-ha-ha!

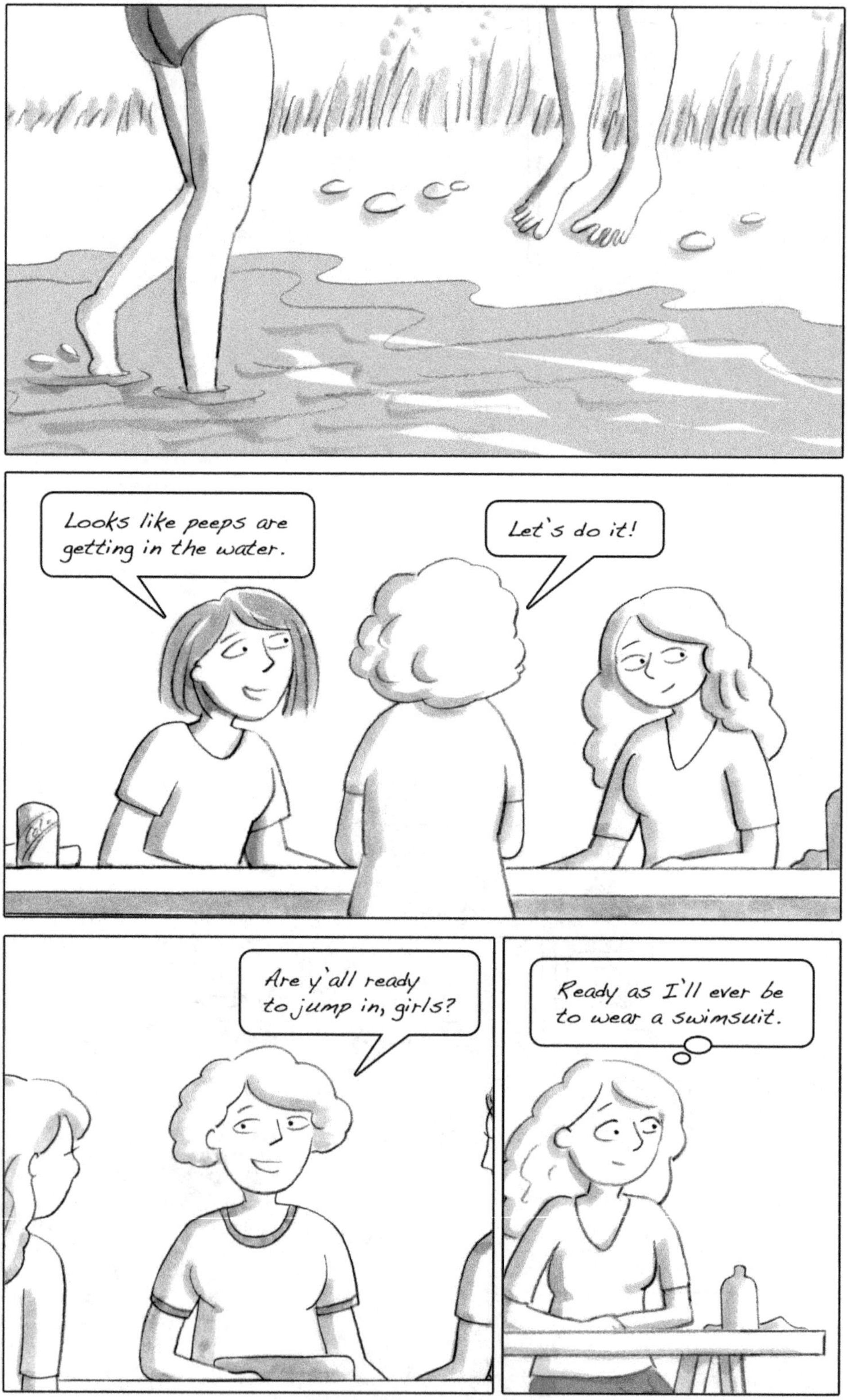
Looks like peeps are getting in the water.
Let's do it!
Are y'all ready to jump in, girls?
Ready as I'll ever be to wear a swimsuit.

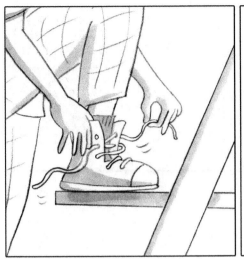

Ugh.

My pre-lunch tummy would've looked way more beach ready.

C'mon, Lily!

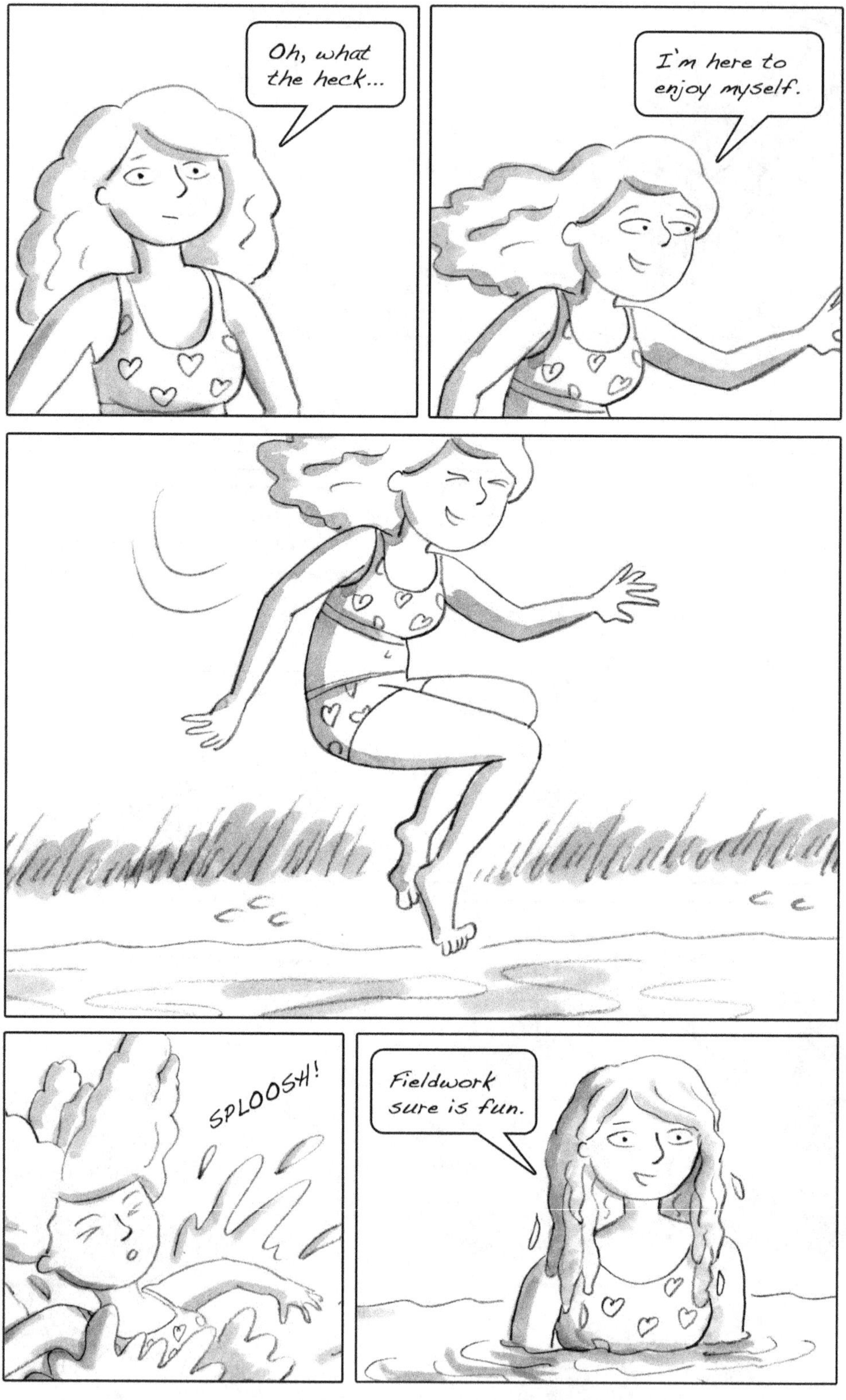
Oh, what the heck...
I'm here to enjoy myself.
SPLOOSH!
Fieldwork sure is fun.

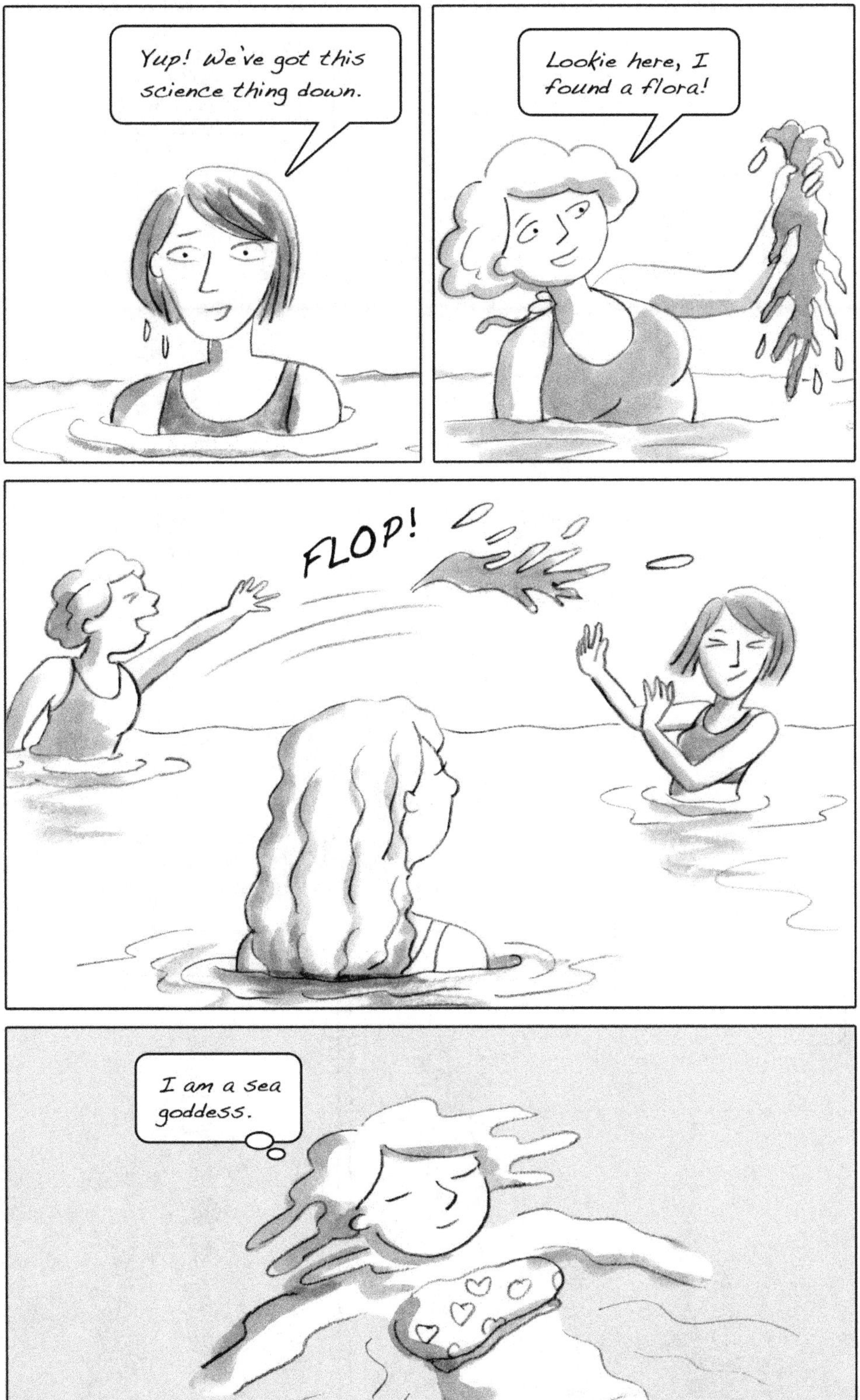
Yup! We've got this science thing down.
Lookie here, I found a flora!
FLOP!
I am a sea goddess.

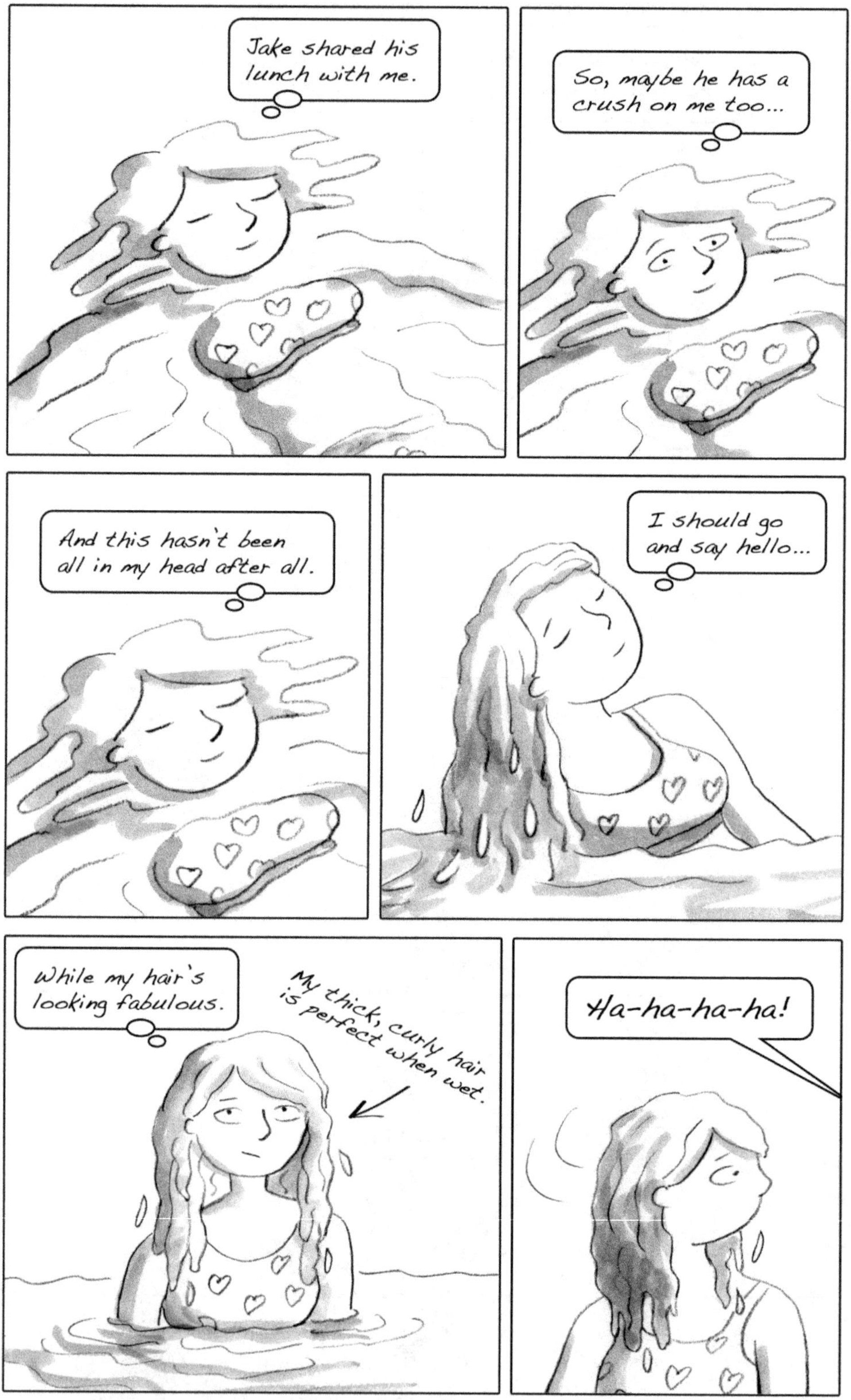

Jake shared his lunch with me.
So, maybe he has a crush on me too...
And this hasn't been all in my head after all.
I should go and say hello...
While my hair's looking fabulous.
My thick, curly hair is perfect when wet.
Ha-ha-ha-ha!

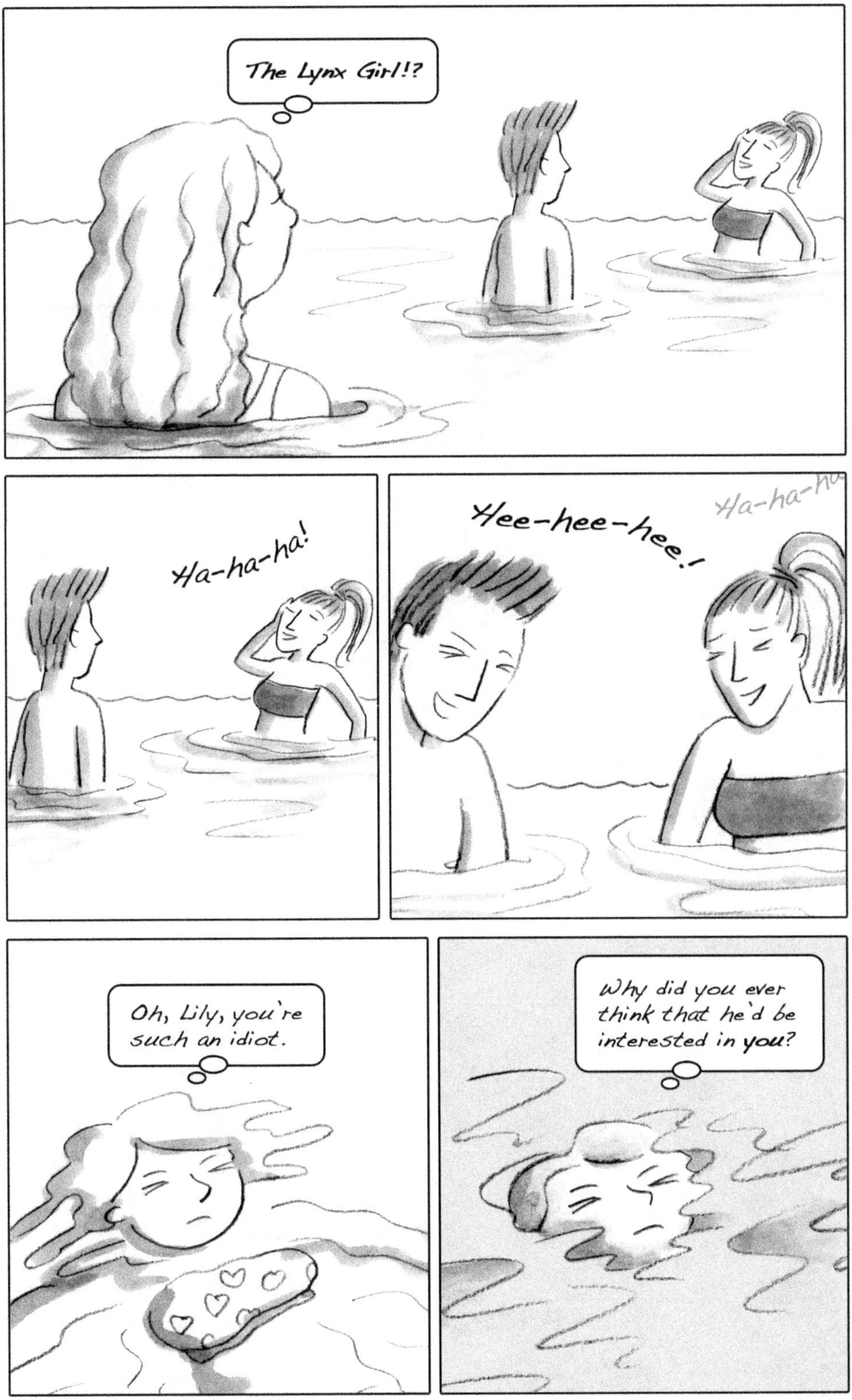

The Lynx Girl!?
Ha-ha-ha!
Hee-hee-hee!
Ha-ha-ha
Oh, Lily, you're such an idiot.
Why did you ever think that he'd be interested in you?

WELCOME TO...

THE COMPARE AND DESPAIR GAME

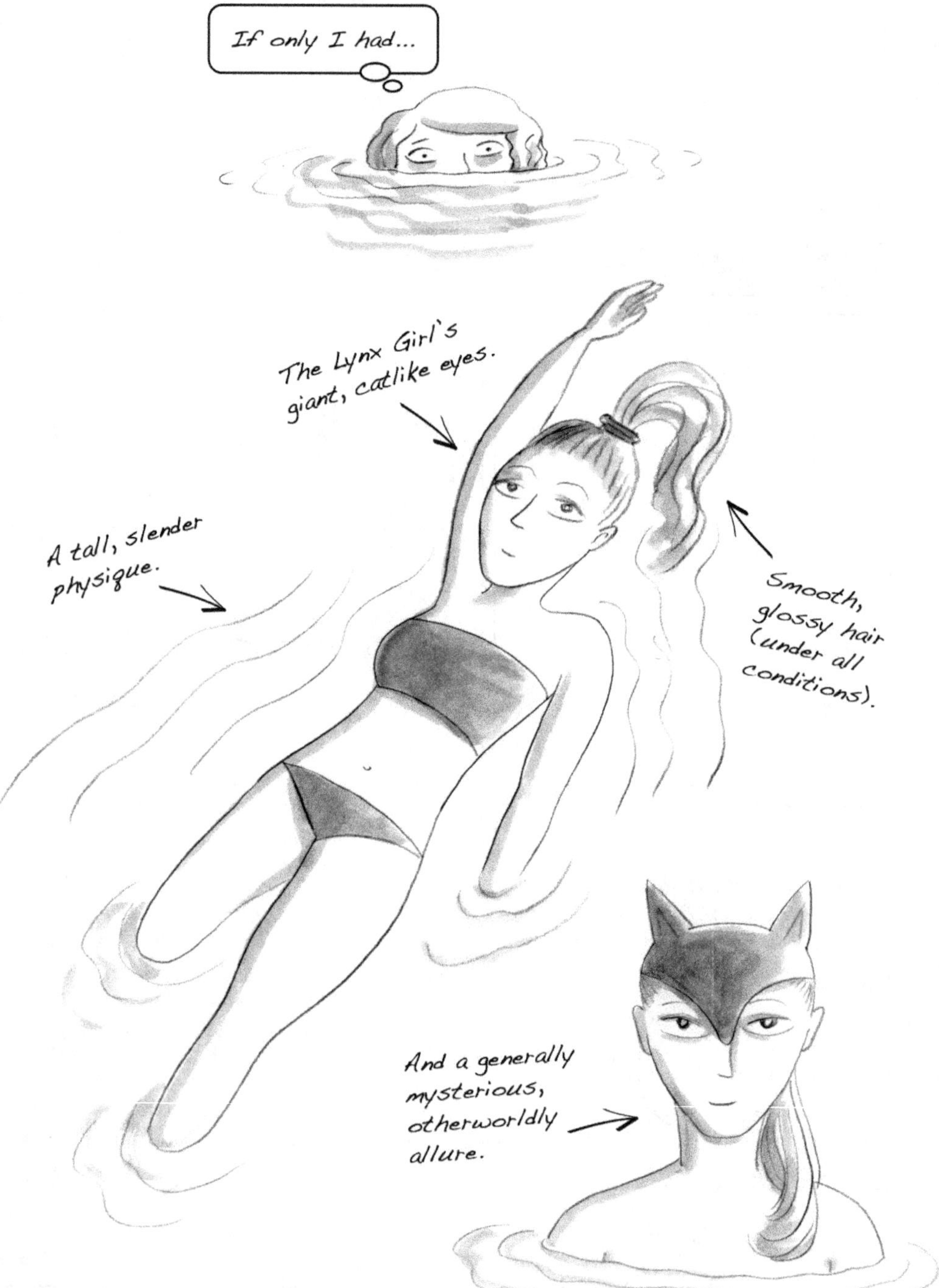
If only I had...
The Lynx Girl's giant, catlike eyes.
A tall, slender physique.
Smooth, glossy hair (under all conditions).
And a generally mysterious, otherworldly allure.

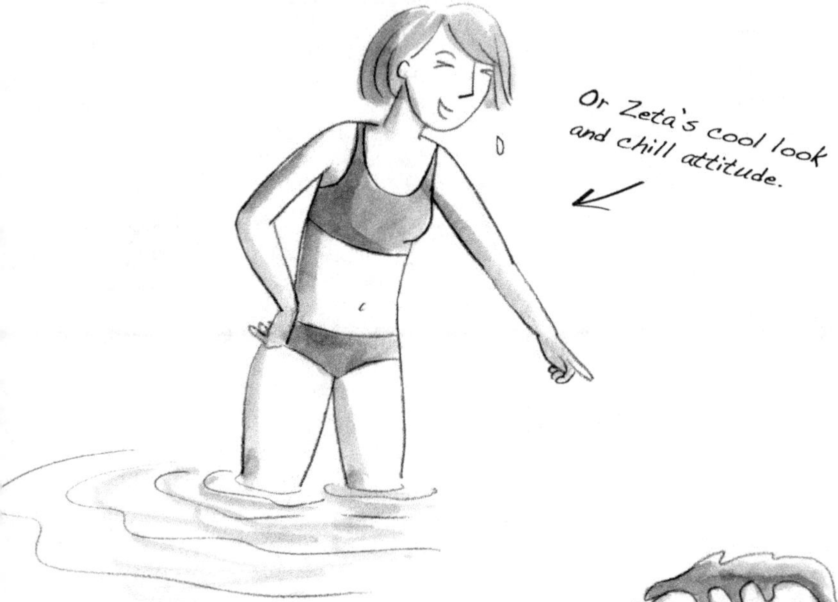
Or Zeta's cool look
and chill attitude.

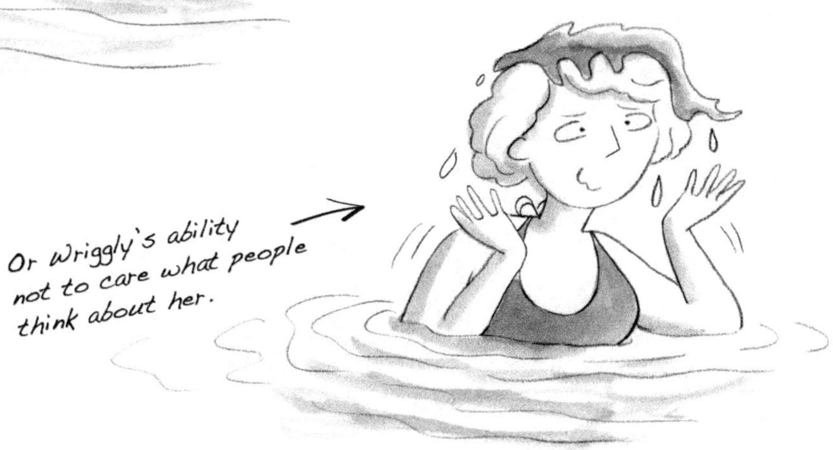
Or Wriggly's ability
not to care what people
think about her.

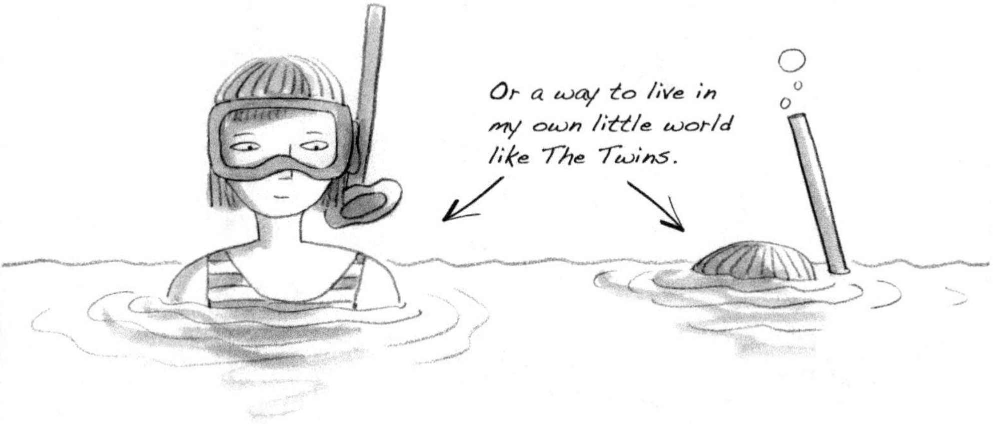
Or a way to live in
my own little world
like The Twins.

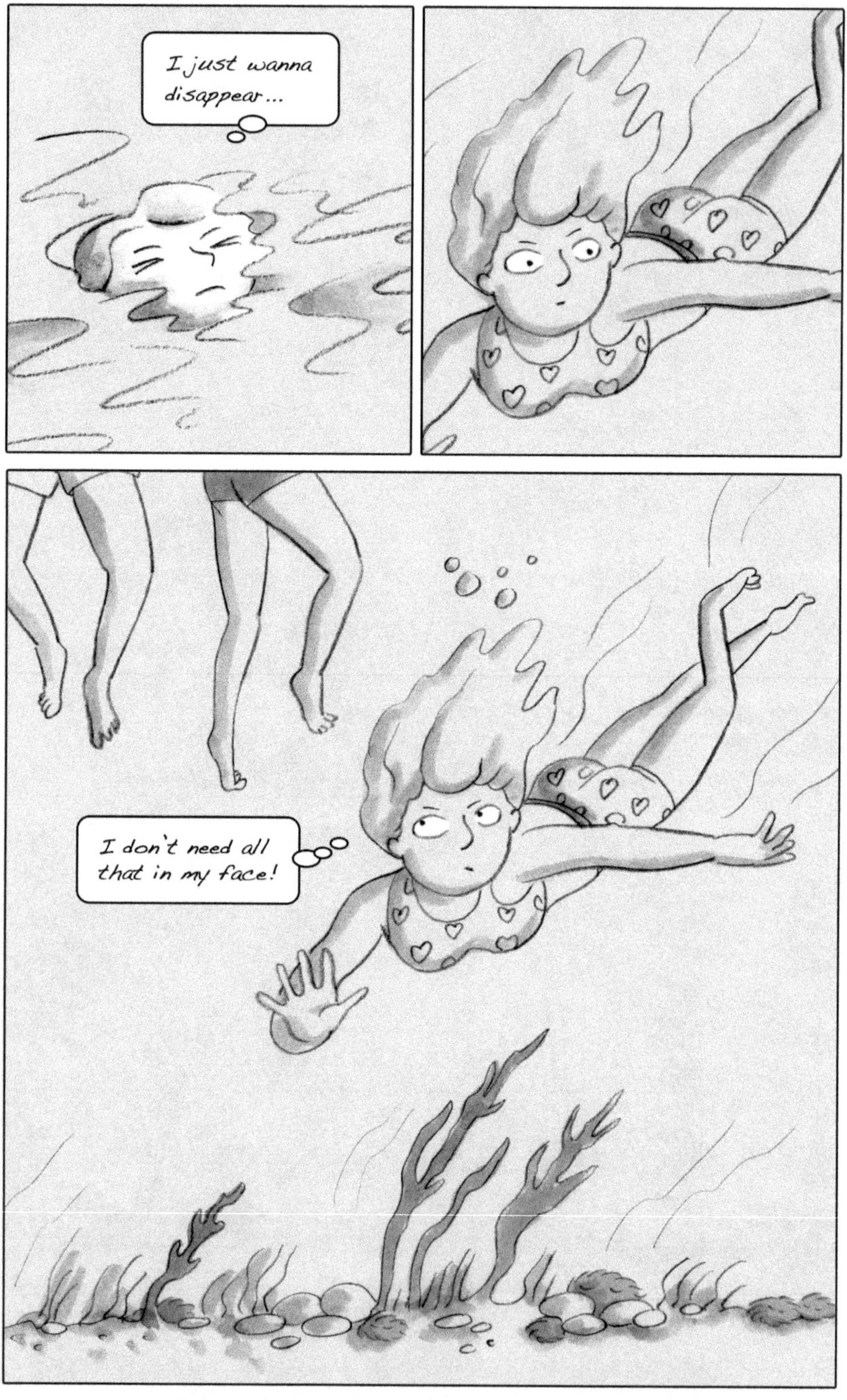
I just wanna disappear...
I don't need all that in my face!

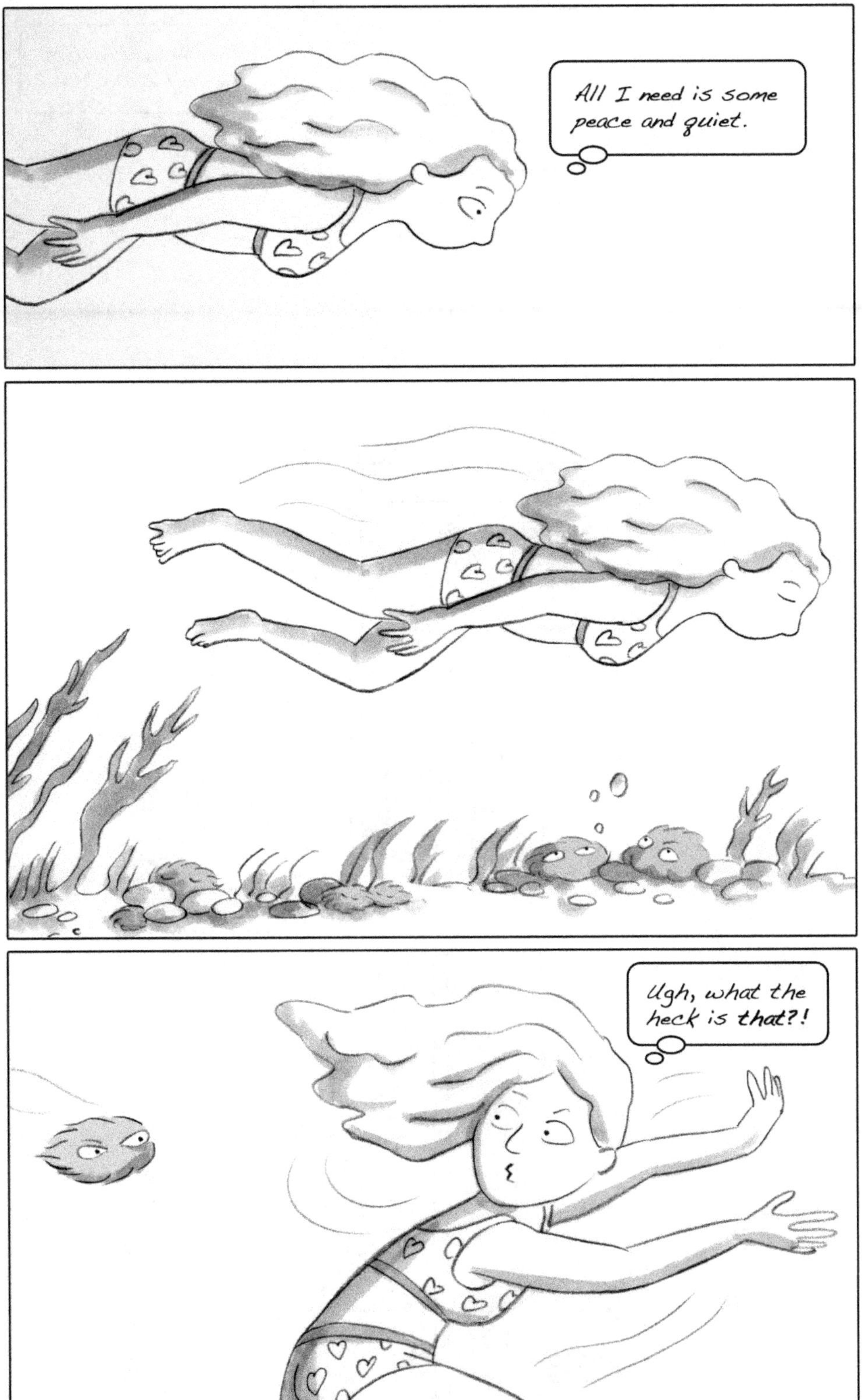
All I need is some peace and quiet.
Ugh, what the heck is that?!

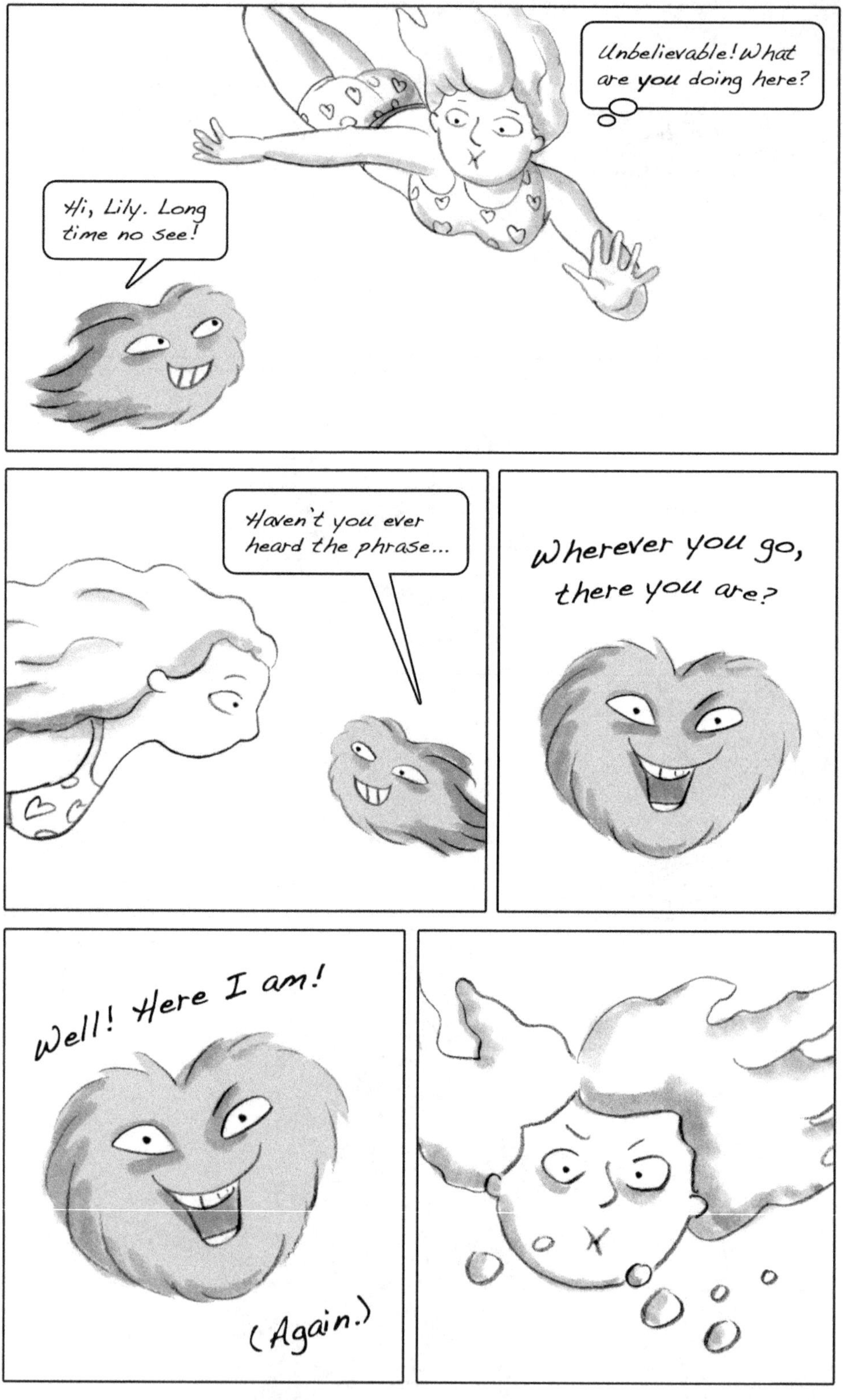

Unbelievable! What are you doing here?
Hi, Lily. Long time no see!
Haven't you ever heard the phrase...
Wherever you go, there you are?
Well! Here I am!
(Again.)

Oh, no. No way. This is nuts.
I'm outta here!
OK, bye then. But just FYI...
That swimsuit's really not doing you any favors!

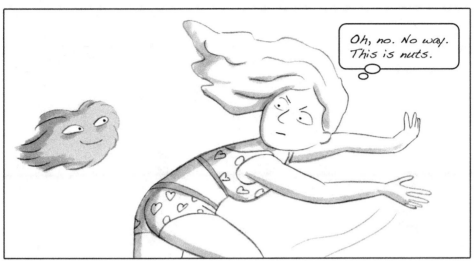

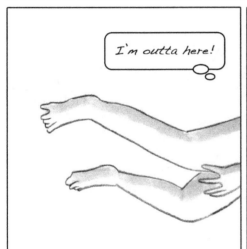

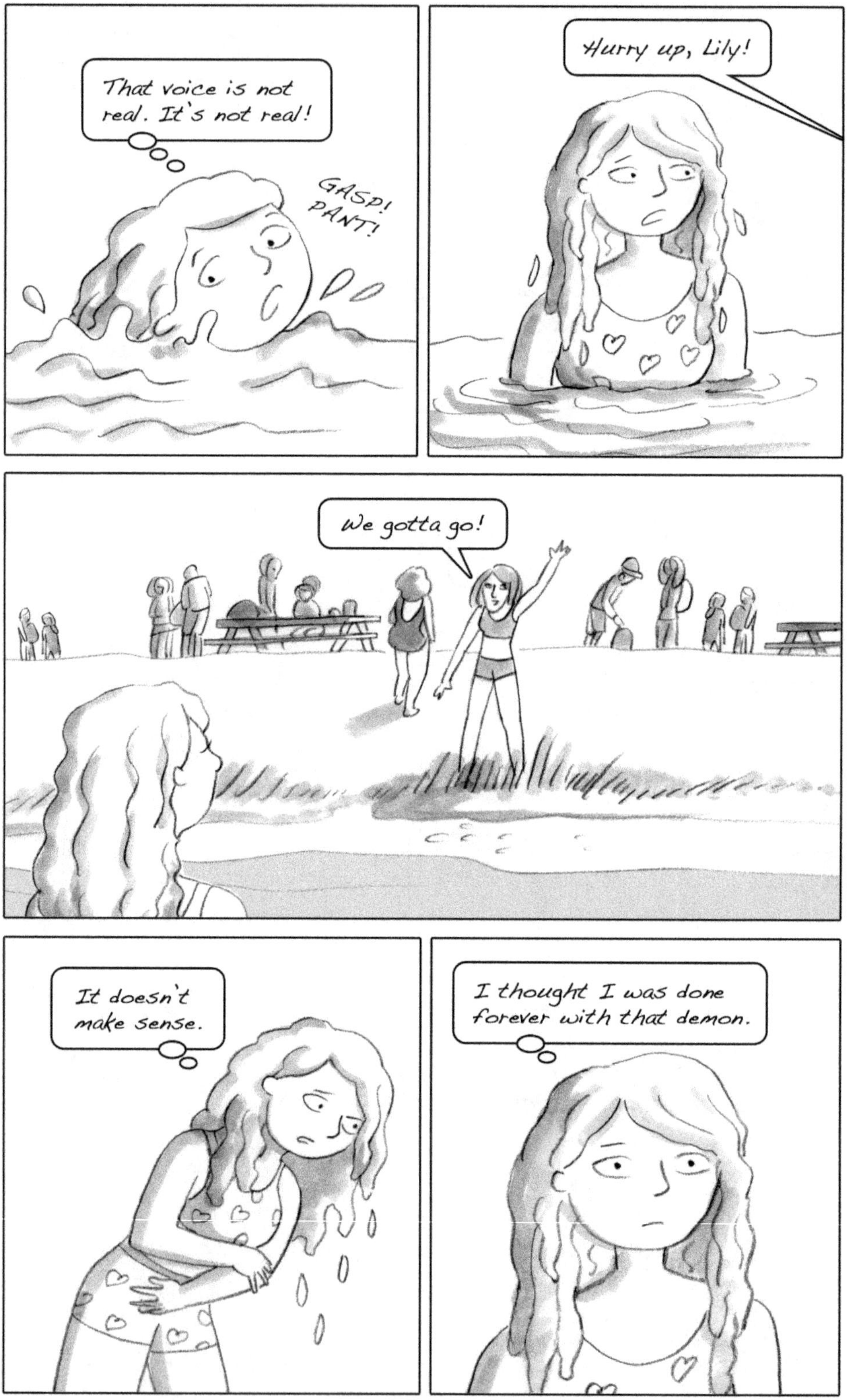
That voice is not real. It's not real!
GASP! PANT!
Hurry up, Lily!
We gotta go!
It doesn't make sense.
I thought I was done forever with that demon.

I was free! I felt good!

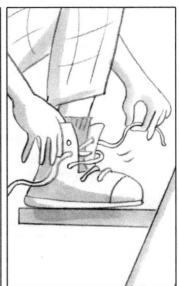

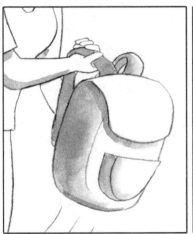

Things were going pretty well, right?

Until I started comparing myself to others.

And wishing I were different.

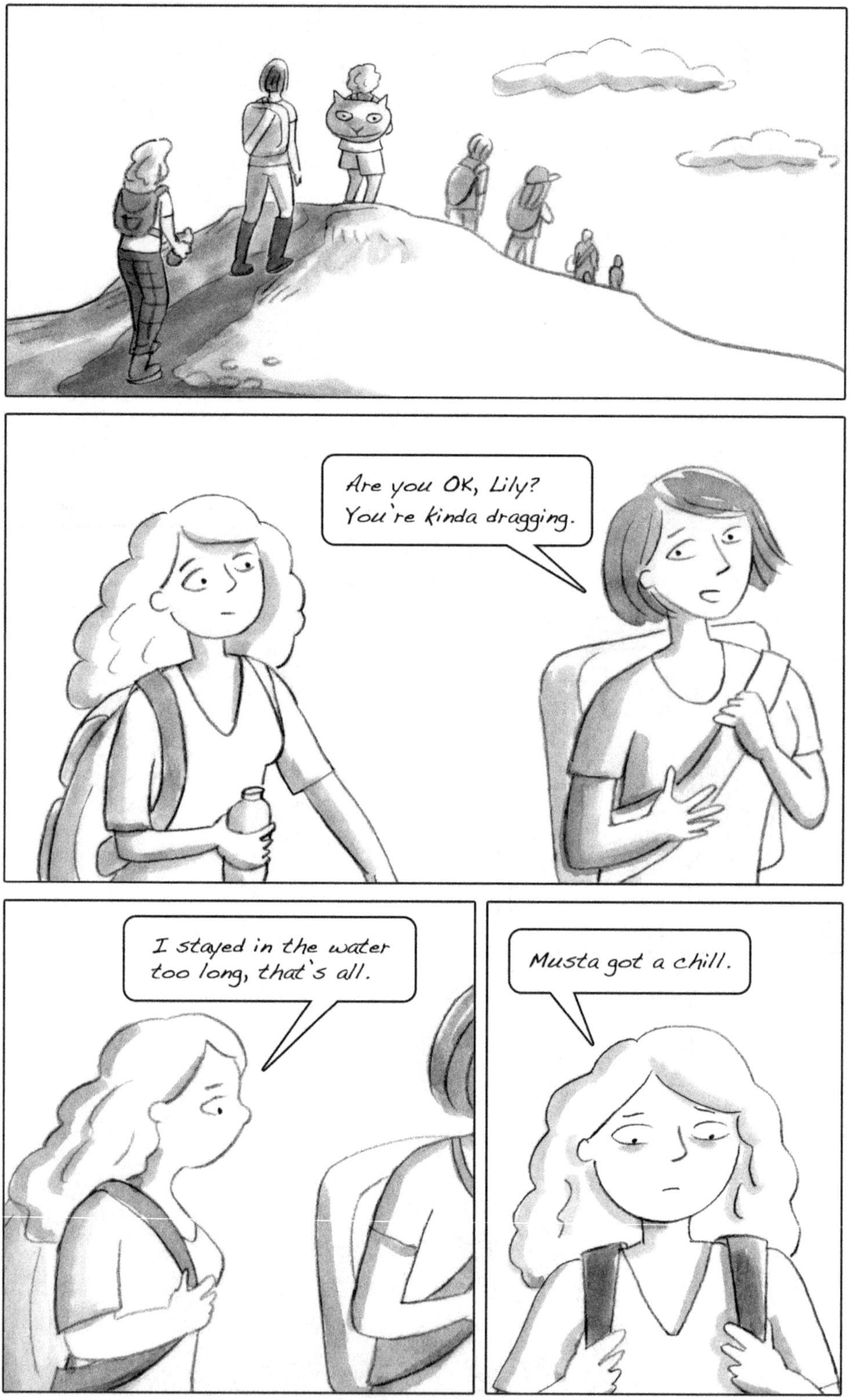
Are you OK, Lily? You're kinda dragging.
I stayed in the water too long, that's all.
Musta got a chill.

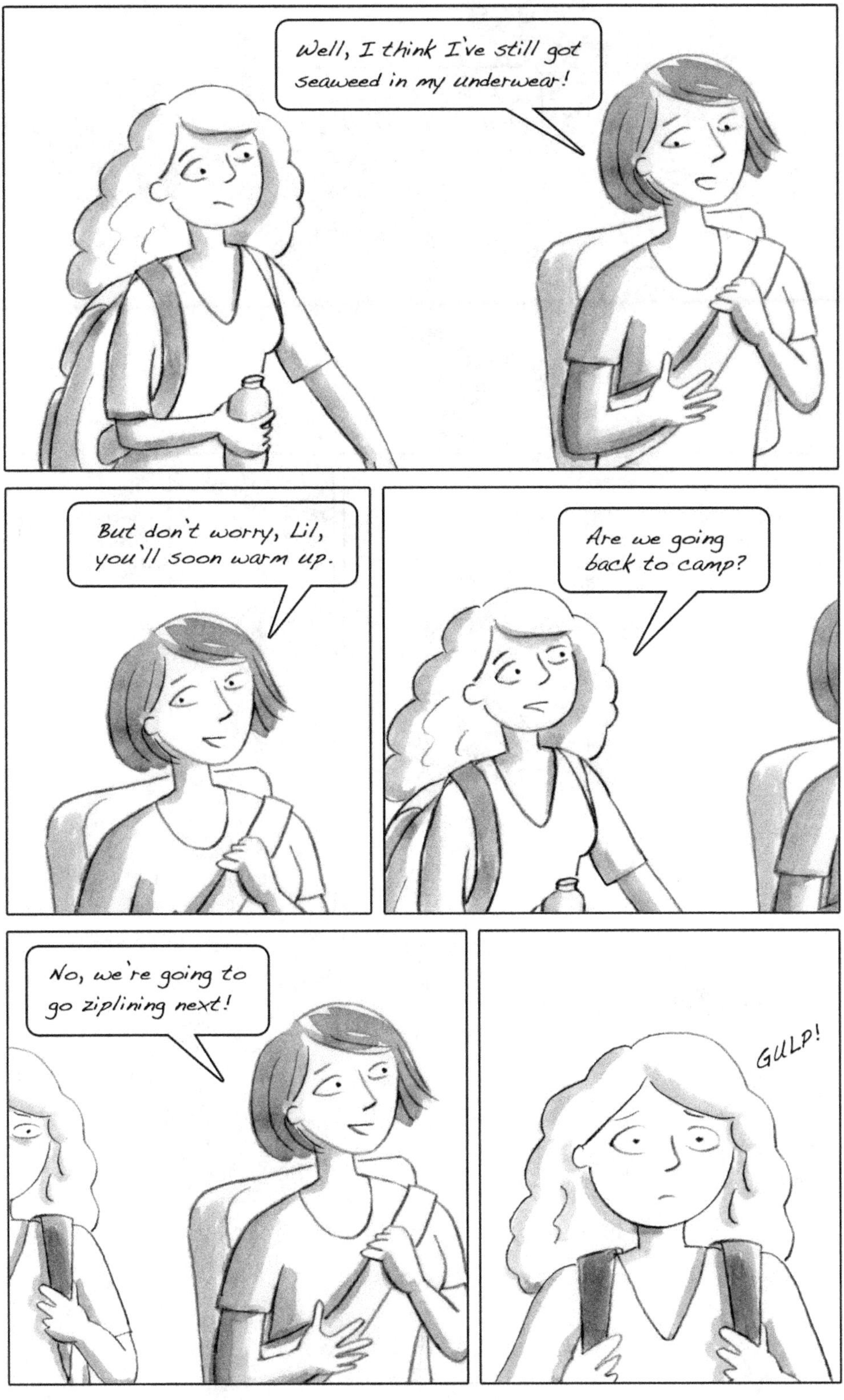
Well, I think I've still got seaweed in my underwear!
But don't worry, Lil, you'll soon warm up.
Are we going back to camp?
No, we're going to go ziplining next!
GULP!

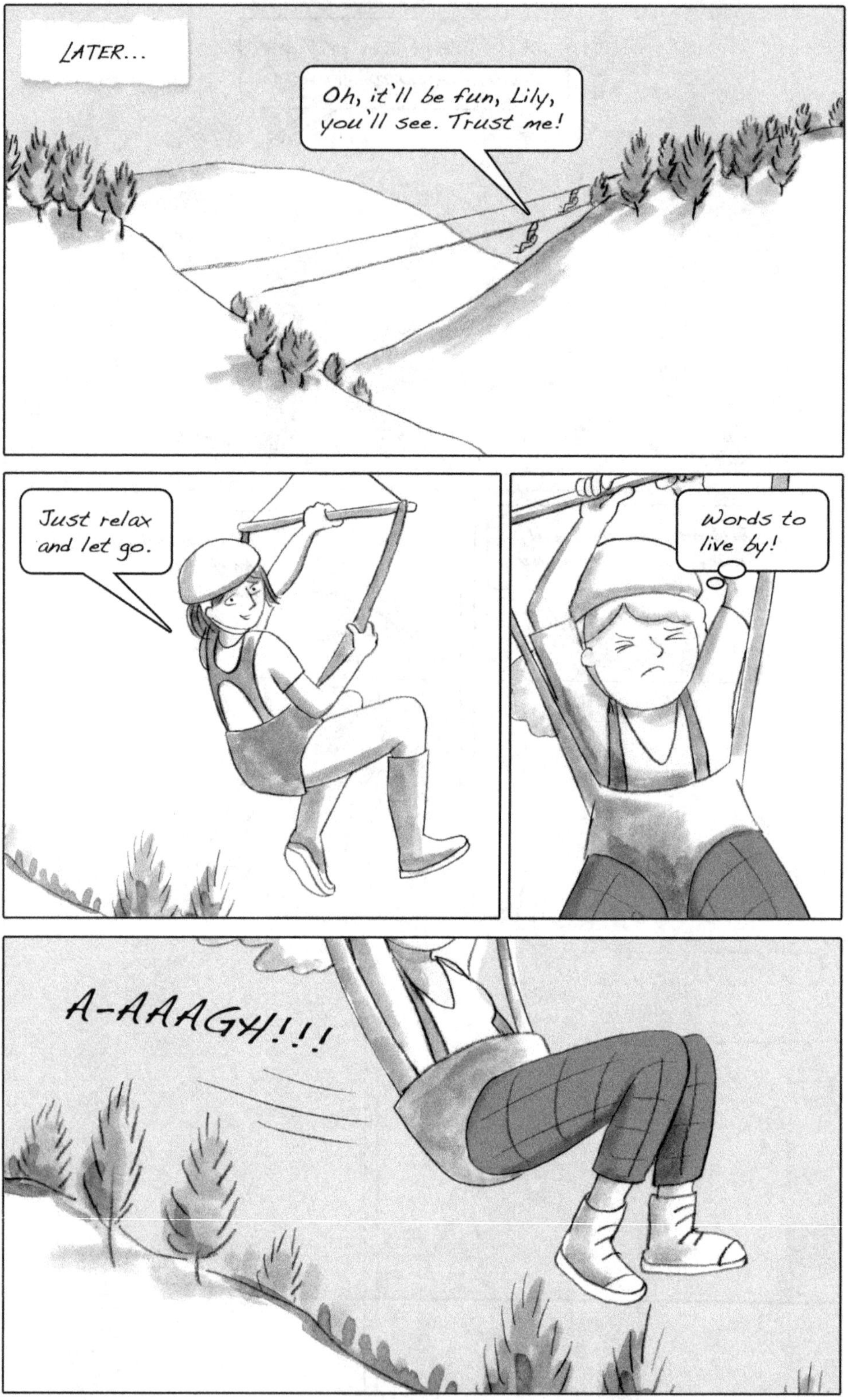
LATER...
Oh, it'll be fun, Lily, you'll see. Trust me!
Just relax and let go.
Words to live by!
A-AAAGH!!!

You can get the monkey
off your back, but the circus
never leaves town.

ANNE LAMOTT

WEDNESDAY

Guess what? The identical princesses opted to go to the lake today. I'm sure they'll be observing aquatic species. NOT!!

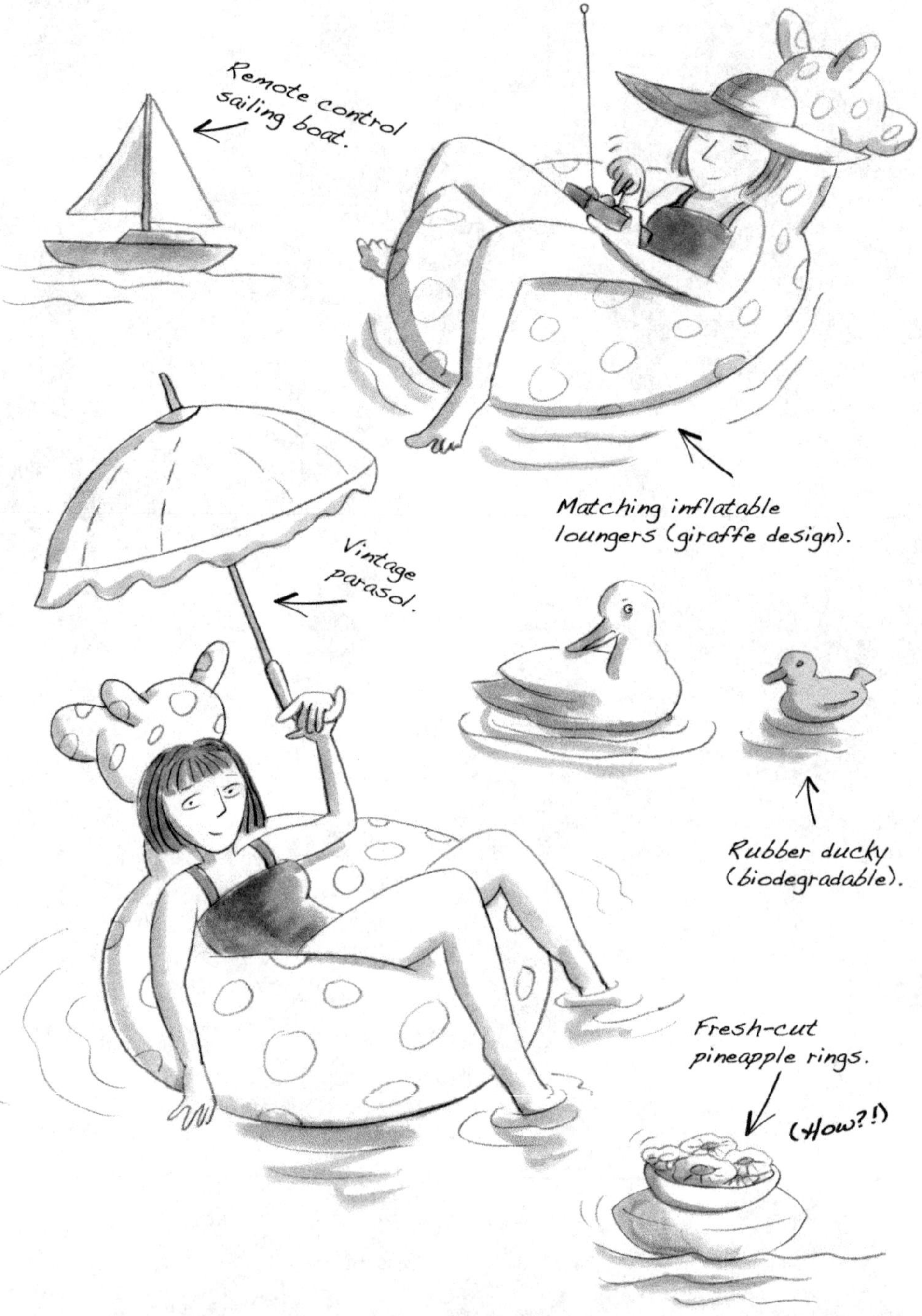
Remote control sailing boat.
Matching inflatable loungers (giraffe design).
Vintage parasol.
Rubber ducky (biodegradable).
Fresh-cut pineapple rings.
(How?!)

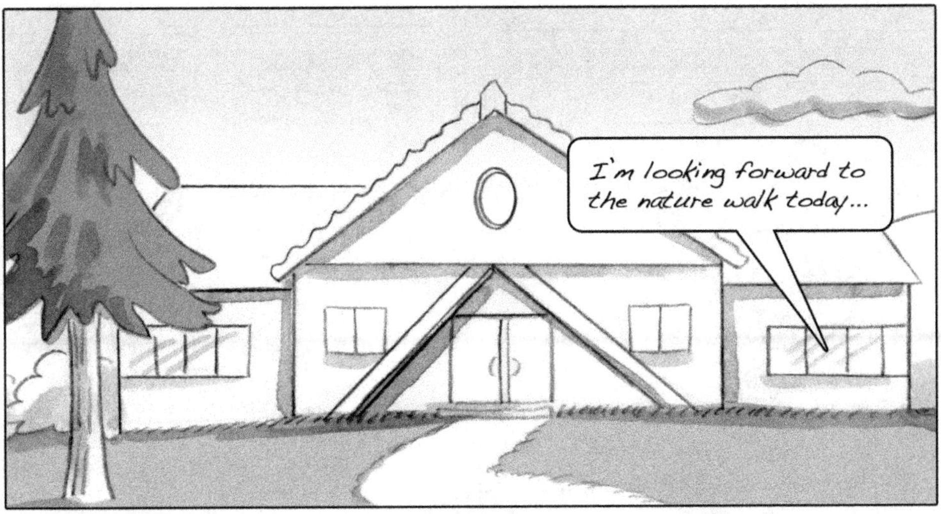
I'm looking forward to the nature walk today...

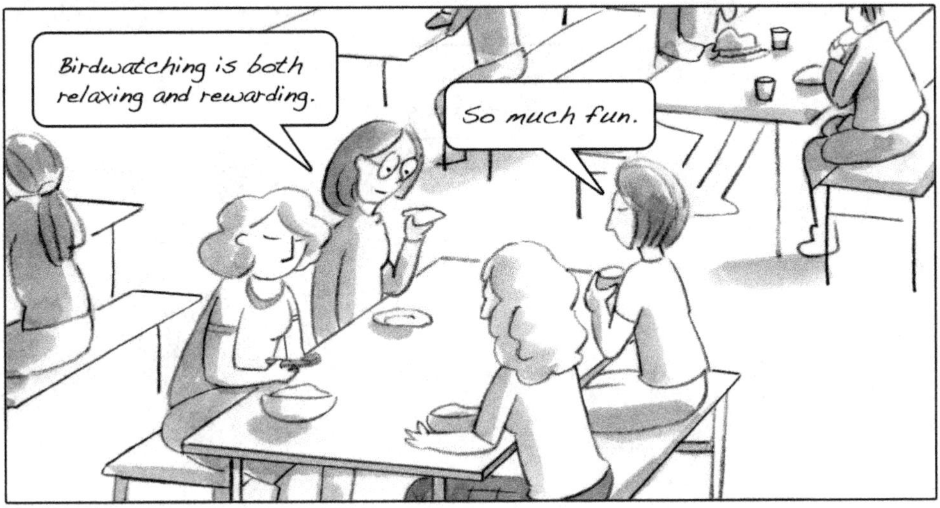
Birdwatching is both relaxing and rewarding.
So much fun.

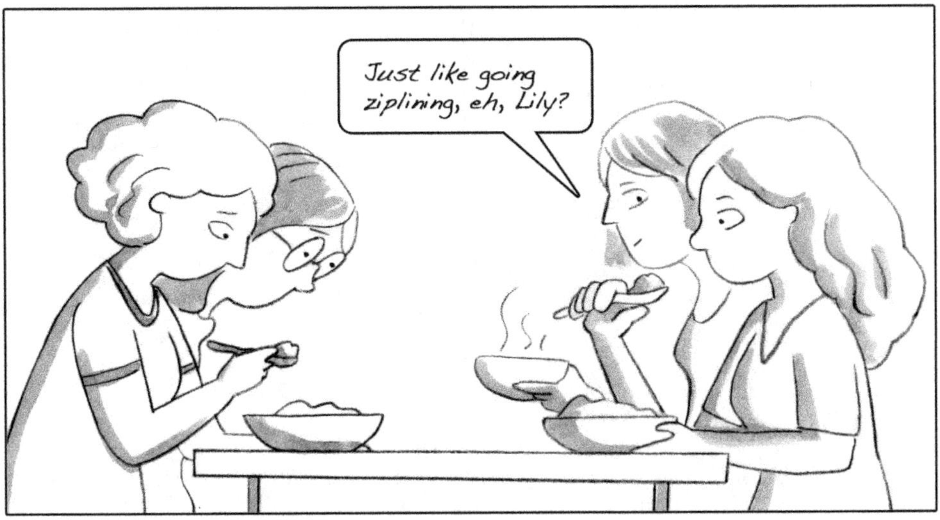
Just like going ziplining, eh, Lily?

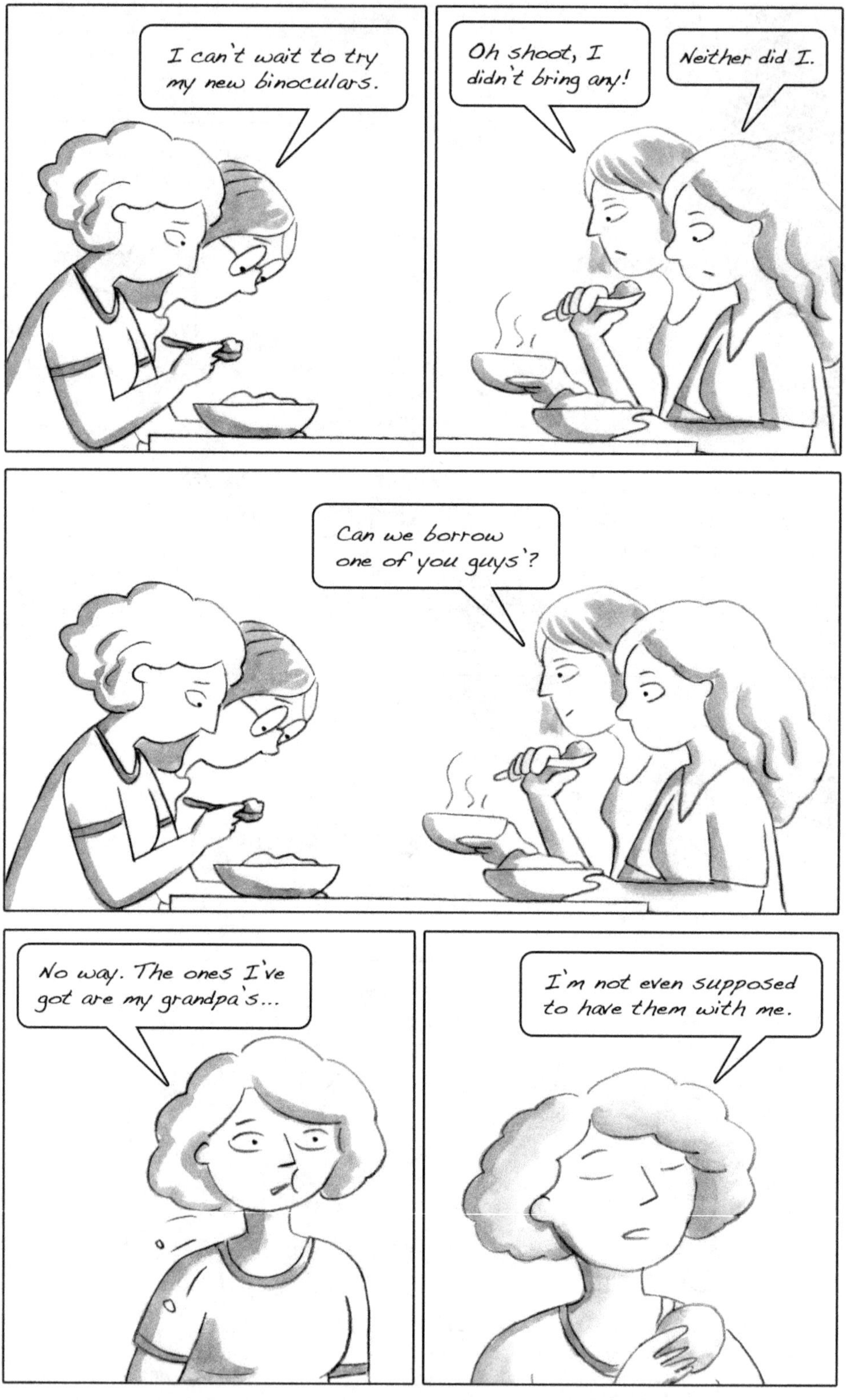
I can't wait to try my new binoculars.
Oh shoot, I didn't bring any!
Neither did I.
Can we borrow one of you guys'?
No way. The ones I've got are my grandpa's...
I'm not even supposed to have them with me.

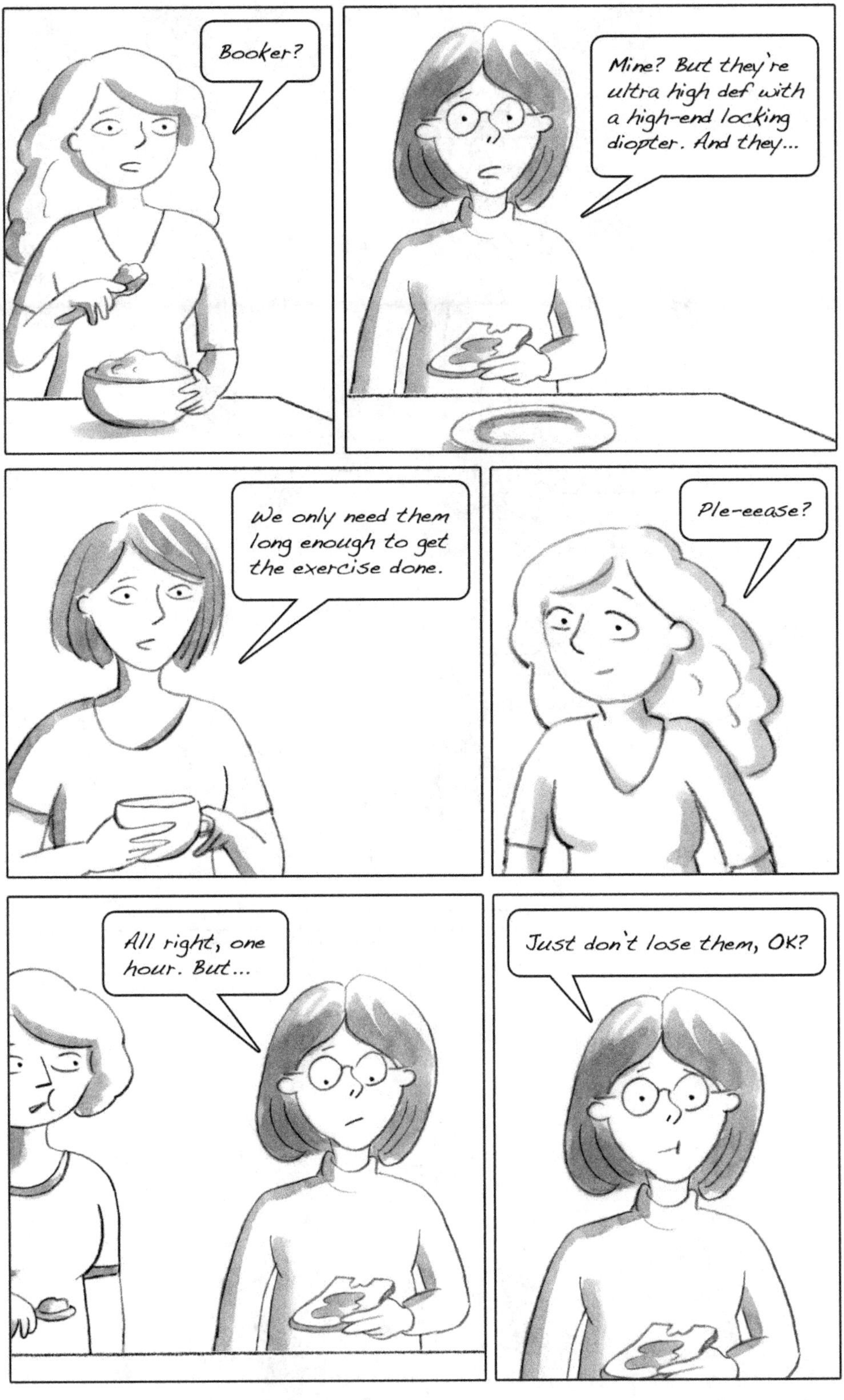
Booker?
Mine? But they're ultra high def with a high-end locking diopter. And they...
We only need them long enough to get the exercise done.
Ple-eease?
All right, one hour. But...
Just don't lose them, OK?

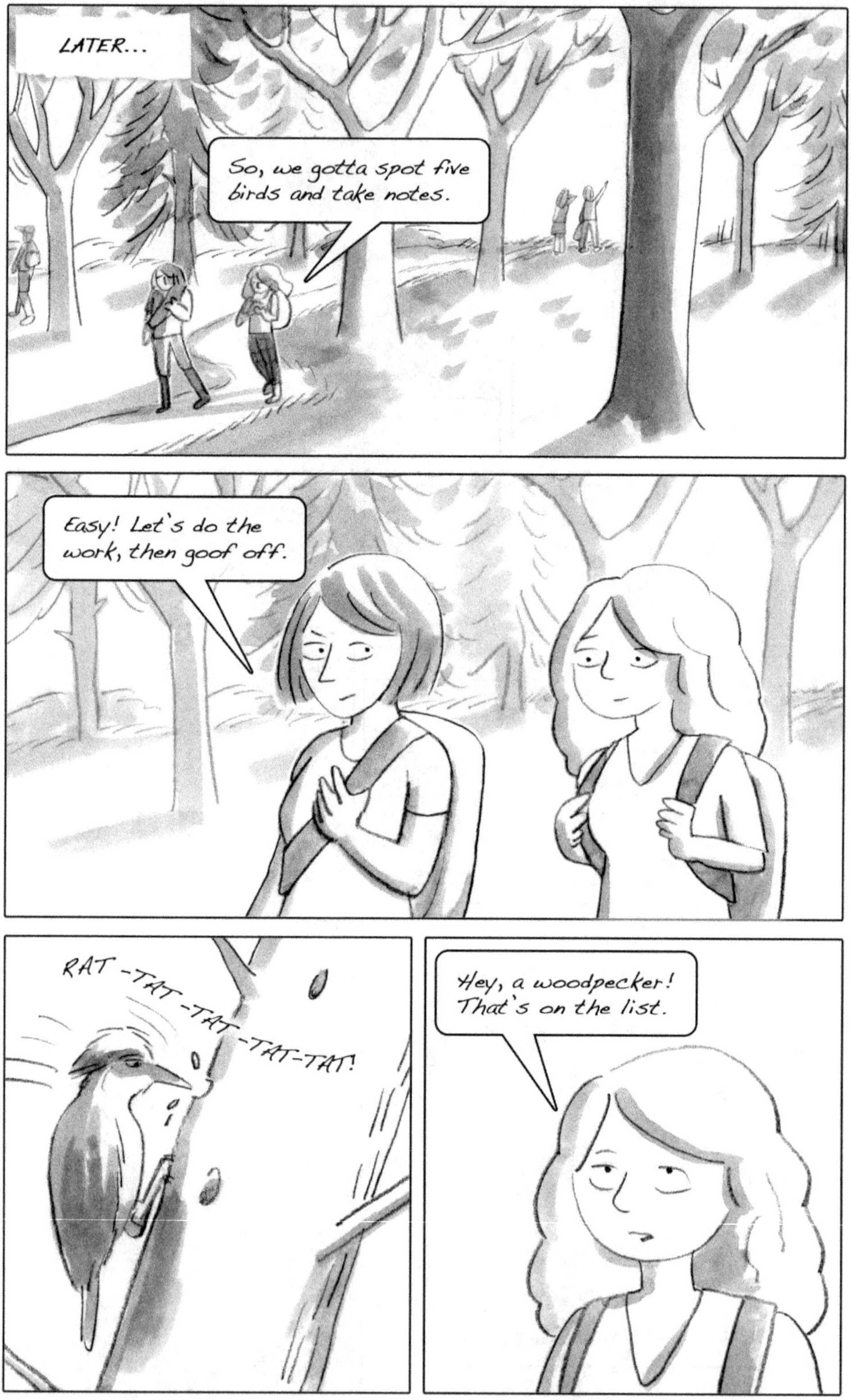
LATER...
So, we gotta spot five birds and take notes.
Easy! Let's do the work, then goof off.
RAT-TAT-TAT-TAT-TAT!
Hey, a woodpecker! That's on the list.

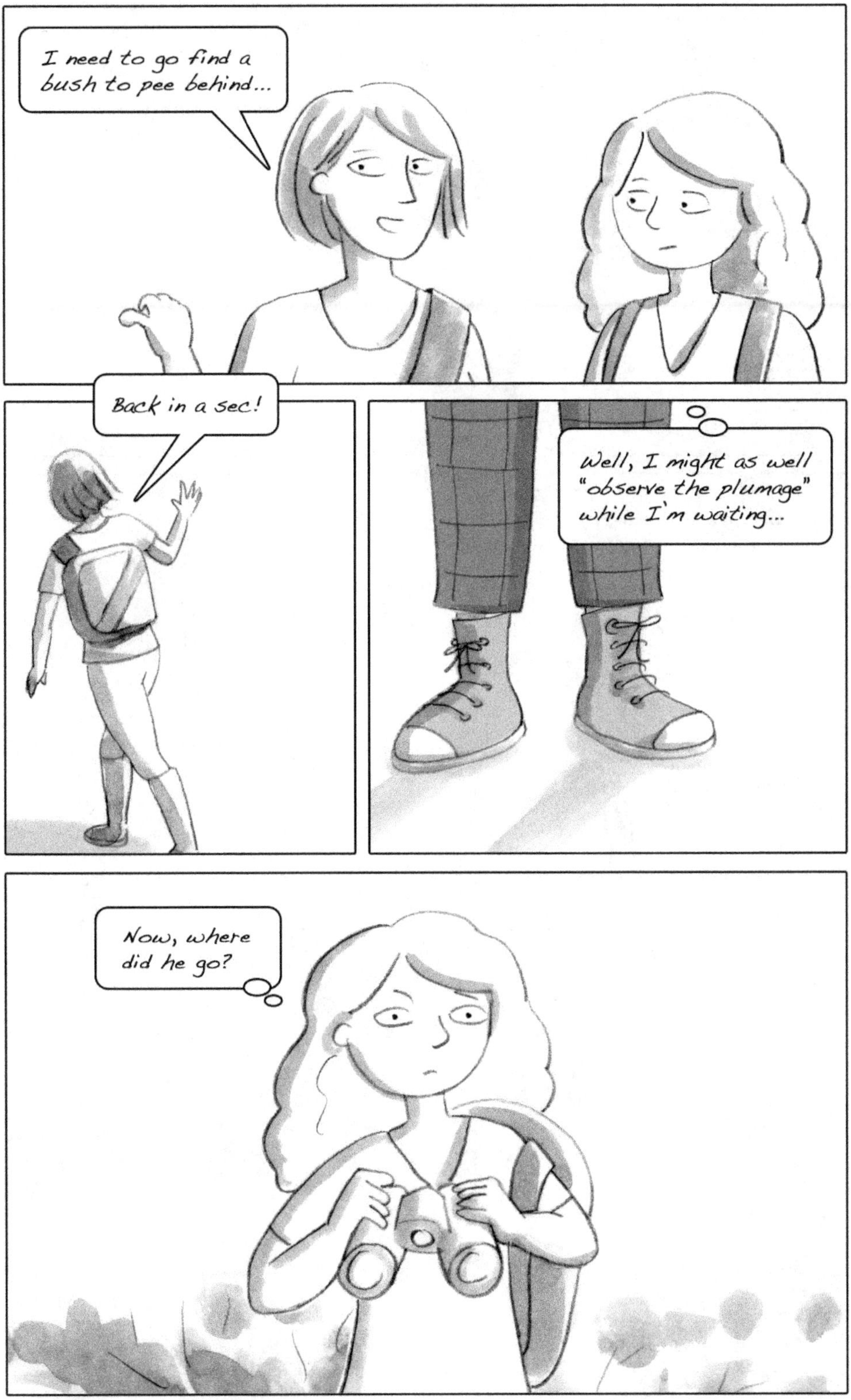
I need to go find a bush to pee behind...
Back in a sec!
Well, I might as well "observe the plumage" while I'm waiting...
Now, where did he go?

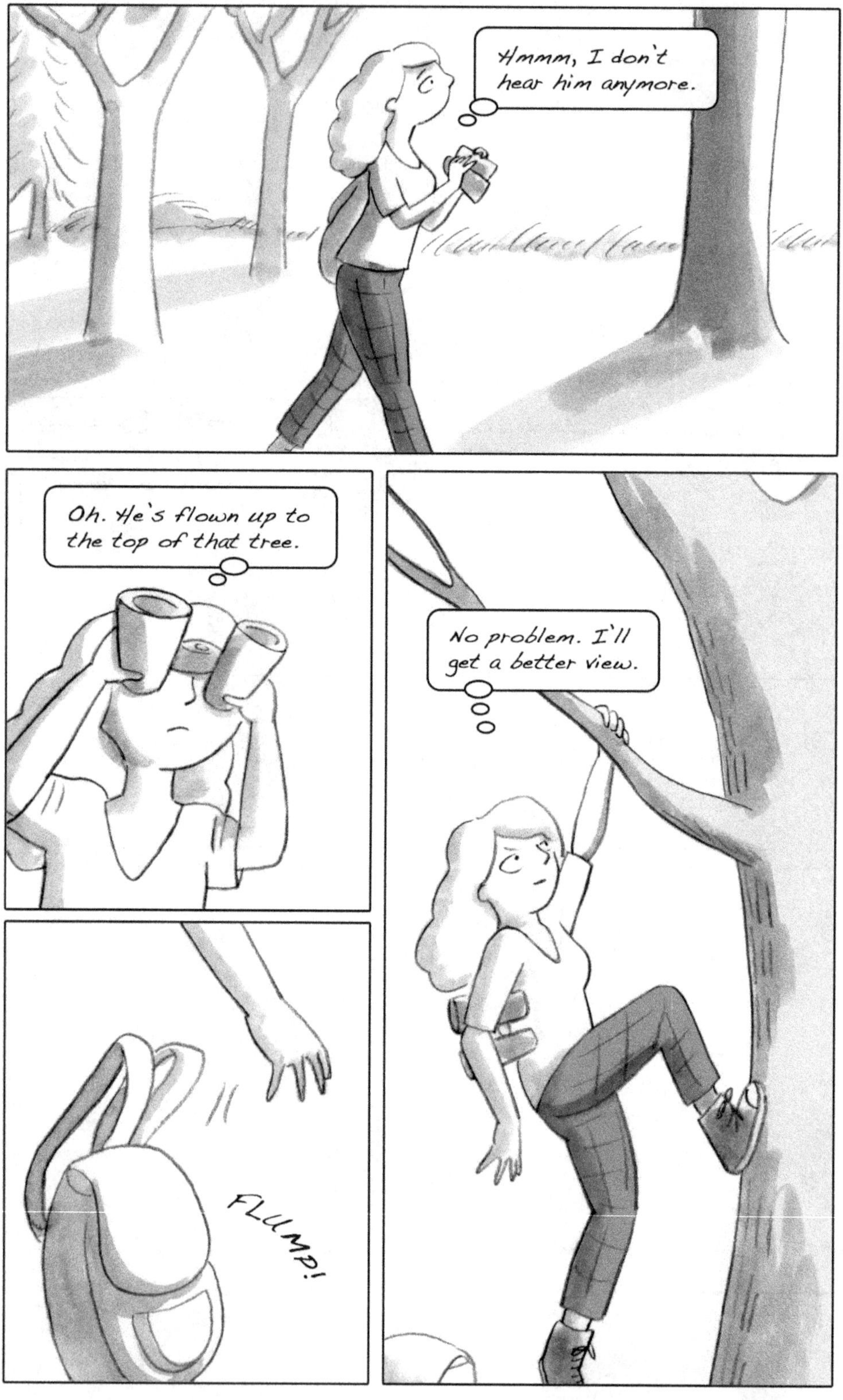
Hmmm, I don't hear him anymore.
Oh. He's flown up to the top of that tree.
No problem. I'll get a better view.
FLUMP!

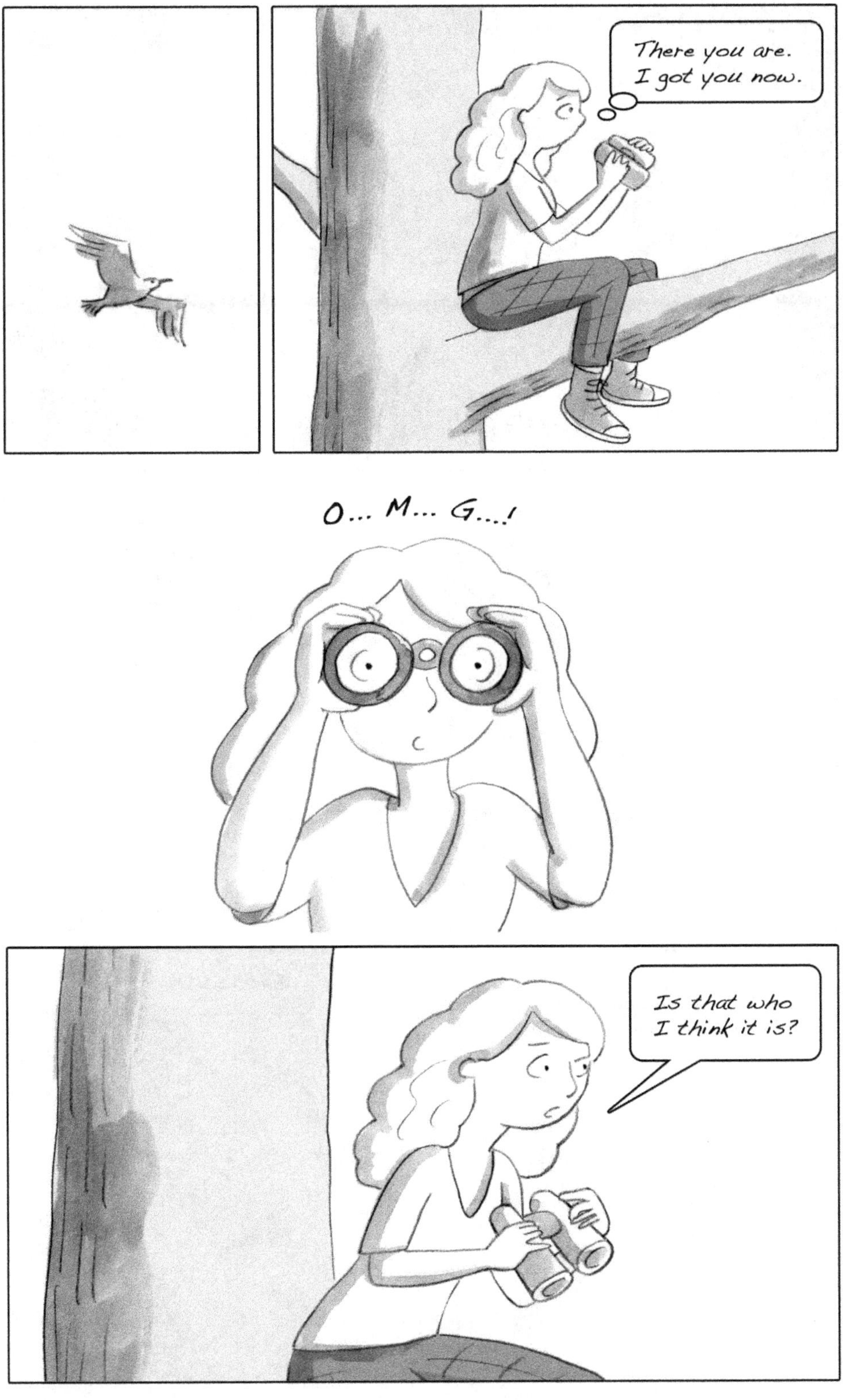
There you are.
I got you now.
O... M... G...!
Is that who
I think it is?

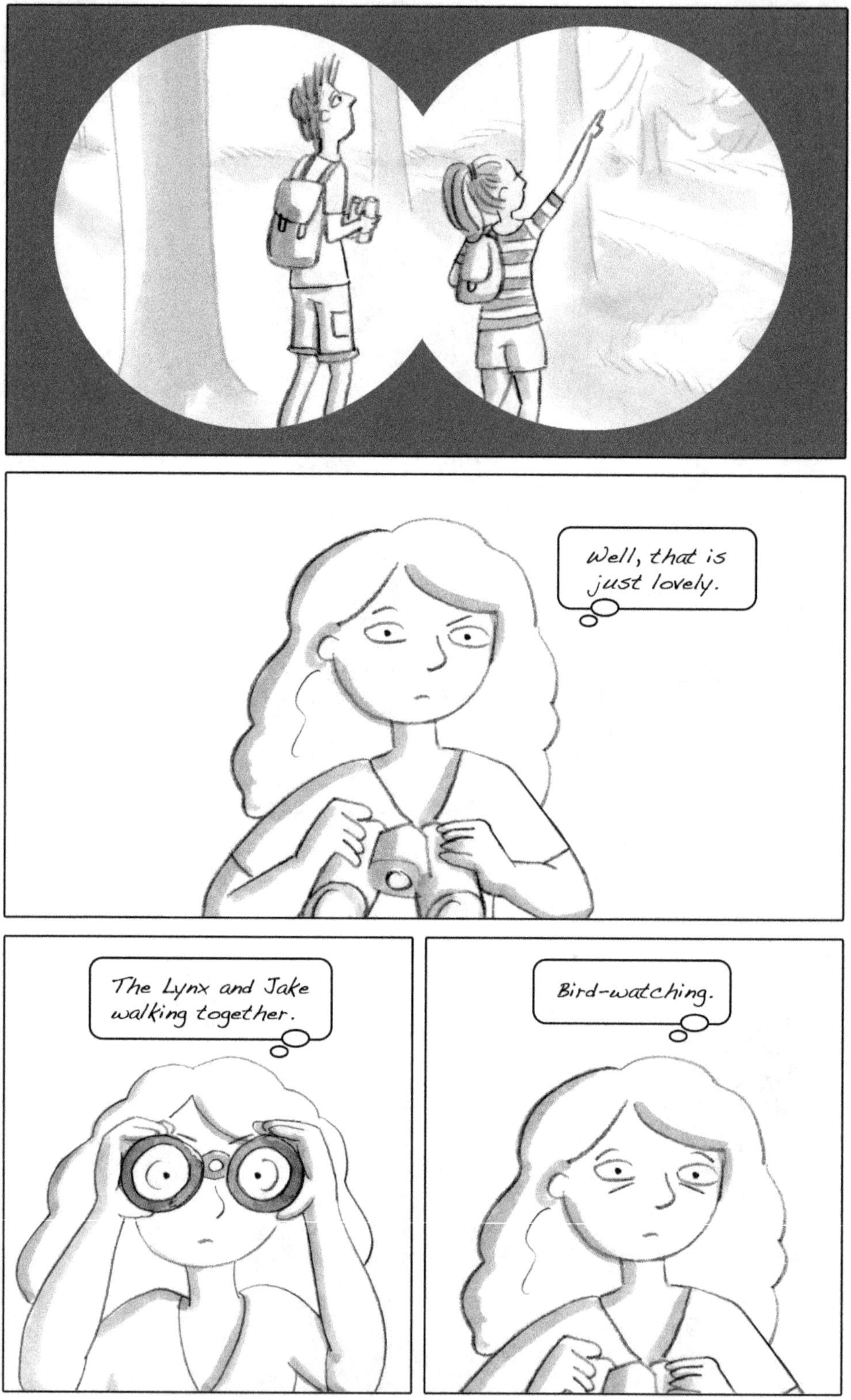
Well, that is just lovely.
The Lynx and Jake walking together.
Bird-watching.

Spotted: lovebirds.

OK, don't be ridiculous, Lily! I'm sure there's a perfectly rational explanation. There's an odd number of girls and boys and we had to pair up with SOMEONE. It was random that Lynx Girl and Jake ended up with each other. You're being oversensitive!

They're just talking and walking. They're probably really bored. I didn't see them laughing or anything! If it were me and Jake, we'd be cracking up the whole time. We'd forget the assignment, lose track of time and get lost. And, putting my survival first, Jake'd give me his fruit.

Anyway, this is just a lousy SCIENCE TRIP...

And they've sure got *chemistry*, eh?

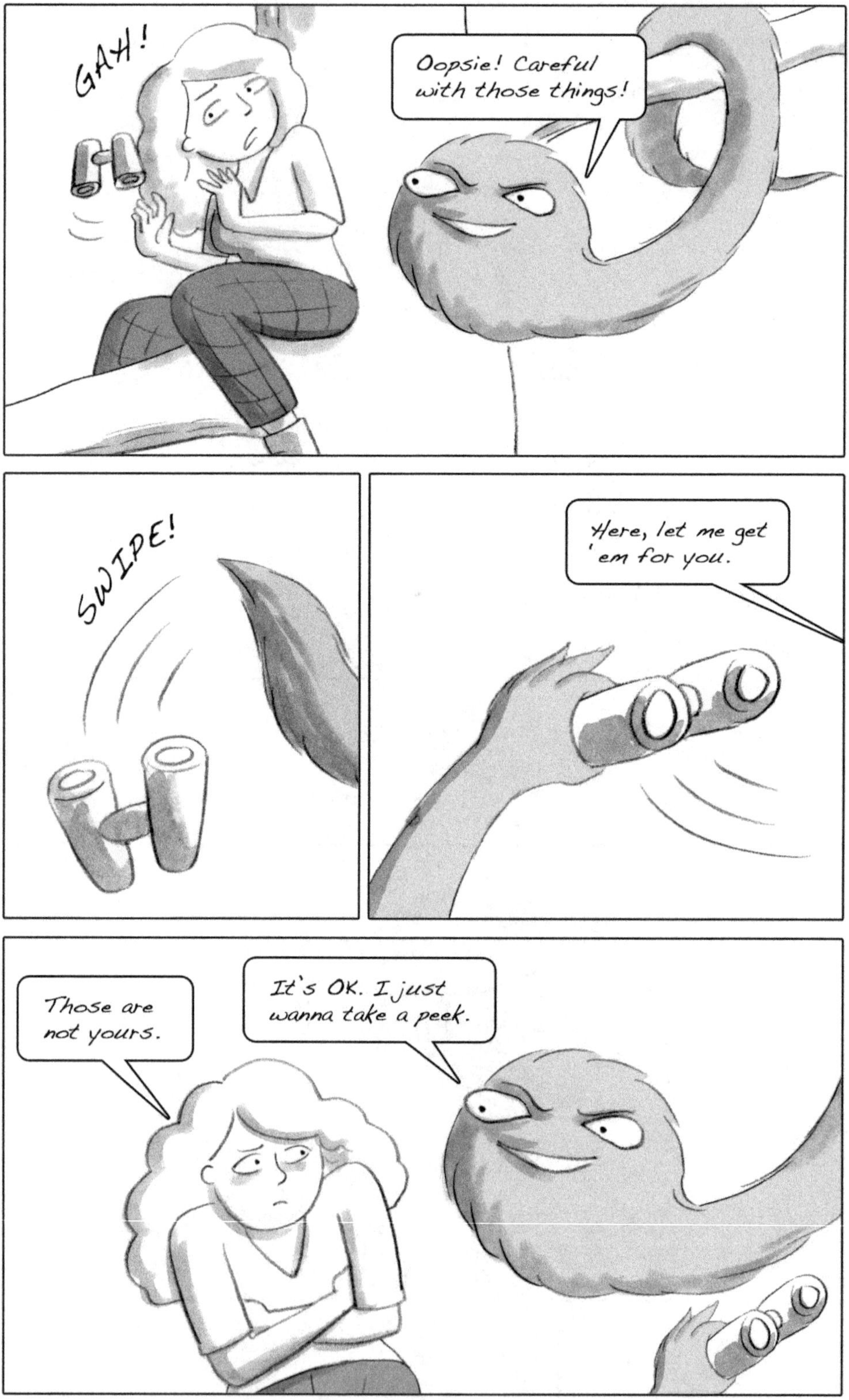
GAH!
Oopsie! Careful with those things!
SWIPE!
Here, let me get 'em for you.
Those are not yours.
It's OK. I just wanna take a peek.

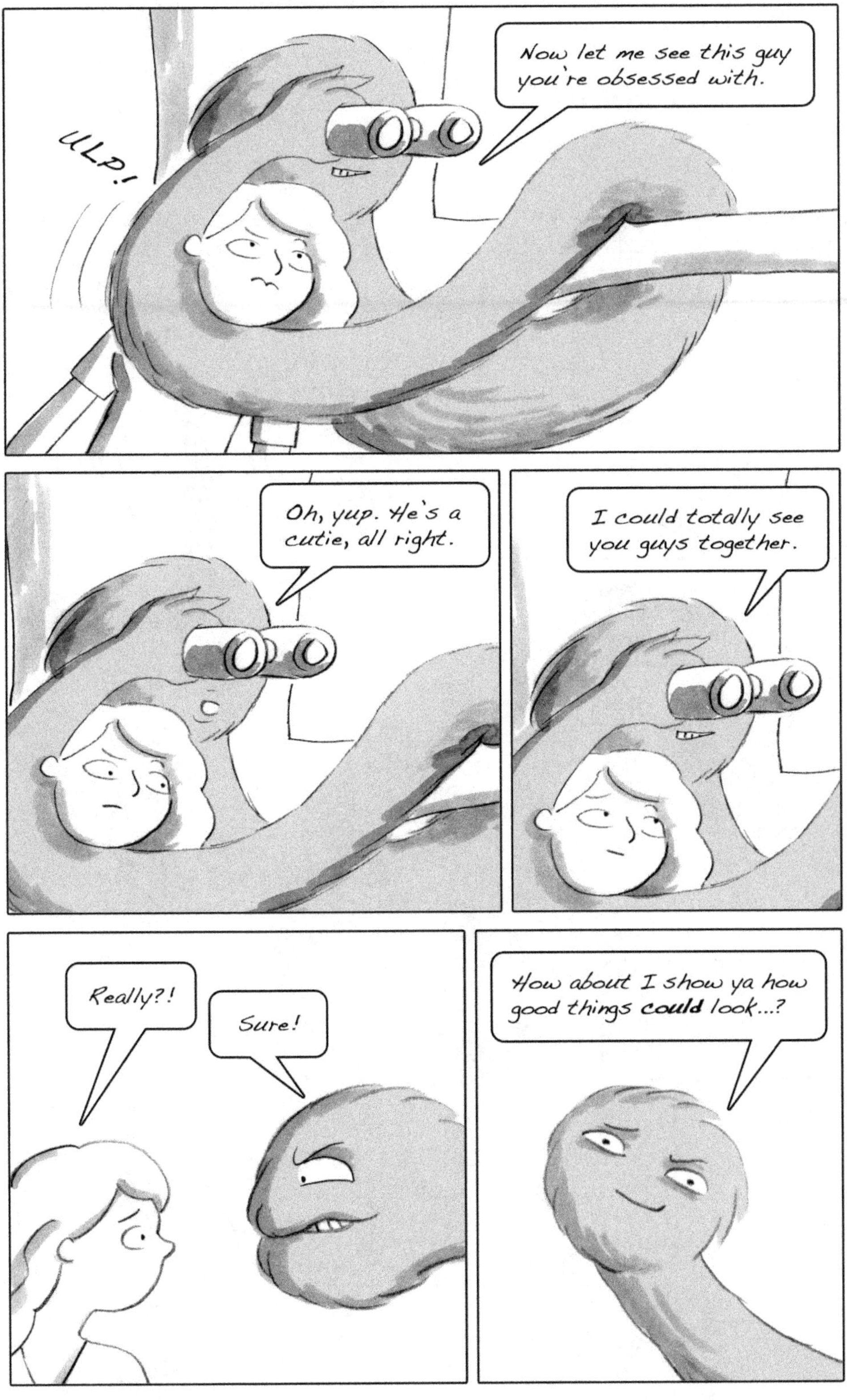
ULP!
Now let me see this guy you're obsessed with.
Oh, yup. He's a cutie, all right.
I could totally see you guys together.
Really?!
Sure!
How about I show ya how good things **could** look...?

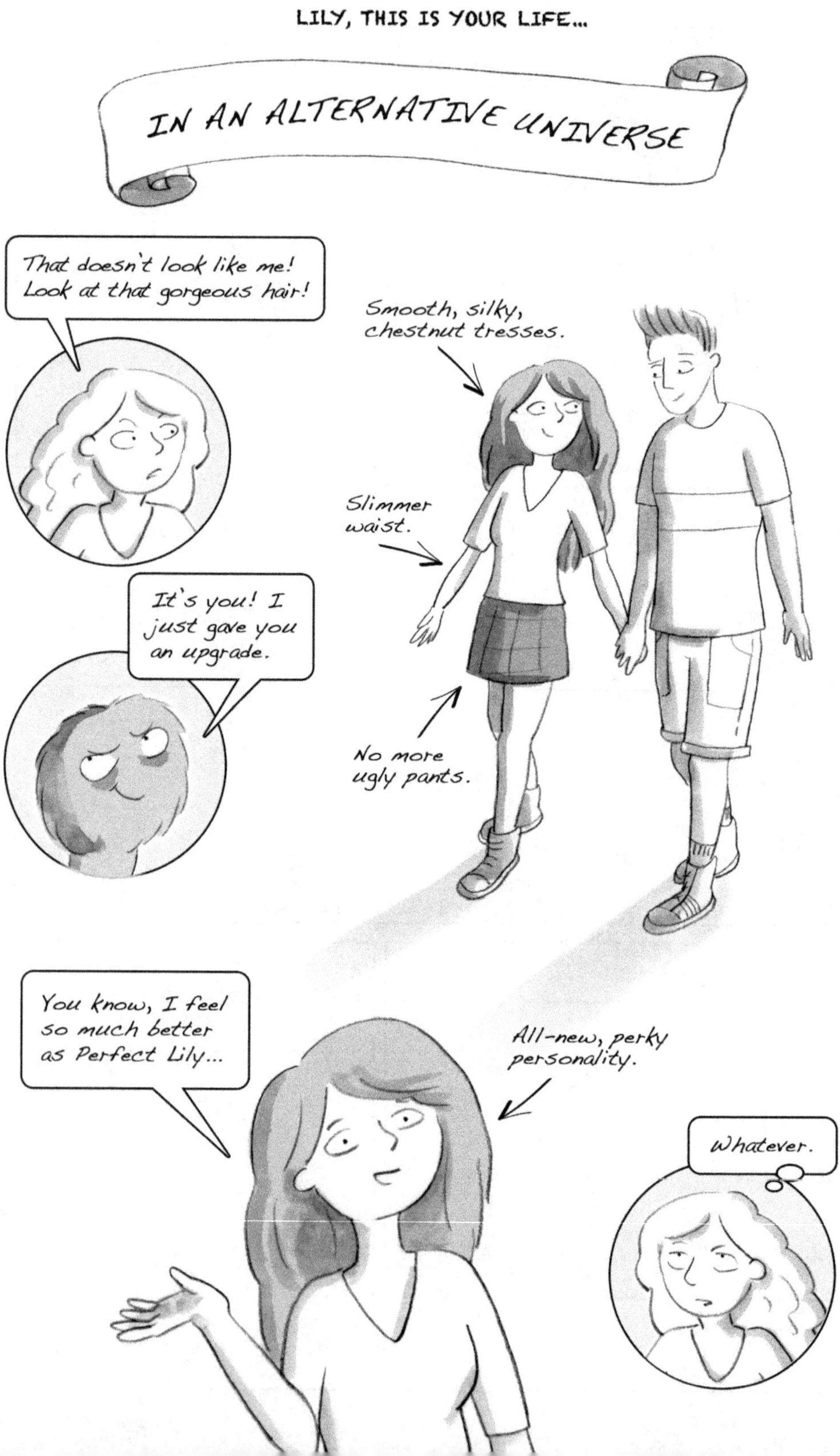
LILY, THIS IS YOUR LIFE...
IN AN ALTERNATIVE UNIVERSE
That doesn't look like me! Look at that gorgeous hair!
Smooth, silky, chestnut tresses.
Slimmer waist.
It's you! I just gave you an upgrade.
No more ugly pants.
You know, I feel so much better as Perfect Lily...
All-new, perky personality.
Whatever.

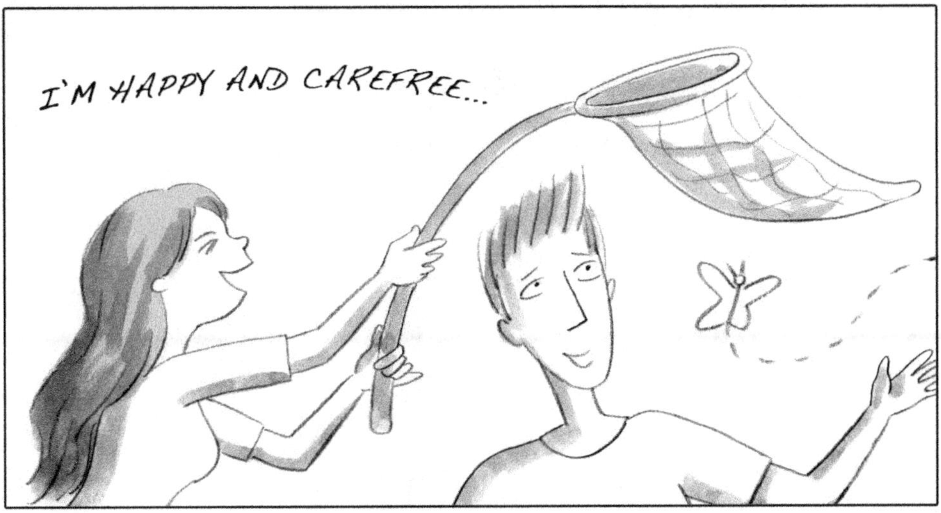
I'M HAPPY AND CAREFREE...

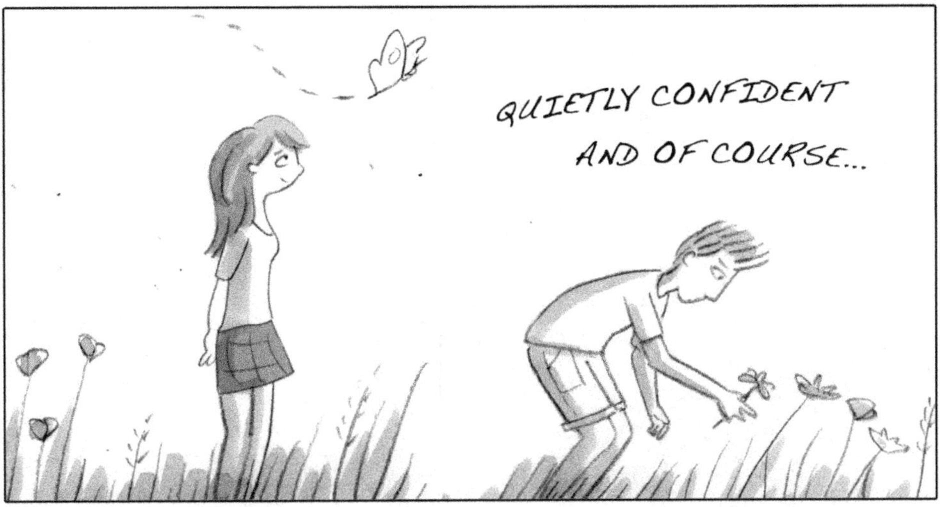
QUIETLY CONFIDENT
AND OF COURSE...

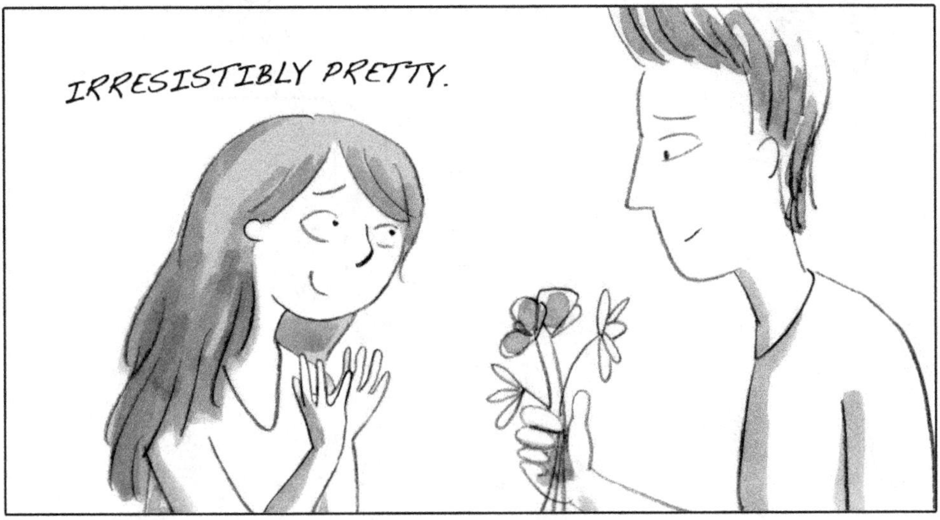
IRRESISTIBLY PRETTY.

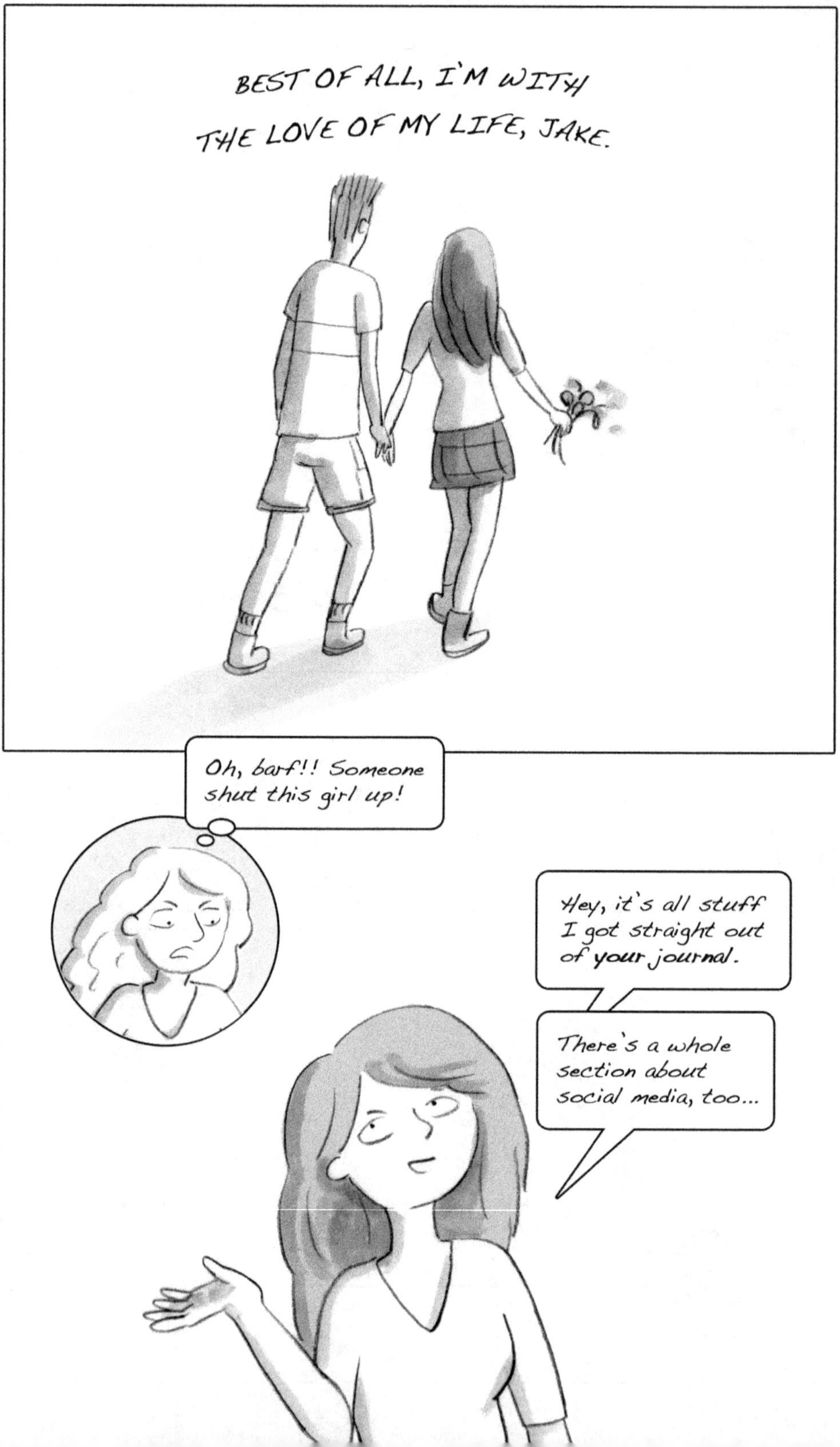
BEST OF ALL, I'M WITH THE LOVE OF MY LIFE, JAKE.
Oh, barf!! Someone shut this girl up!
Hey, it's all stuff I got straight out of **your** journal.
There's a whole section about social media, too...

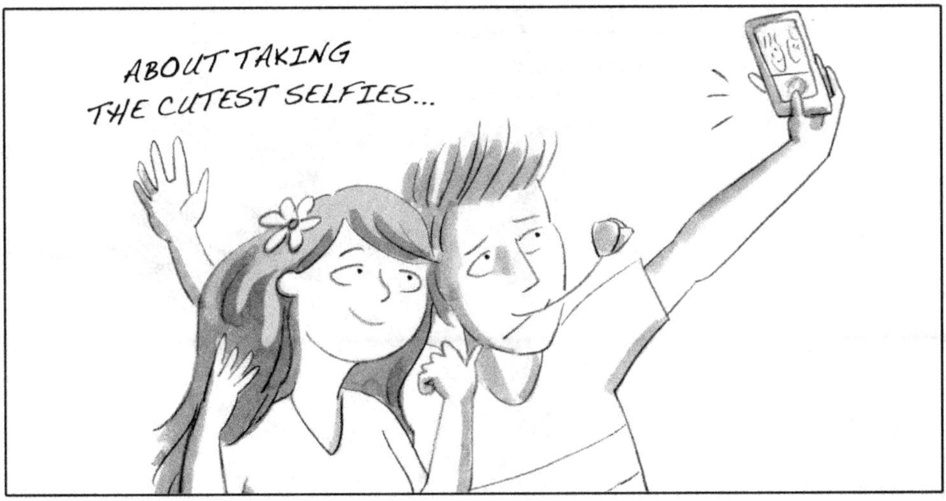
ABOUT TAKING
THE CUTEST SELFIES...

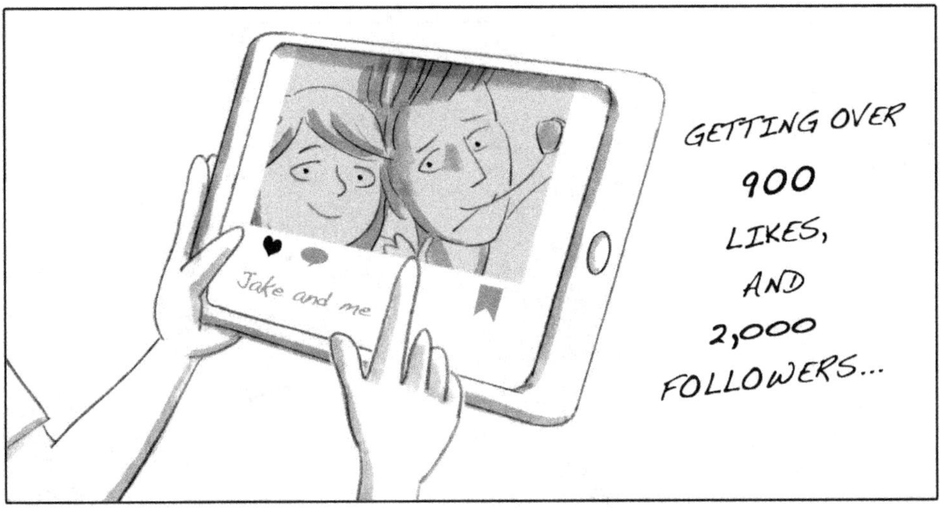
Jake and me
GETTING OVER
900
LIKES,
AND
2,000
FOLLOWERS...

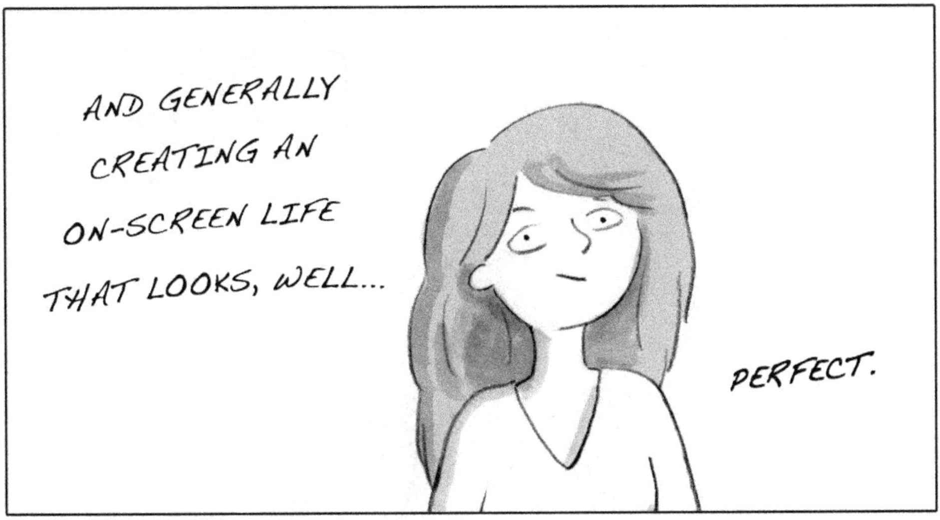
AND GENERALLY
CREATING AN
ON-SCREEN LIFE
THAT LOOKS, WELL...
PERFECT.

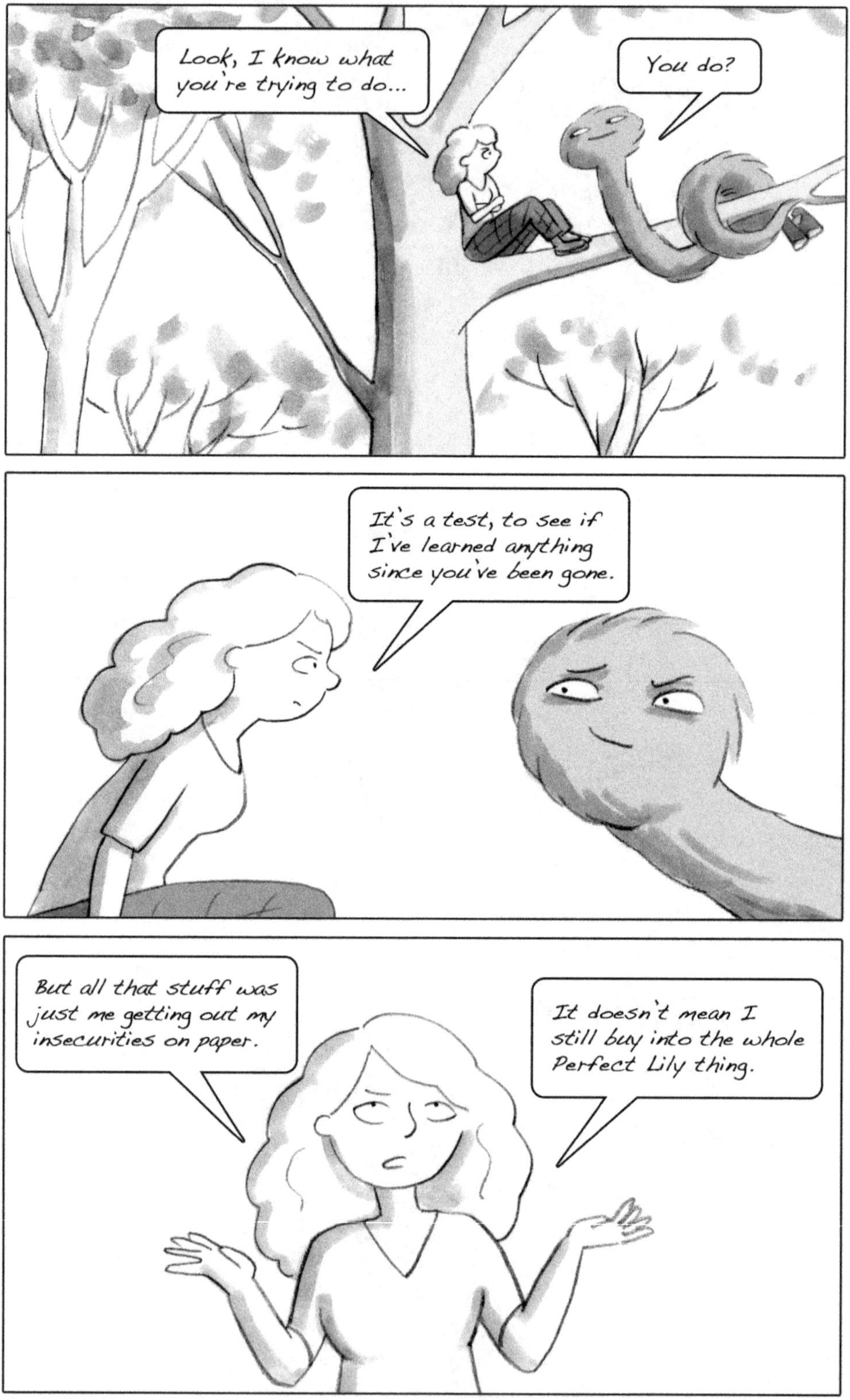
Look, I know what you're trying to do...
You do?
It's a test, to see if I've learned anything since you've been gone.
But all that stuff was just me getting out my insecurities on paper.
It doesn't mean I still buy into the whole Perfect Lily thing.

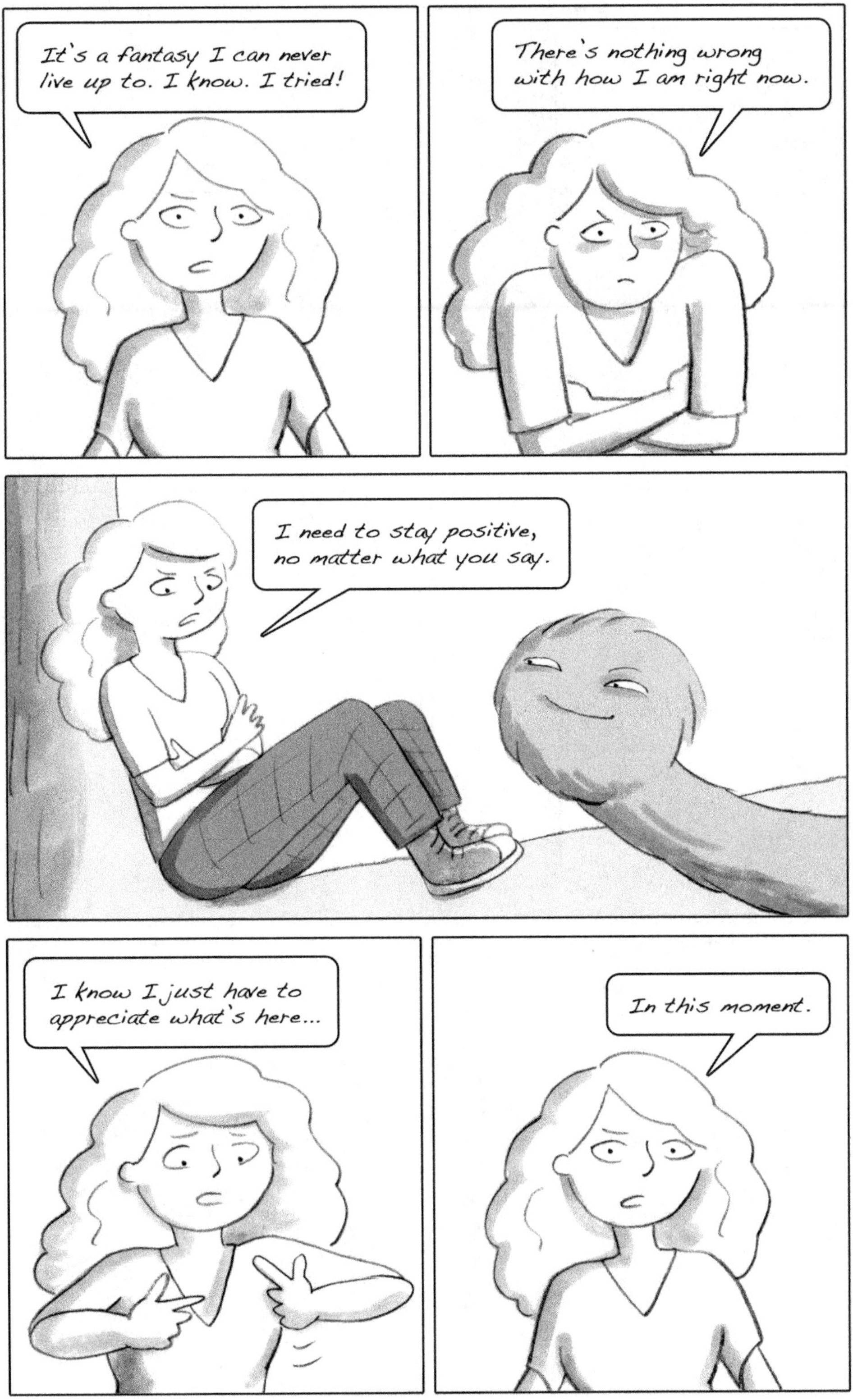
It's a fantasy I can never live up to. I know. I tried!
There's nothing wrong with how I am right now.
I need to stay positive, no matter what you say.
I know I just have to appreciate what's here...
In this moment.

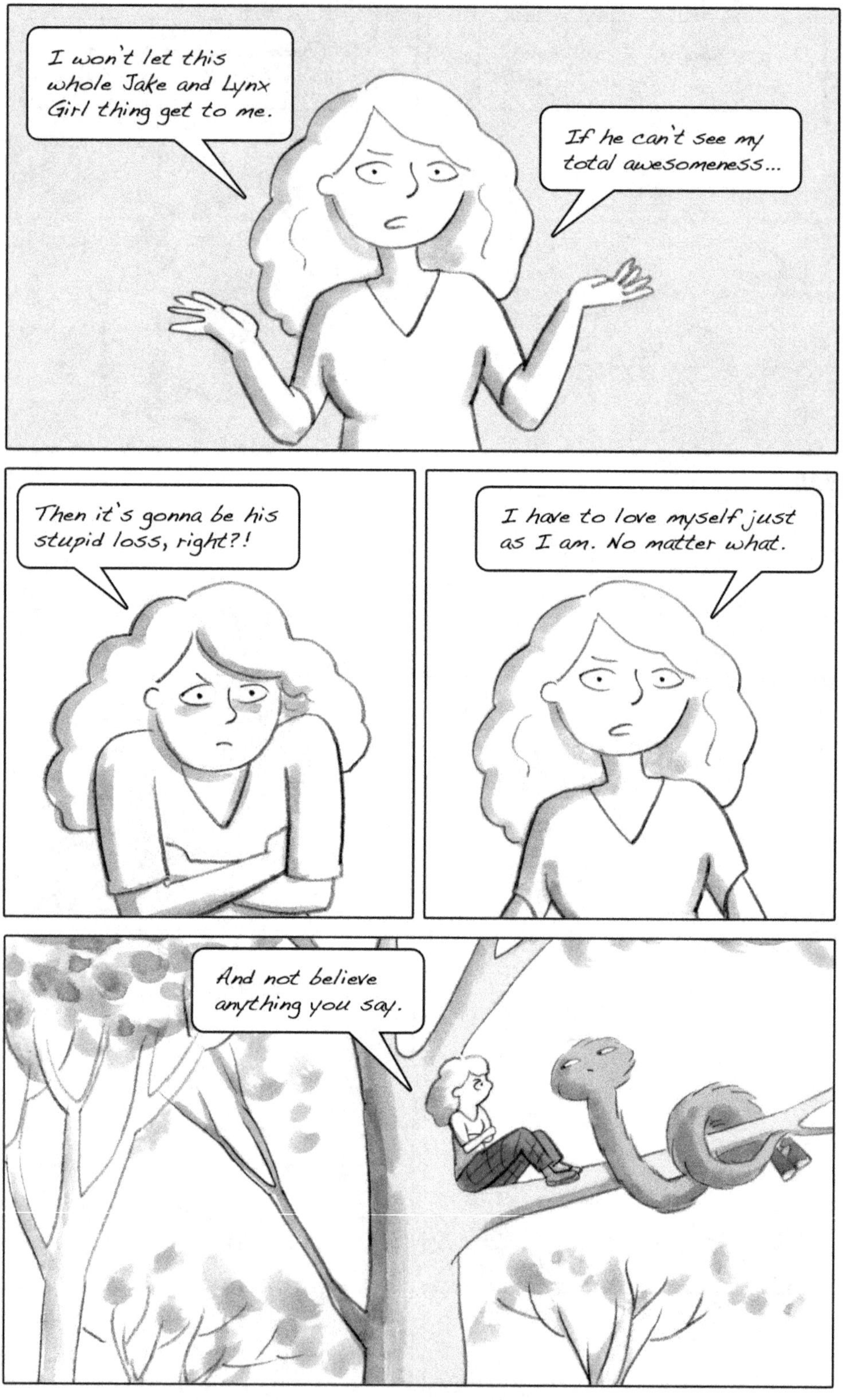

I won't let this whole Jake and Lynx Girl thing get to me.
If he can't see my total awesomeness...
Then it's gonna be his stupid loss, right?!
I have to love myself just as I am. No matter what.
And not believe anything you say.

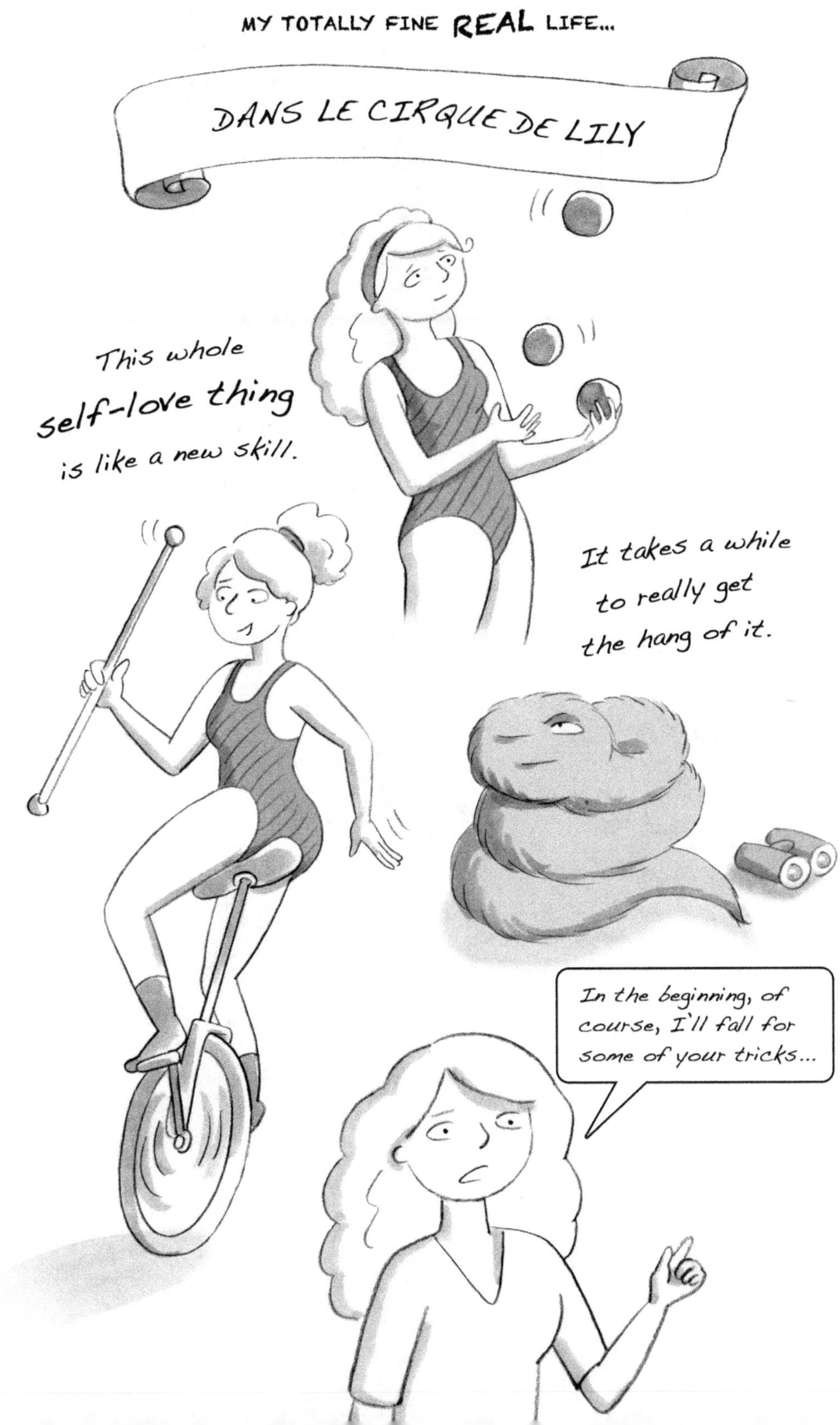
MY TOTALLY FINE REAL LIFE...
DANS LE CIRQUE DE LILY
This whole self-love thing is like a new skill.
It takes a while to really get the hang of it.
In the beginning, of course, I'll fall for some of your tricks...

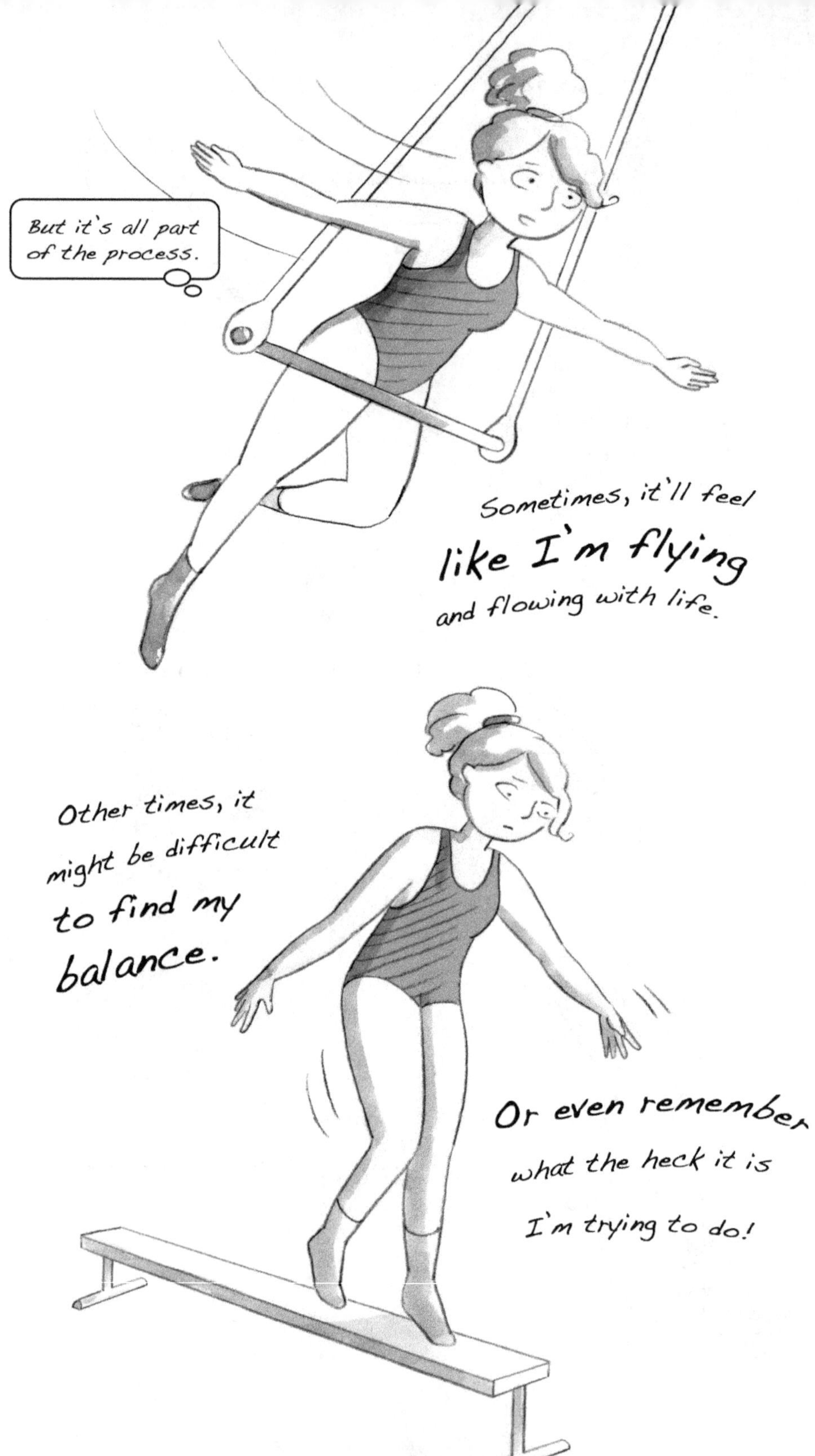
But it's all part of the process.
Sometimes, it'll feel
like I'm flying
and flowing with life.
Other times, it might be difficult
to find my
balance.
Or even remember
what the heck it is
I'm trying to do!

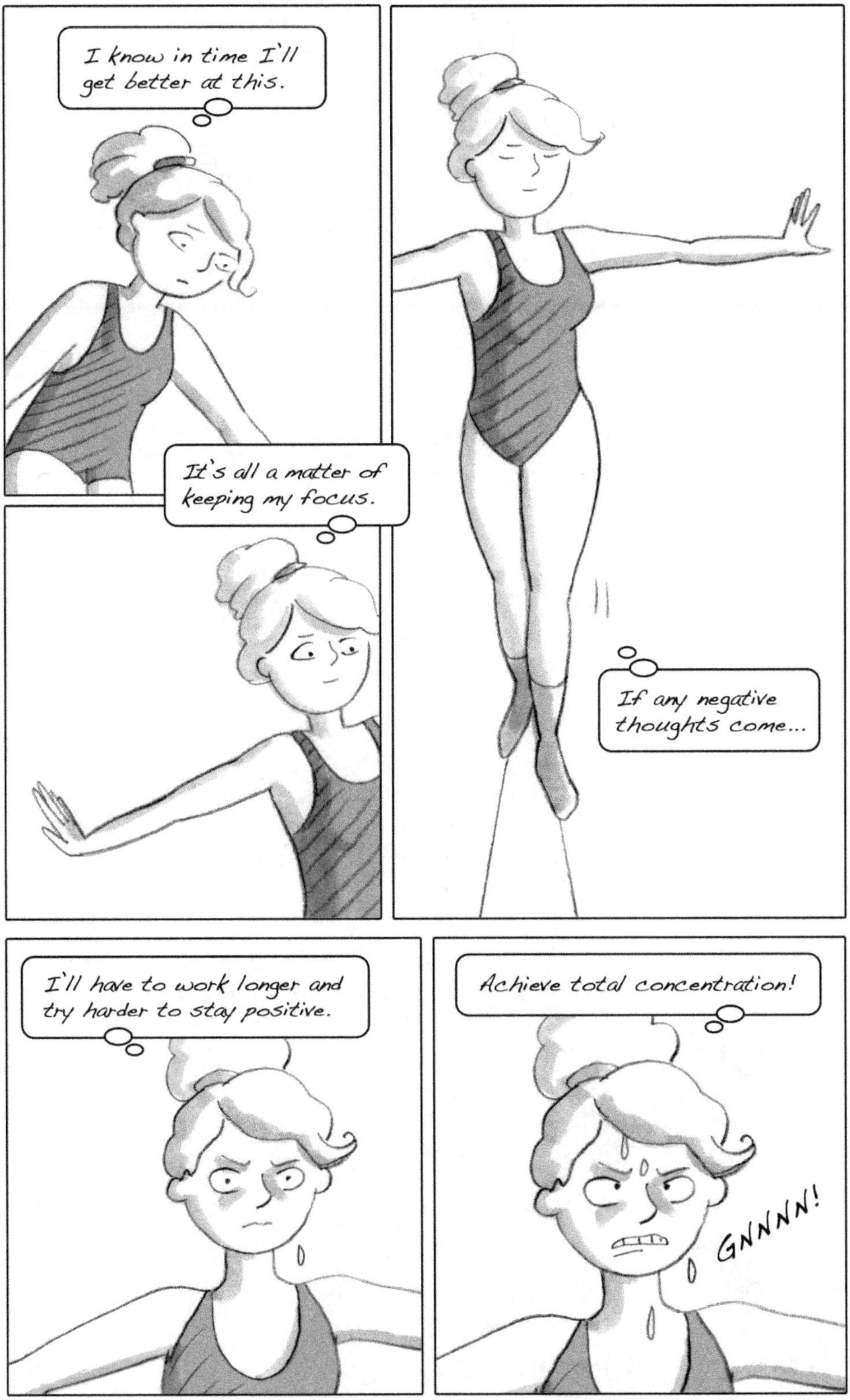
I know in time I'll get better at this.
It's all a matter of keeping my focus.
If any negative thoughts come...
I'll have to work longer and try harder to stay positive.
Achieve total concentration!
GNNNN!

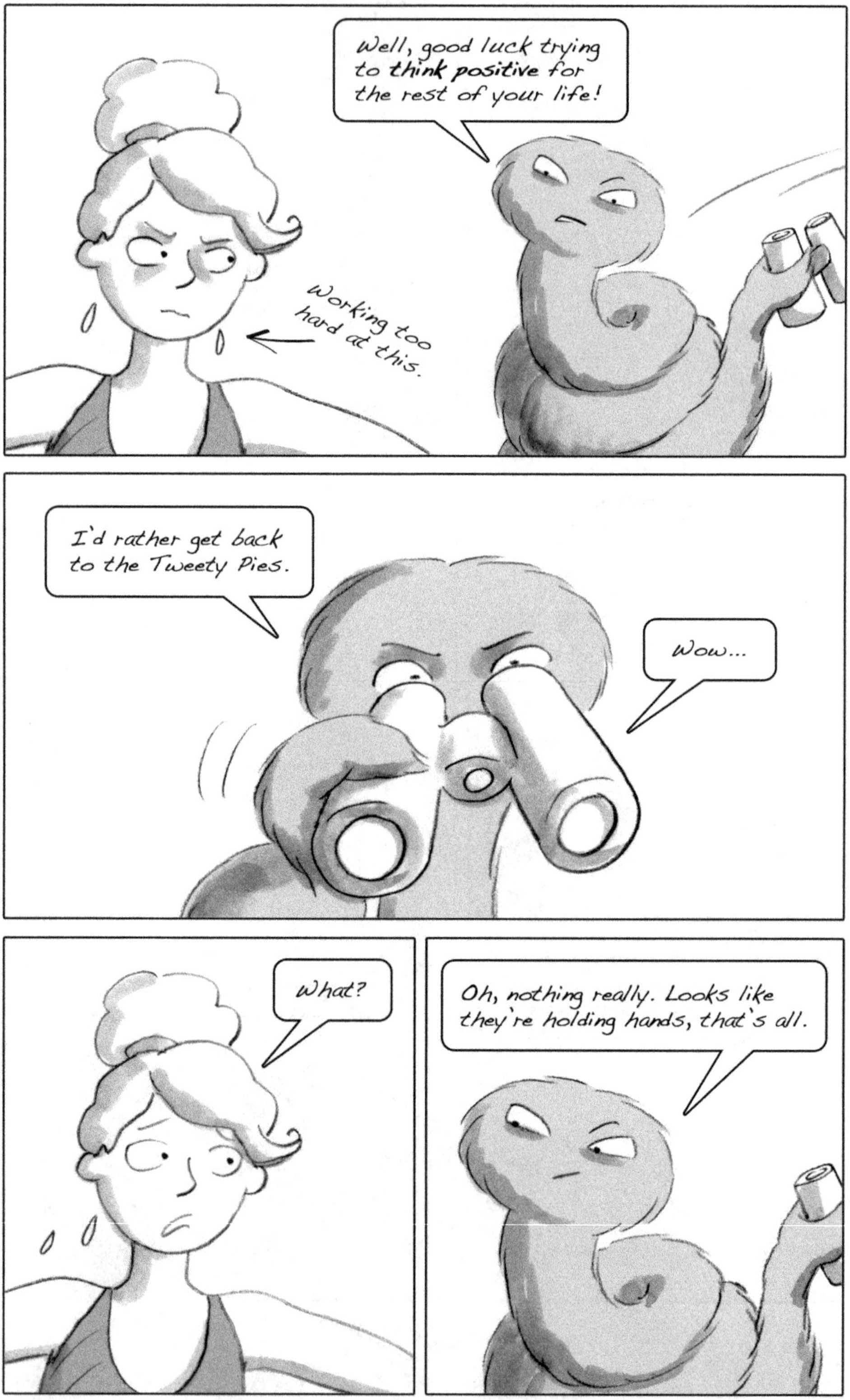
Well, good luck trying to **think positive** for the rest of your life!
Working too hard at this.
I'd rather get back to the Tweety Pies.
Wow...
What?
Oh, nothing really. Looks like they're holding hands, that's all.

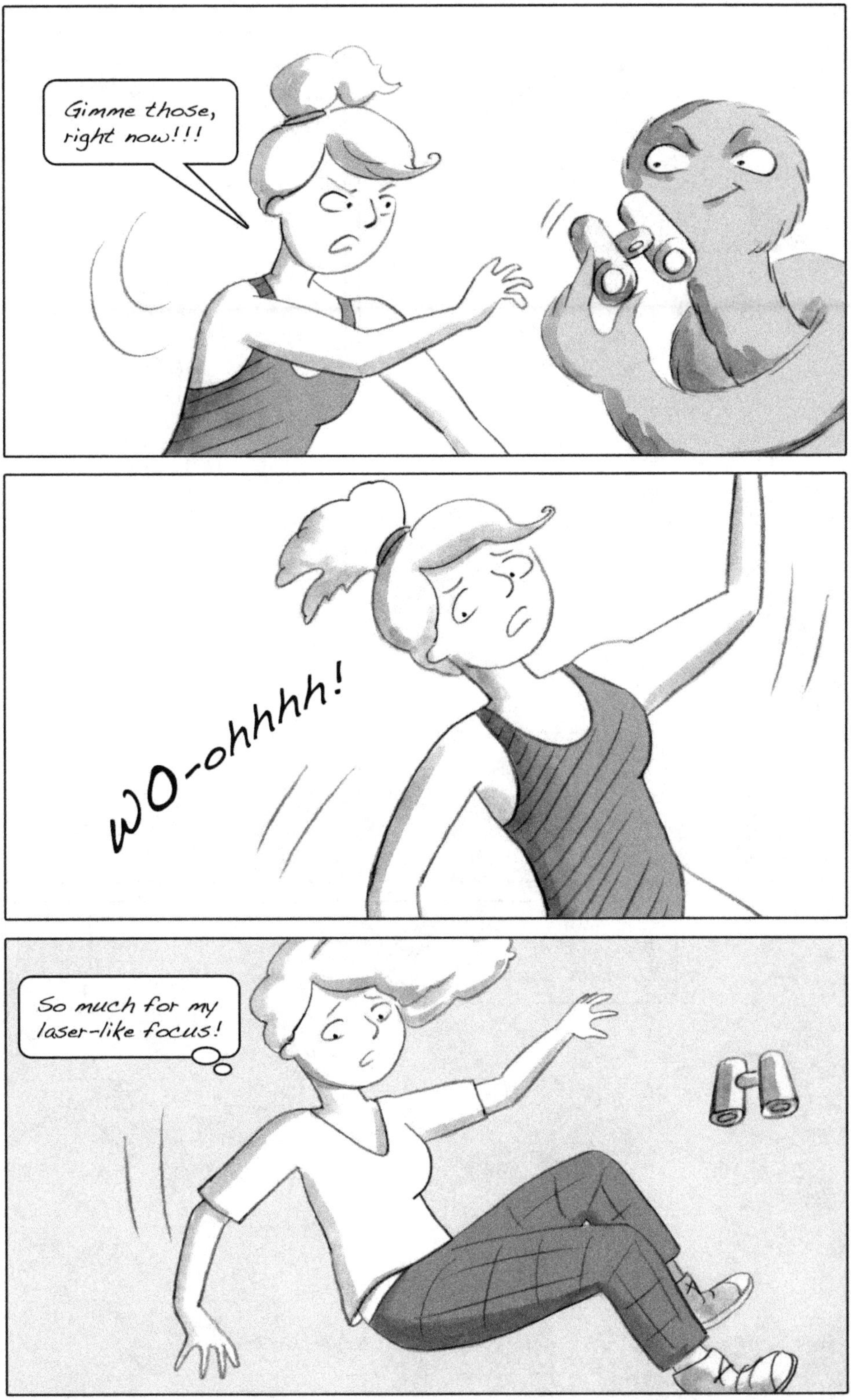
Gimme those, right now!!!
WO-ohhhh!
So much for my laser-like focus!

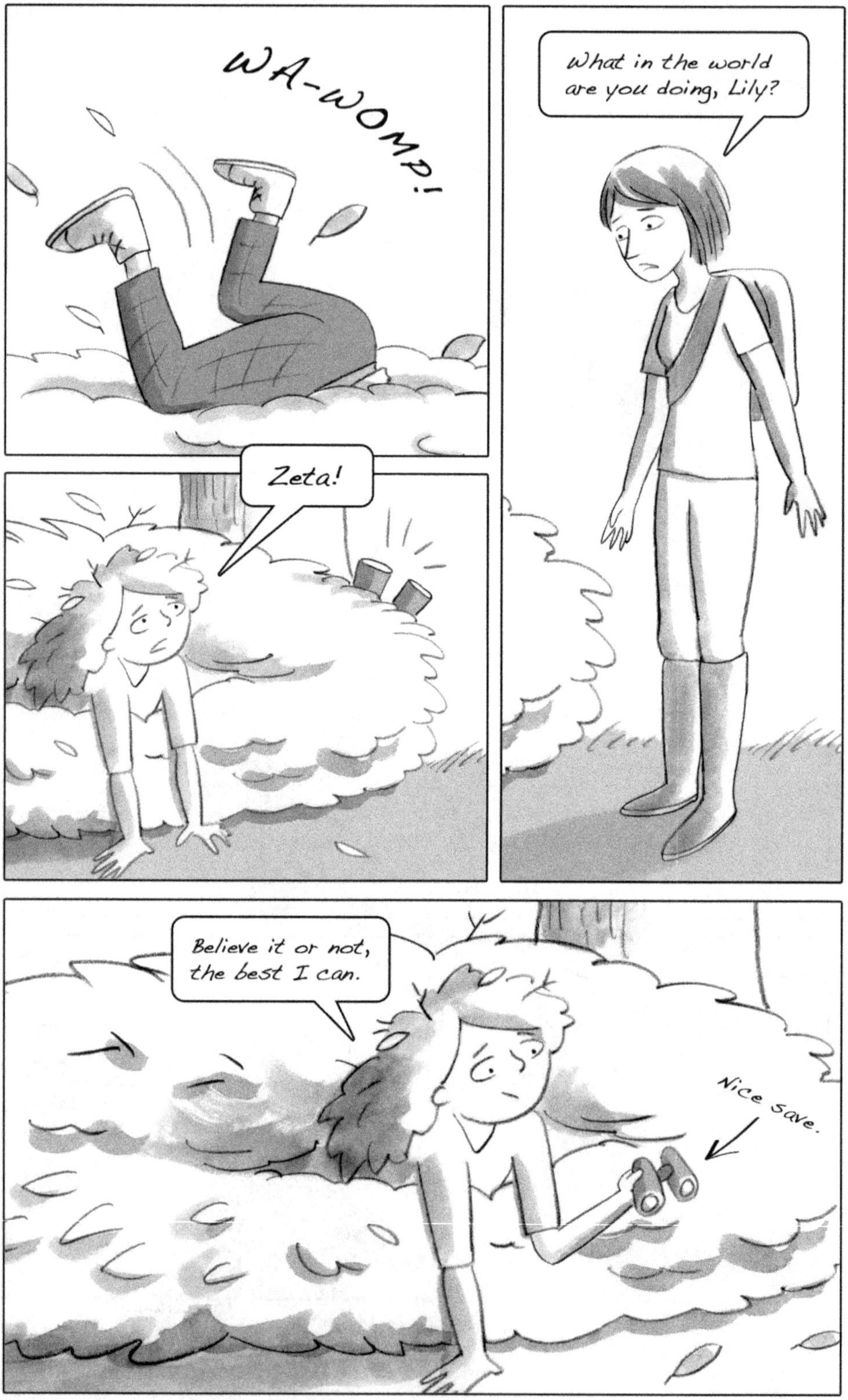
WA-WOMP!
What in the world are you doing, Lily?
Zeta!
Believe it or not, the best I can.
Nice save.

If you try to win the

war with your mind, you'll

be at war forever.

ADYASHANTI

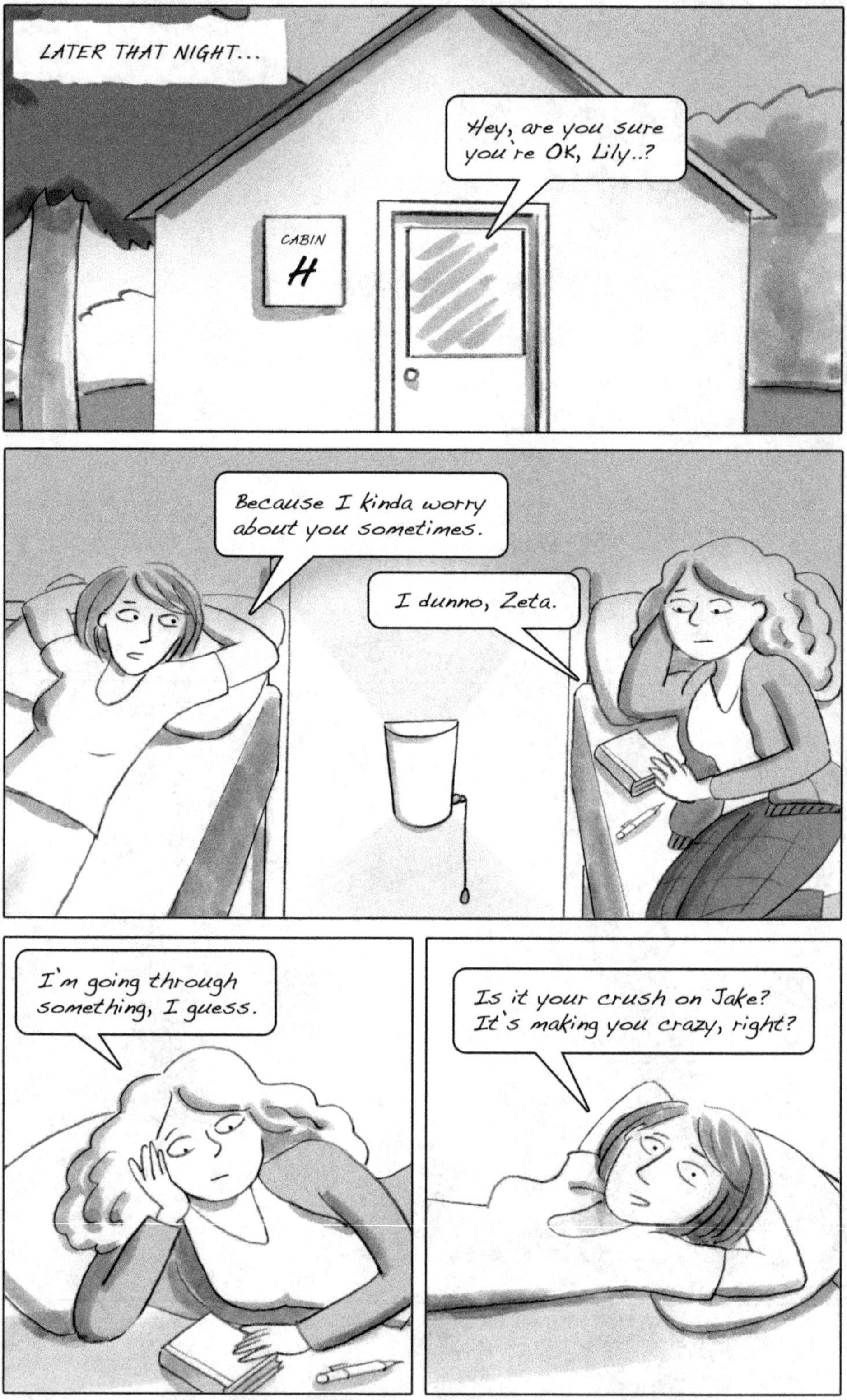
LATER THAT NIGHT...
Hey, are you sure you're OK, Lily..?
CABIN H
Because I kinda worry about you sometimes.
I dunno, Zeta.
I'm going through something, I guess.
Is it your crush on Jake? It's making you crazy, right?

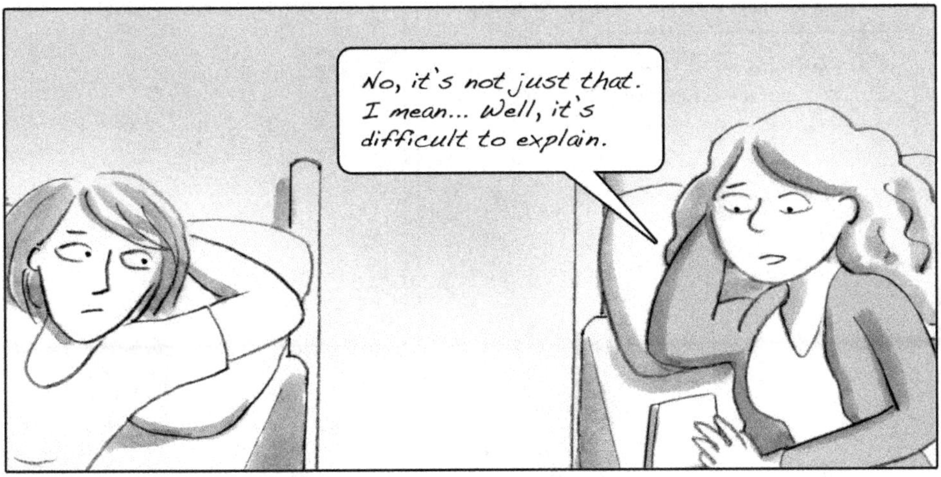
No, it's not just that. I mean... Well, it's difficult to explain.

WEDNESDAY p.m.

What can I say? That I have a demon? That I'm possessed? And I've tried everything under the sun to deal with this thing? Zeta will think I'm nuts. Or worse, she'll make a big joke of it. And somehow everyone will find out and they'll think I'm super weird. Then they'll laugh at me or avoid me. Cuz nobody likes a party pooper.

And the worst part is, I've already seen through this whole thing. I know it's not real. But it gets me every time. One little thought and I get sucked back in all over again.

Maybe I'll feel better if I just talk about it. What's the worst that can happen? Burst out crying, go red as a beet and have snot running down my chin?

In that case, I have nothing to lose but my dignity!

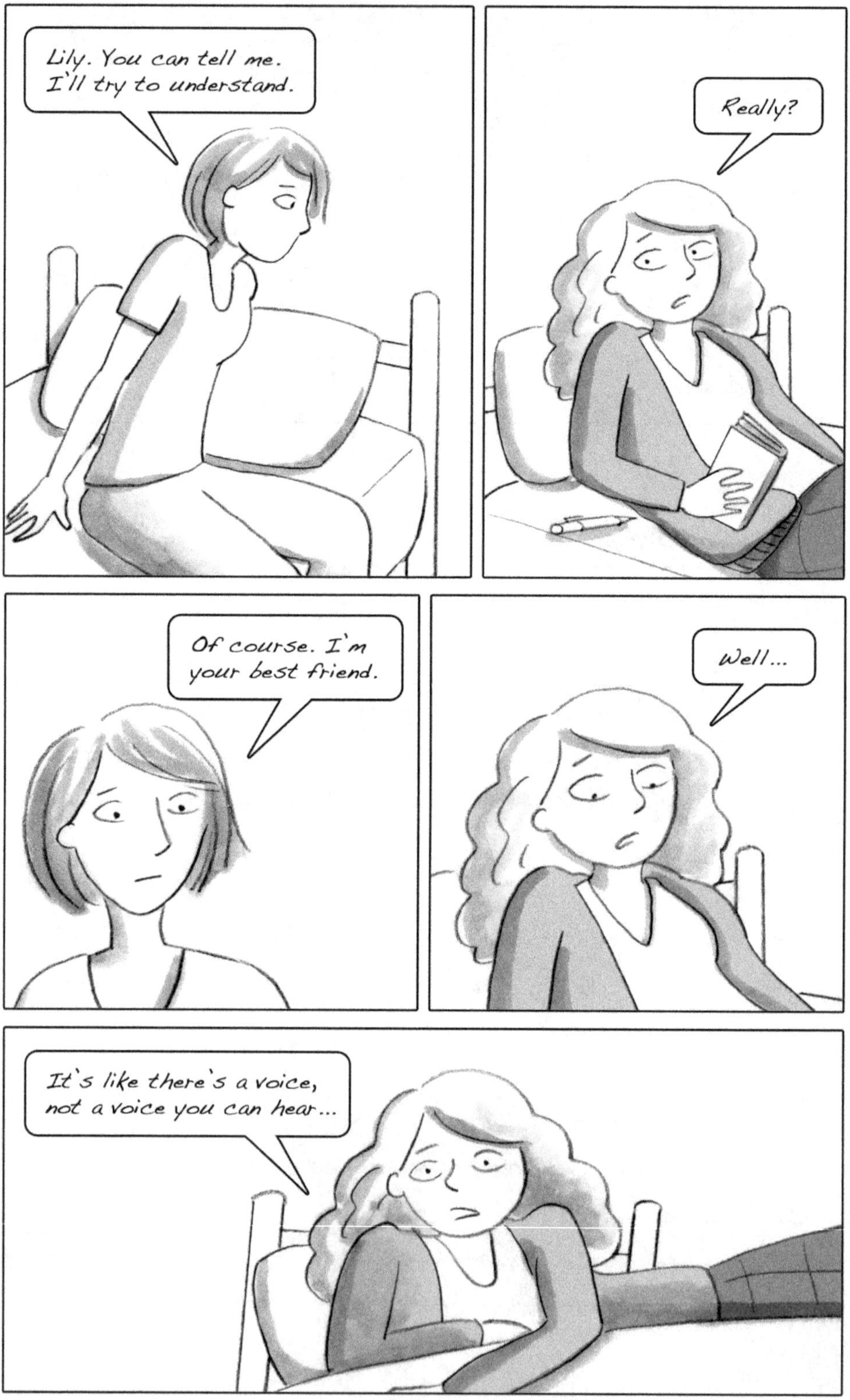
Lily. You can tell me. I'll try to understand.
Really?
Of course. I'm your best friend.
Well...
It's like there's a voice, not a voice you can hear...

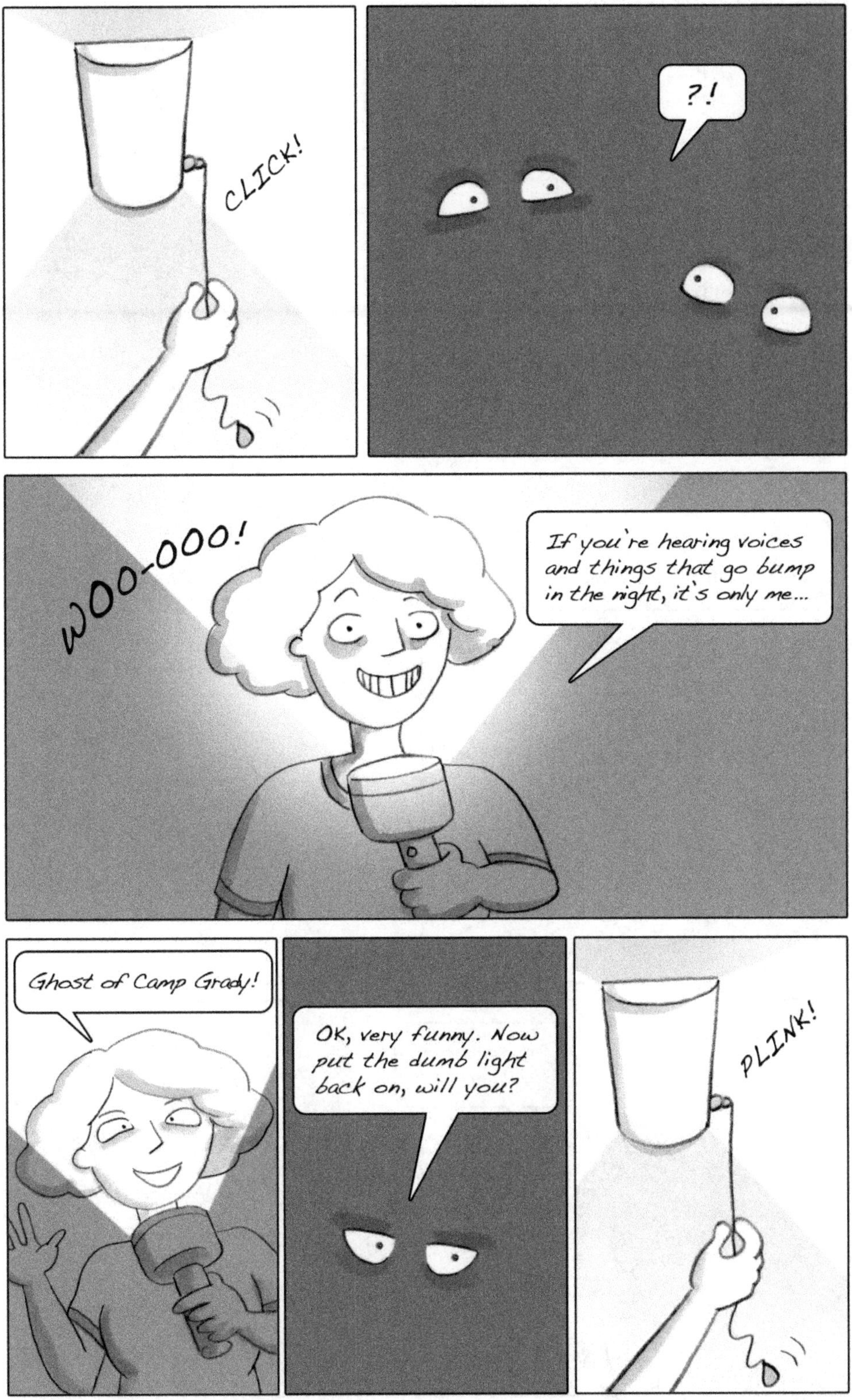
CLICK!
?!
WOO-OOO!
If you're hearing voices and things that go bump in the night, it's only me...
Ghost of Camp Grady!
OK, very funny. Now put the dumb light back on, will you?
PLINK!

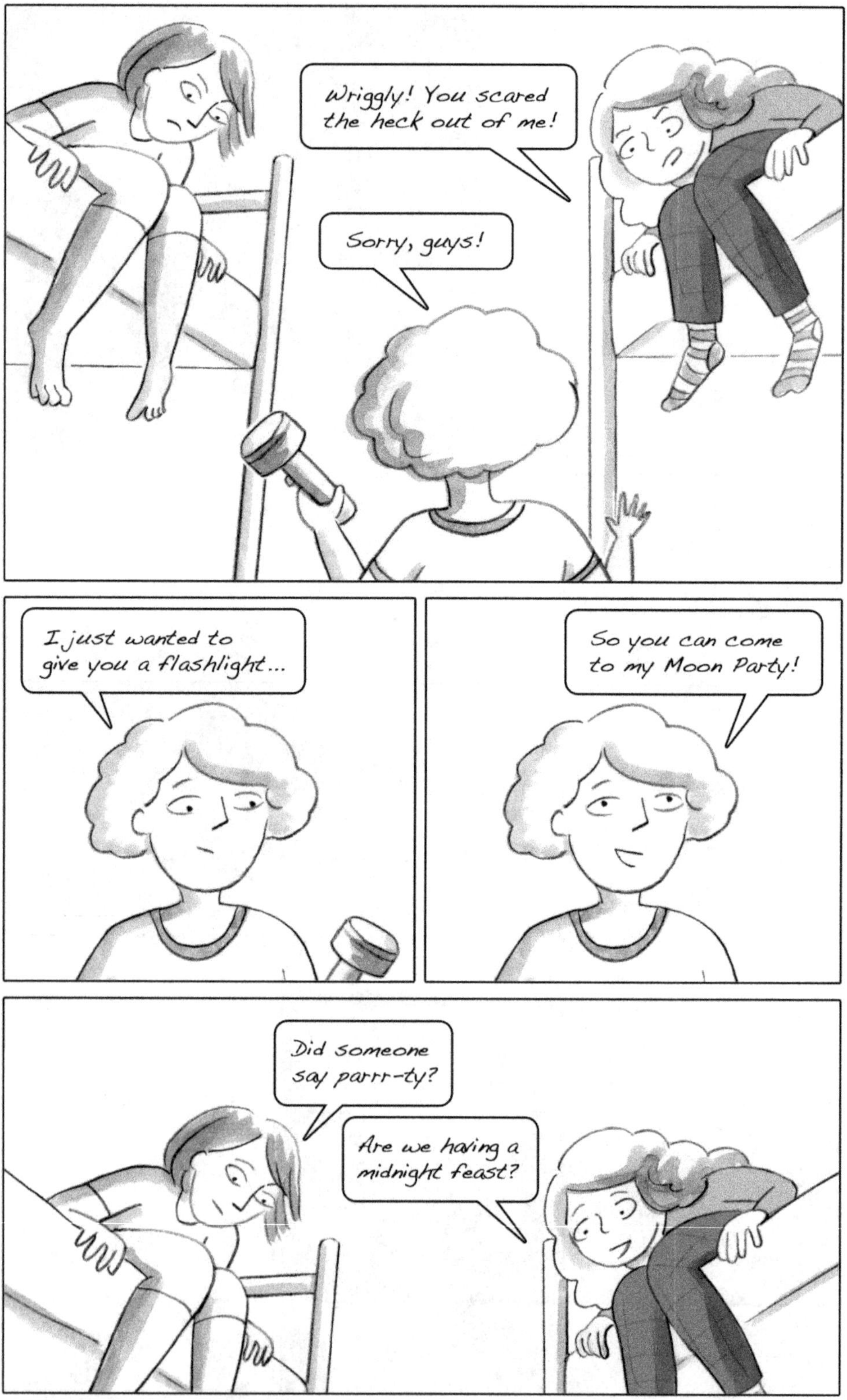
Wriggly! You scared the heck out of me!
Sorry, guys!
I just wanted to give you a flashlight...
So you can come to my Moon Party!
Did someone say parrr-ty?
Are we having a midnight feast?

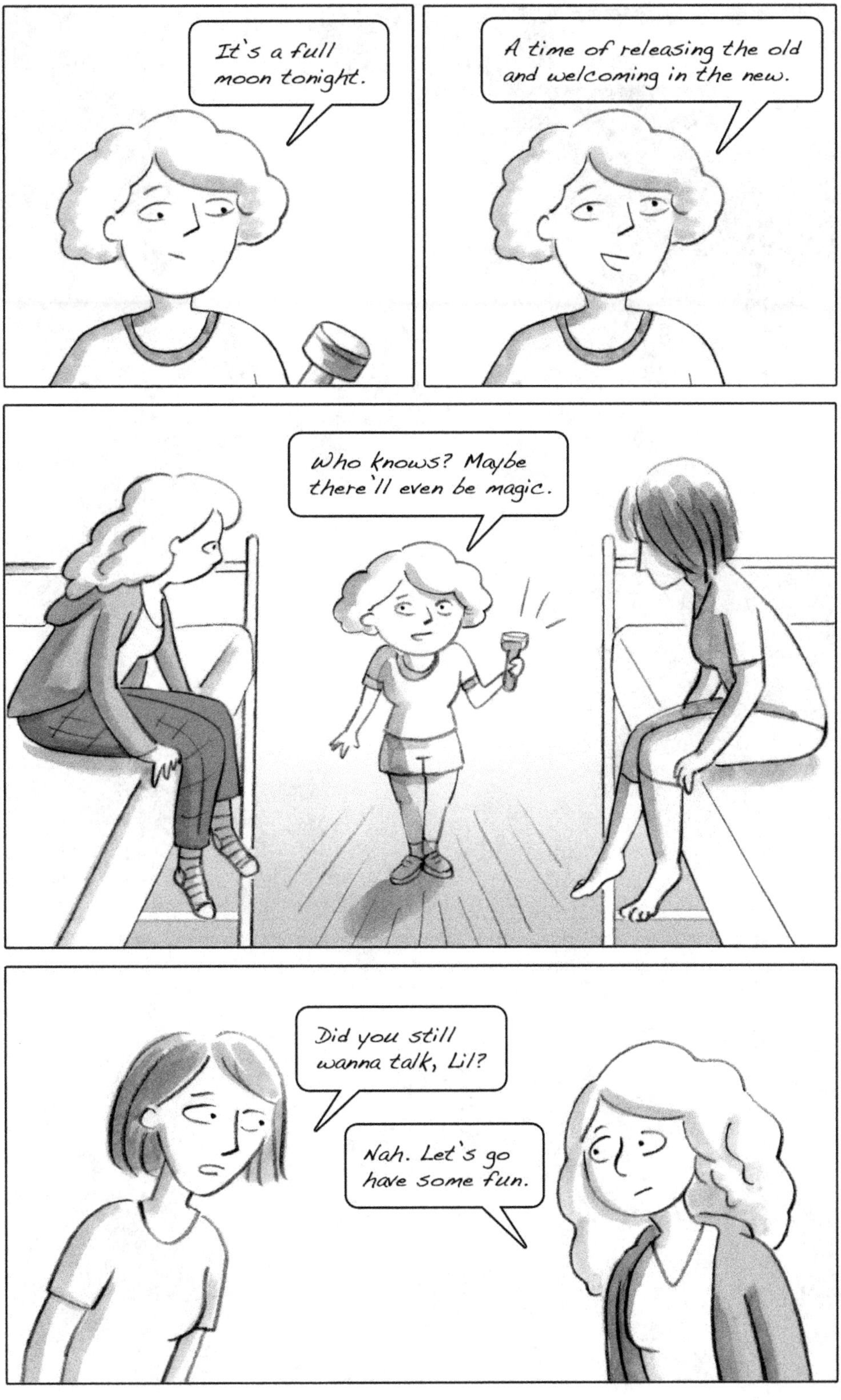
It's a full moon tonight.
A time of releasing the old and welcoming in the new.
Who knows? Maybe there'll even be magic.
Did you still wanna talk, Lil?
Nah. Let's go have some fun.

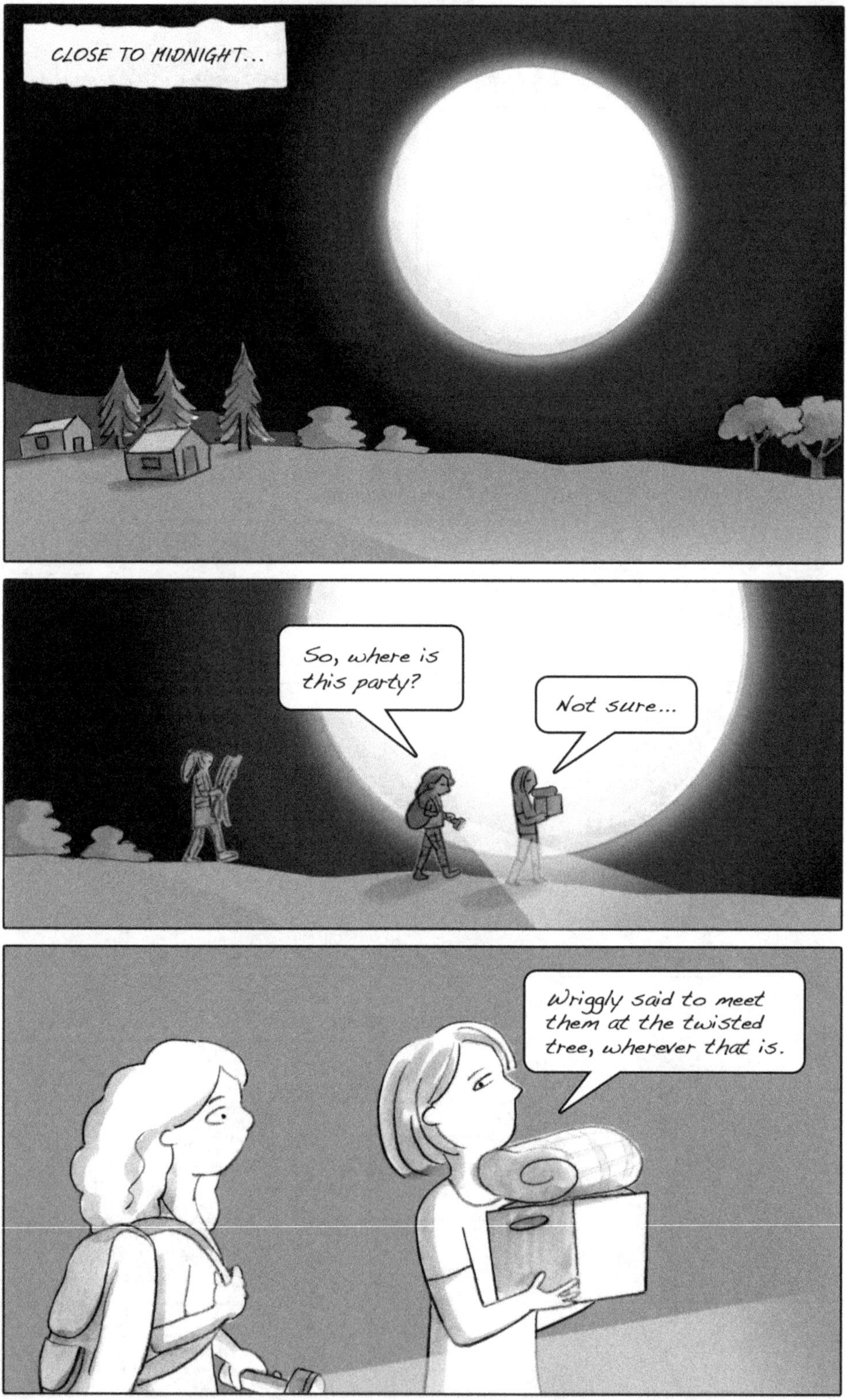
CLOSE TO MIDNIGHT...
So, where is this party?
Not sure...
Wriggly said to meet them at the twisted tree, wherever that is.

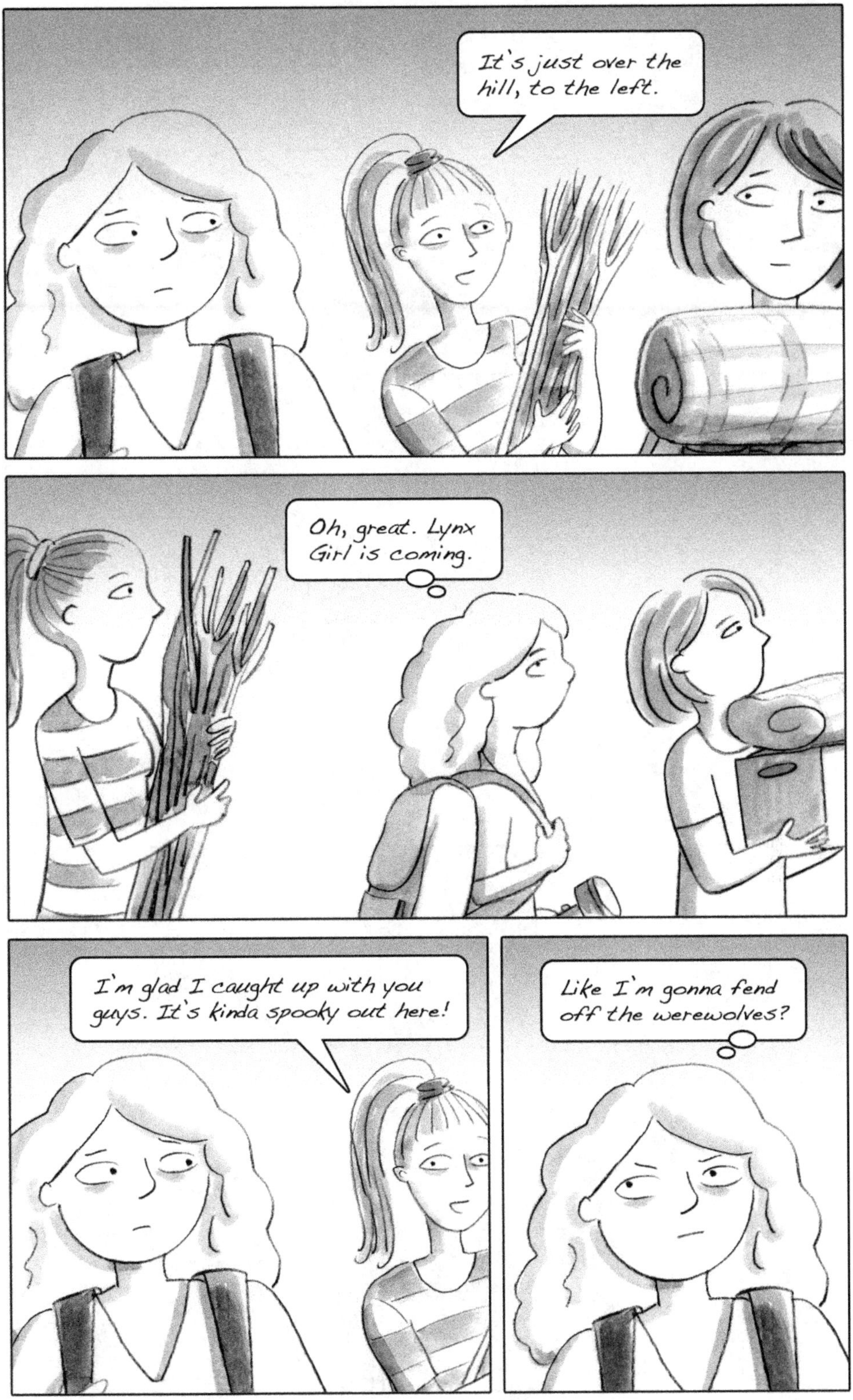
It's just over the hill, to the left.
Oh, great. Lynx Girl is coming.
I'm glad I caught up with you guys. It's kinda spooky out here!
Like I'm gonna fend off the werewolves?

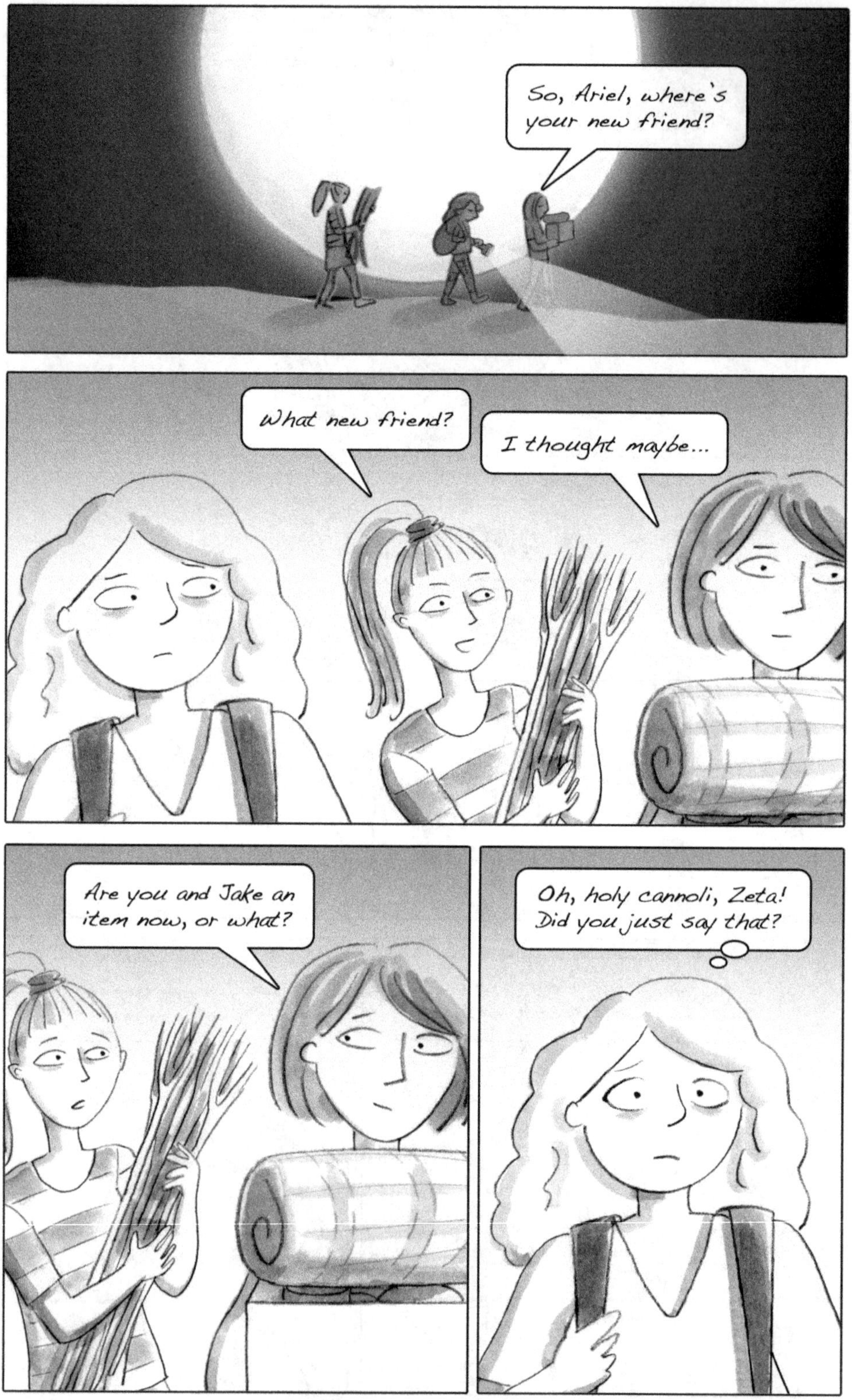
So, Ariel, where's your new friend?
What new friend?
I thought maybe...
Are you and Jake an item now, or what?
Oh, holy cannoli, Zeta! Did you just say that?

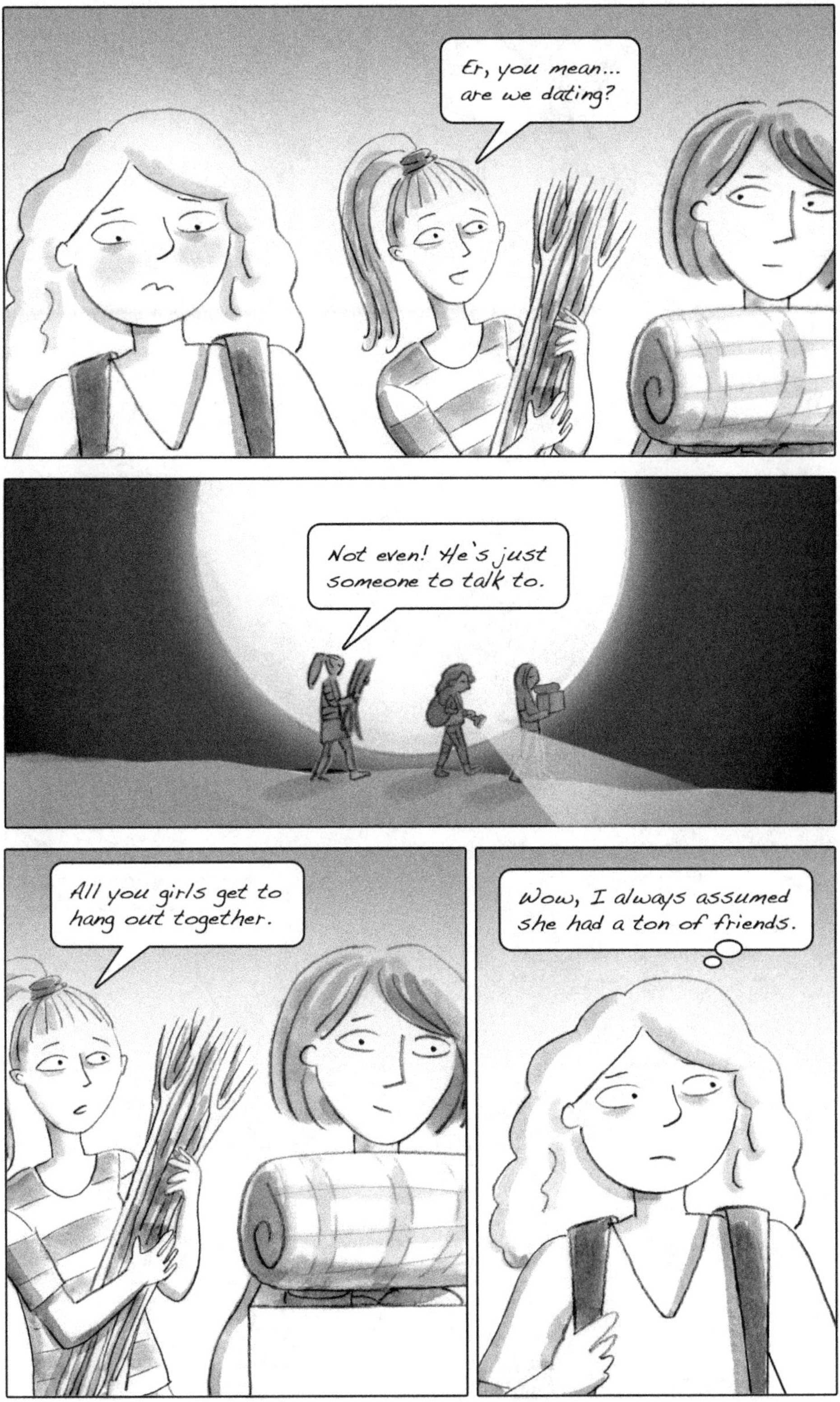
Er, you mean...
are we dating?
Not even! He's just someone to talk to.
All you girls get to hang out together.
Wow, I always assumed she had a ton of friends.

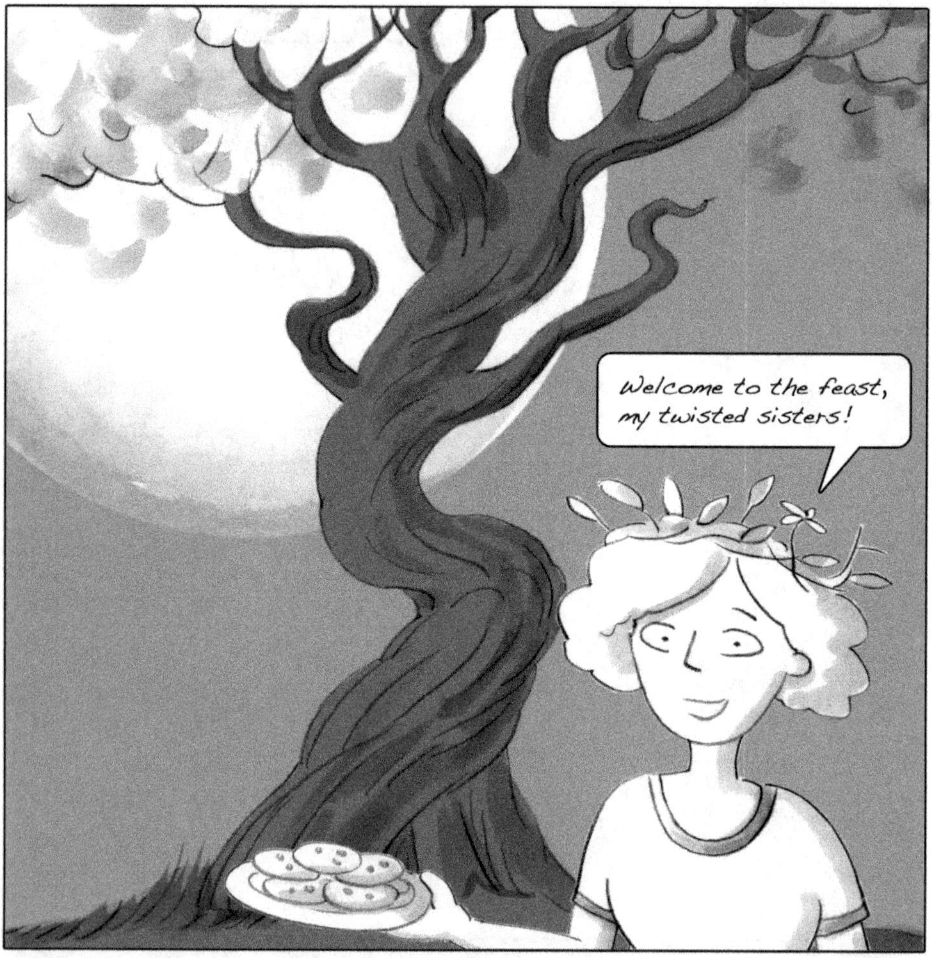
Welcome to the feast, my twisted sisters!

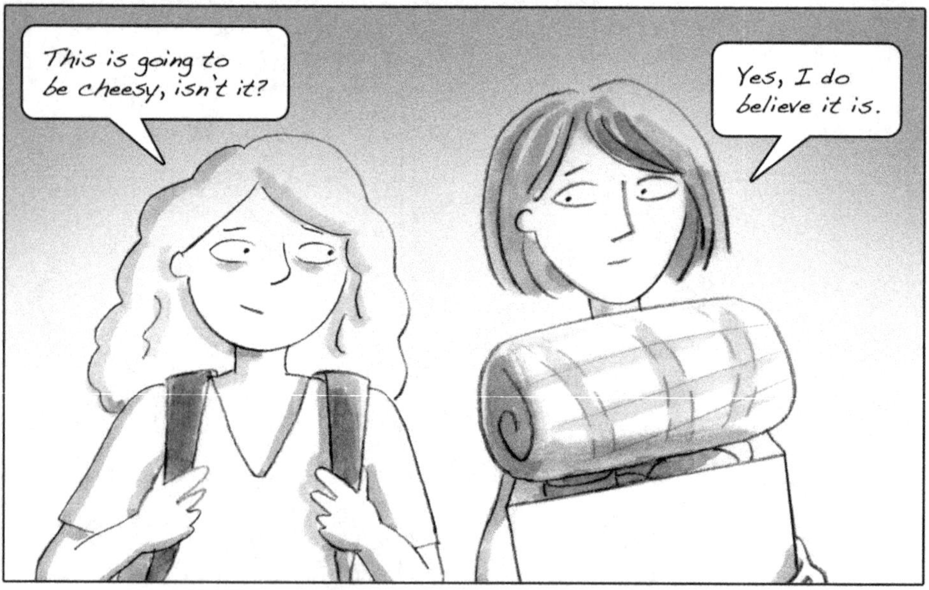
This is going to be cheesy, isn't it?
Yes, I do believe it is.

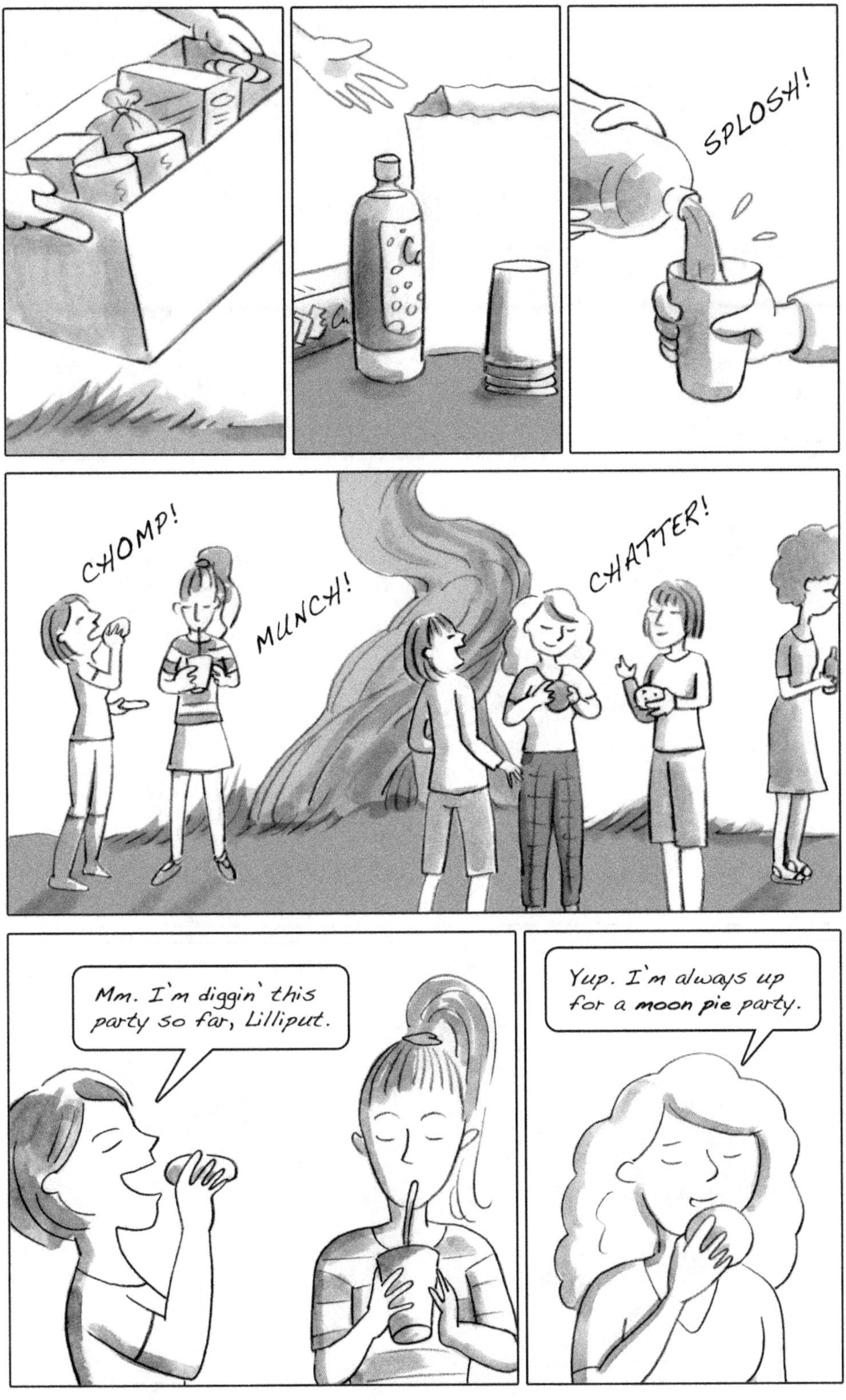
SPLOSH!
CHOMP!
MUNCH!
CHATTER!
Mm. I'm diggin' this party so far, Lilliput.
Yup. I'm always up for a **moon pie** party.

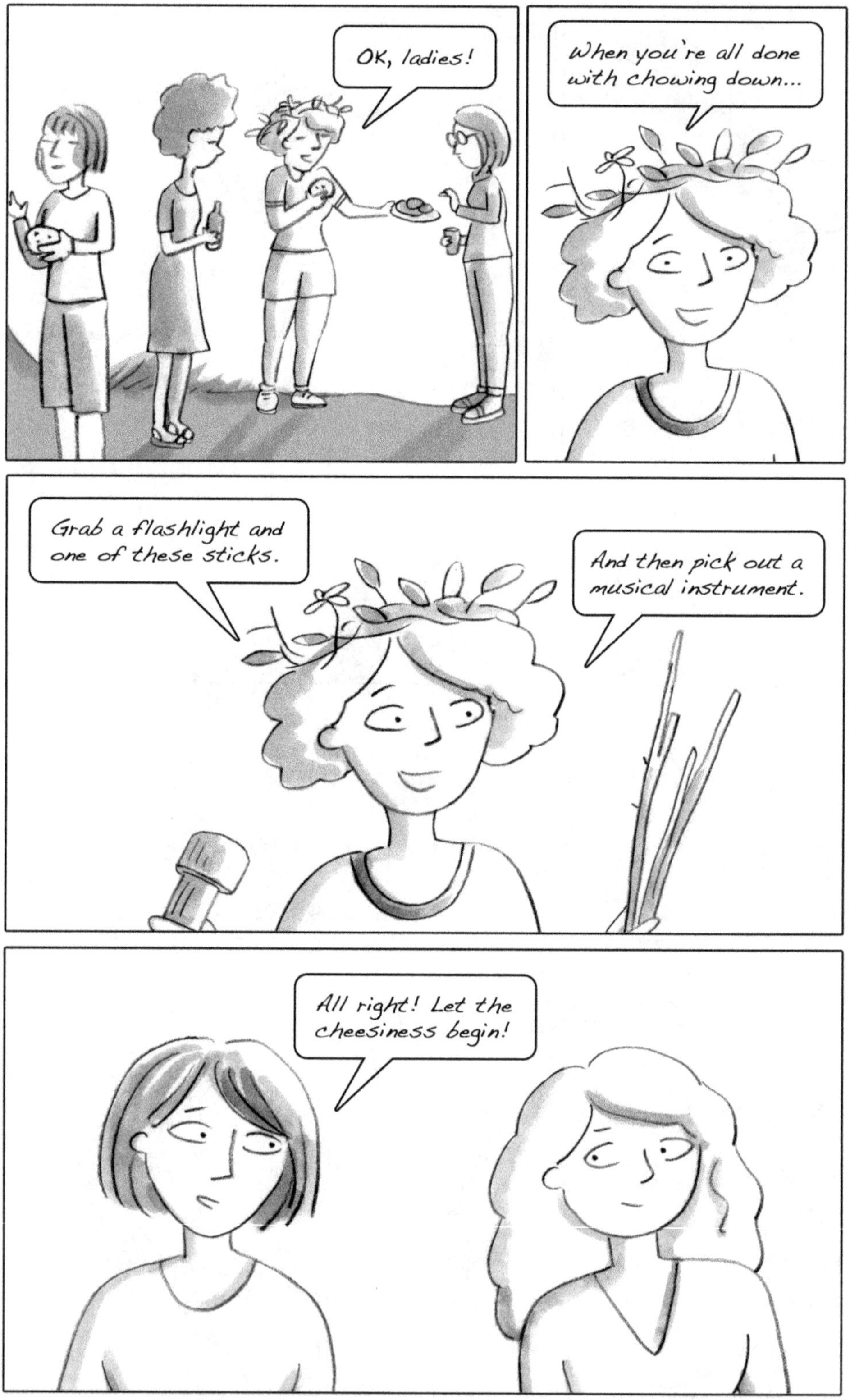
OK, ladies!
When you're all done with chowing down...
Grab a flashlight and one of these sticks.
And then pick out a musical instrument.
All right! Let the cheesiness begin!

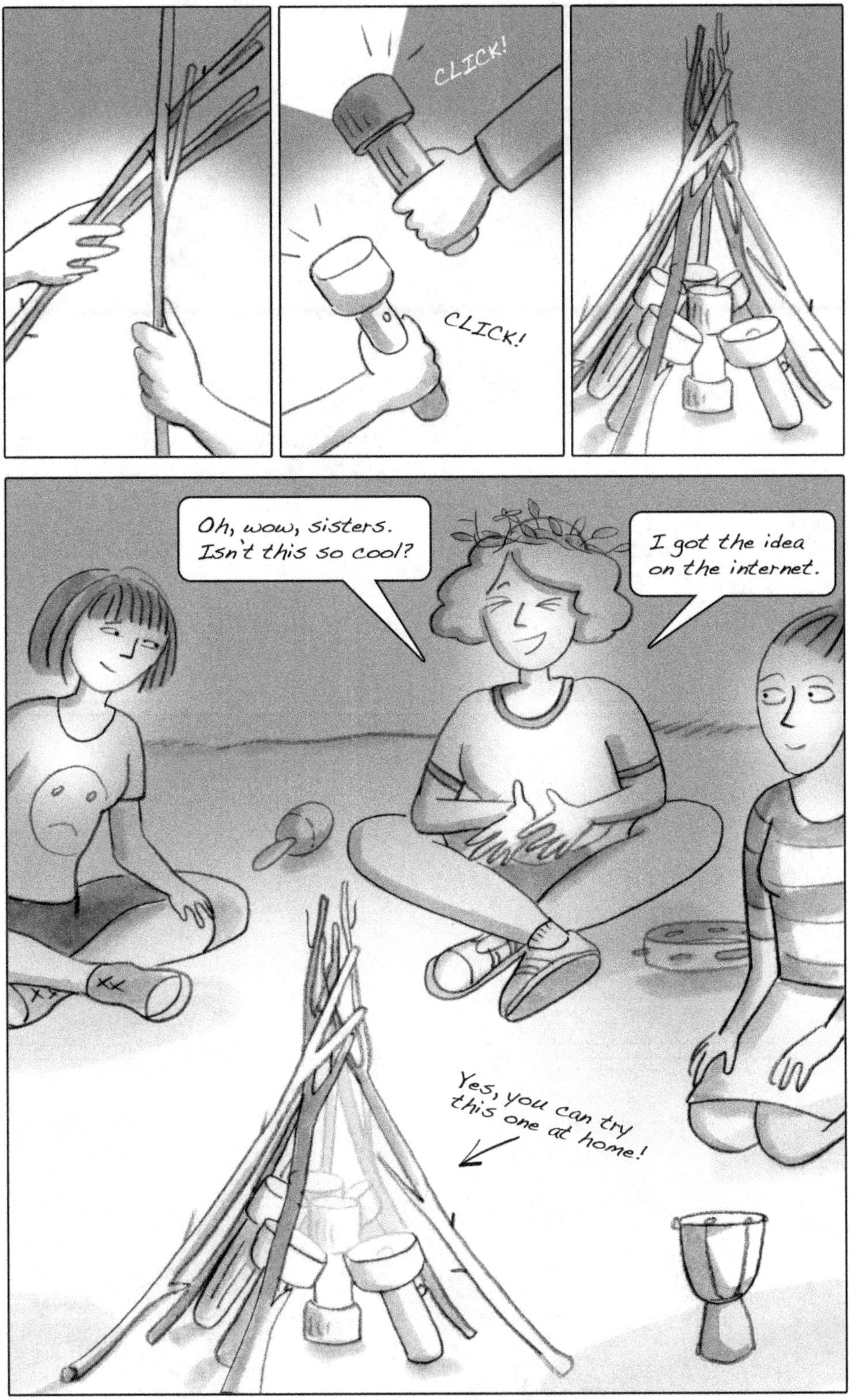
CLICK!
CLICK!
Oh, wow, sisters. Isn't this so cool?
I got the idea on the internet.
Yes, you can try this one at home!

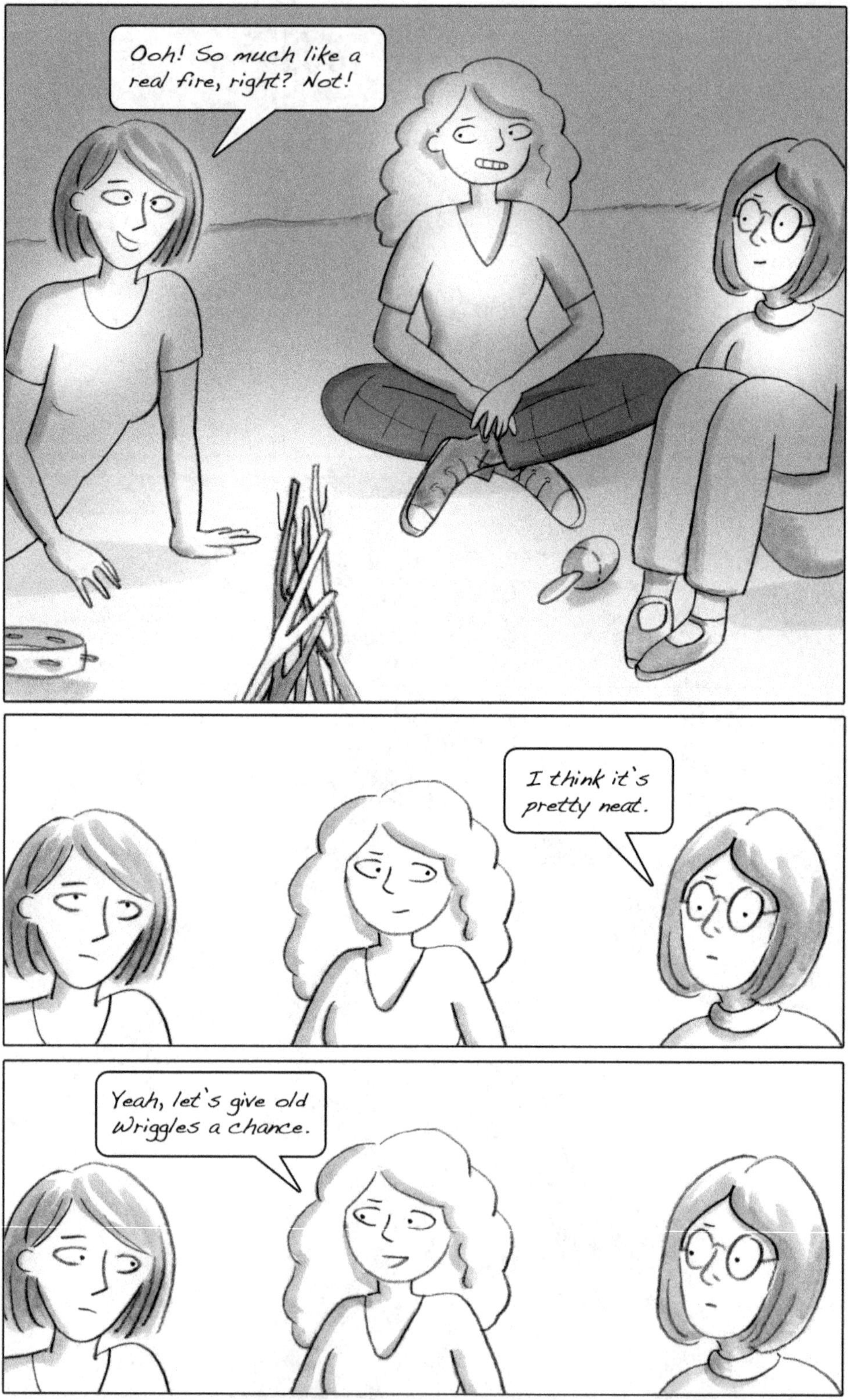
Ooh! So much like a real fire, right? Not!
I think it's pretty neat.
Yeah, let's give old Wriggles a chance.

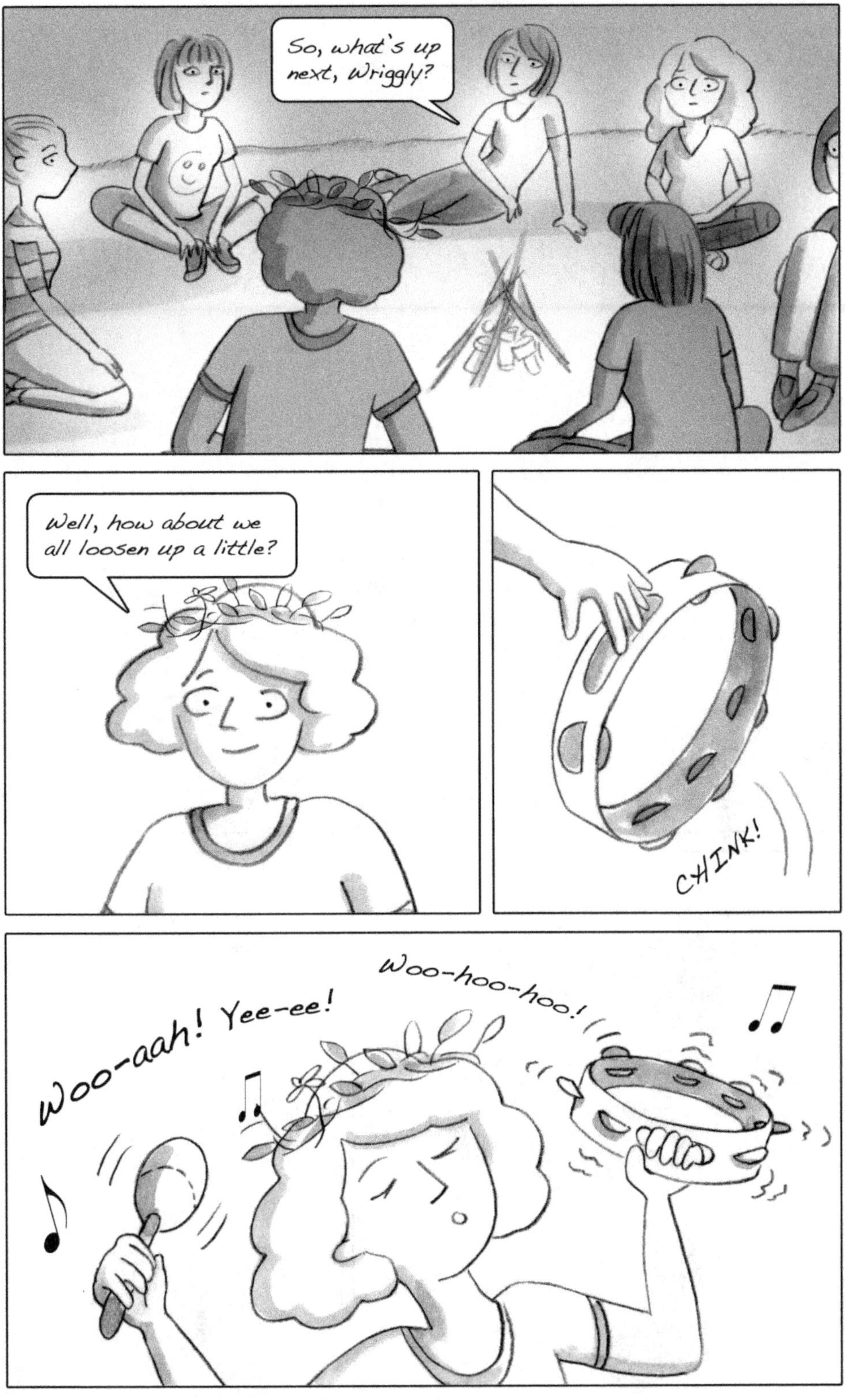
So, what's up next, Wriggly?
Well, how about we all loosen up a little?
CHINK!
Woo-hoo-hoo!
Woo-aah! Yee-ee!

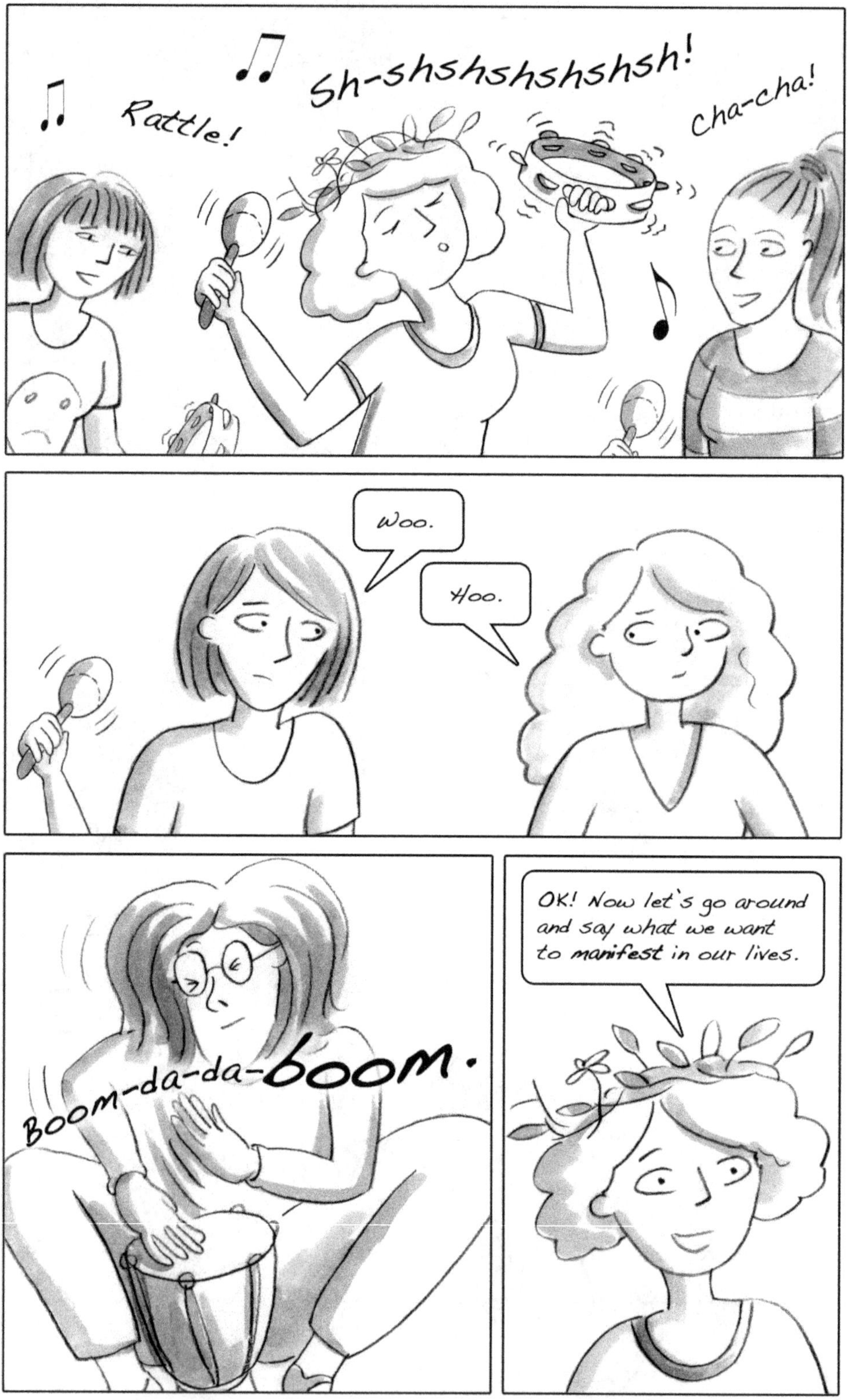
Rattle!
Sh-shshshshshsh!
Cha-cha!
Woo.
Hoo.
Boom-da-da-boom.
OK! Now let's go around and say what we want to manifest in our lives.

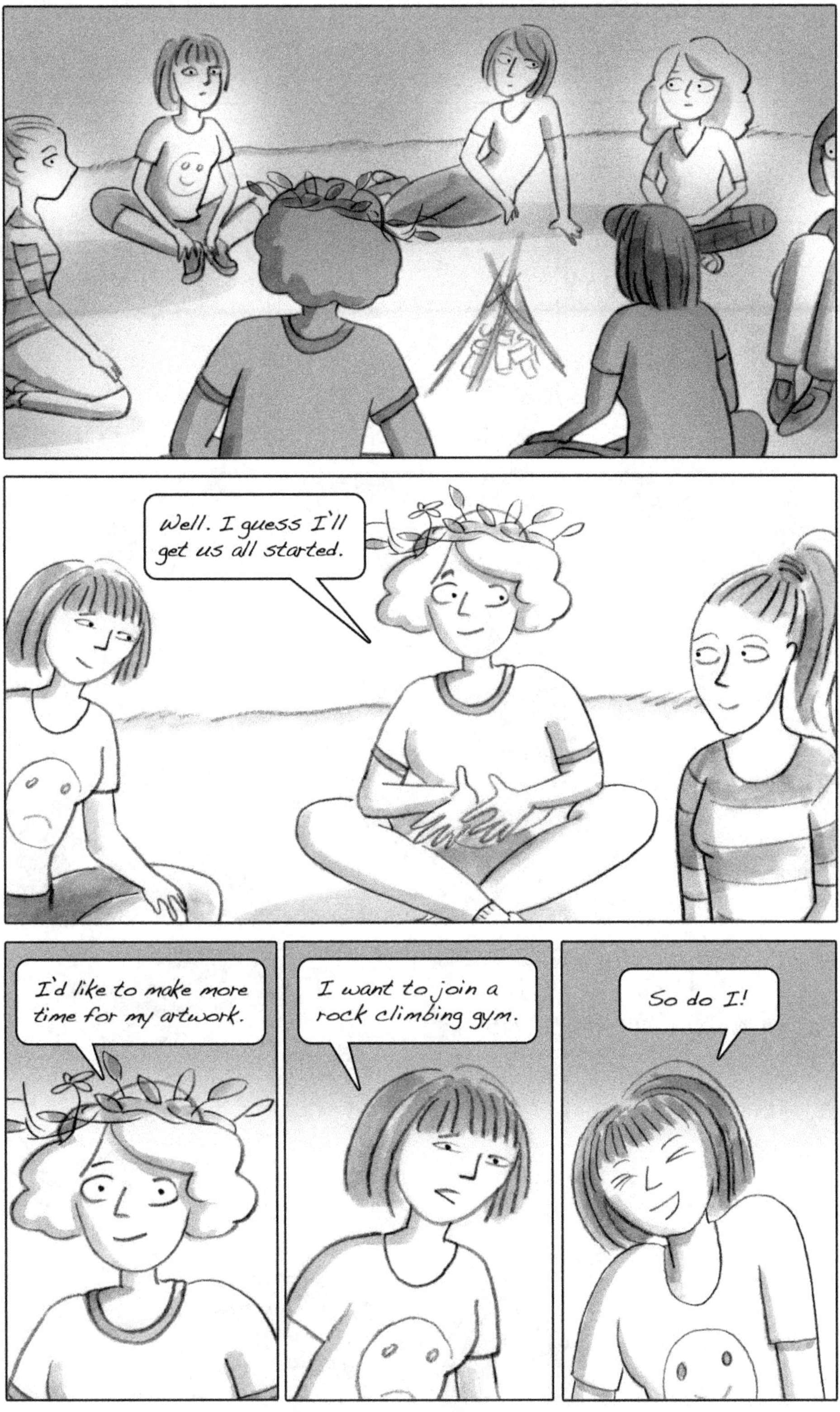
Well. I guess I'll get us all started.
I'd like to make more time for my artwork.
I want to join a rock climbing gym.
So do I!

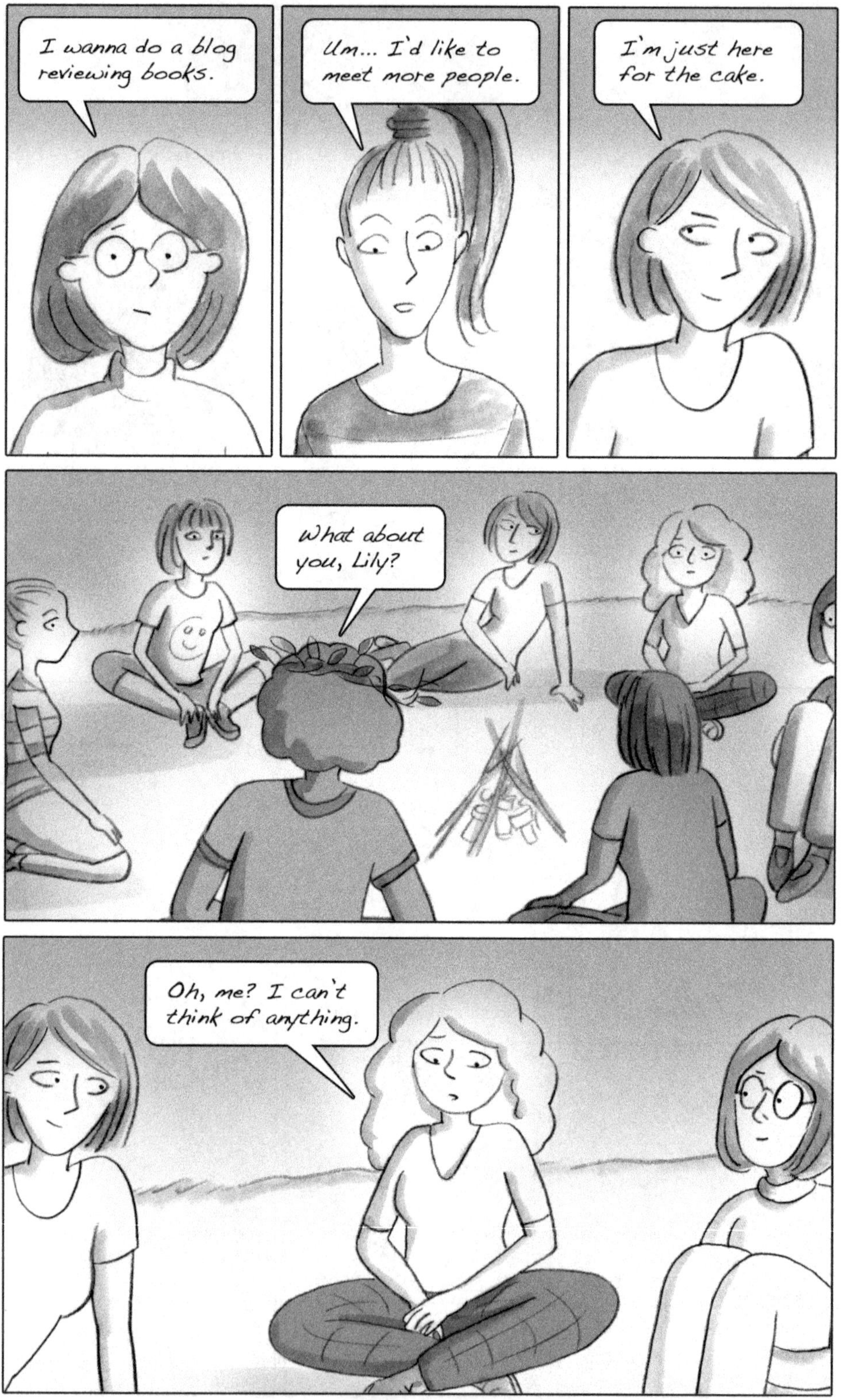
I wanna do a blog reviewing books.
Um... I'd like to meet more people.
I'm just here for the cake.
What about you, Lily?
Oh, me? I can't think of anything.

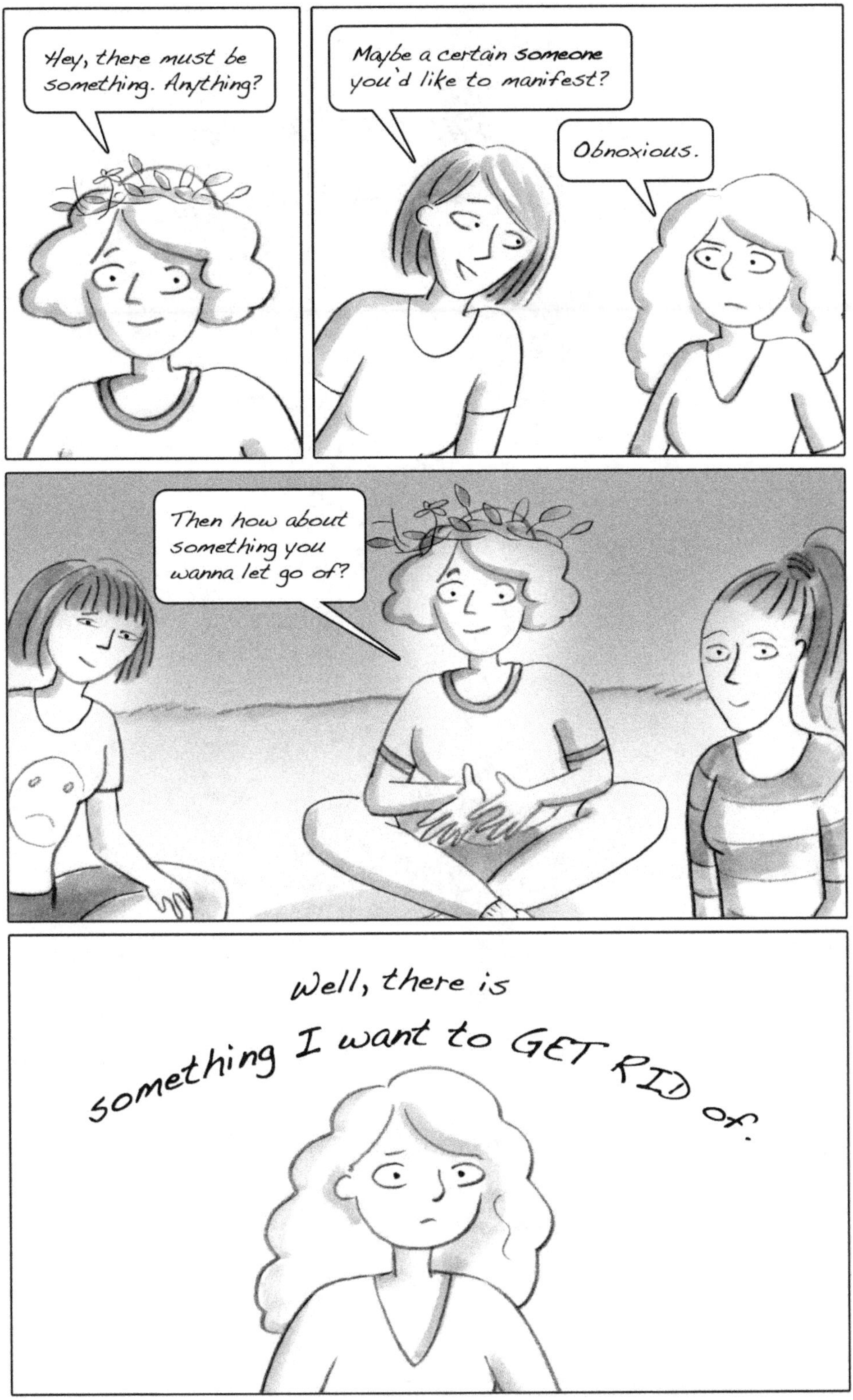
Hey, there must be something. Anything?
Maybe a certain someone you'd like to manifest?
Obnoxious.
Then how about something you wanna let go of?
Well, there is something I want to GET RID of.

IT'S THE ONE THING

I want gone forever and ever.

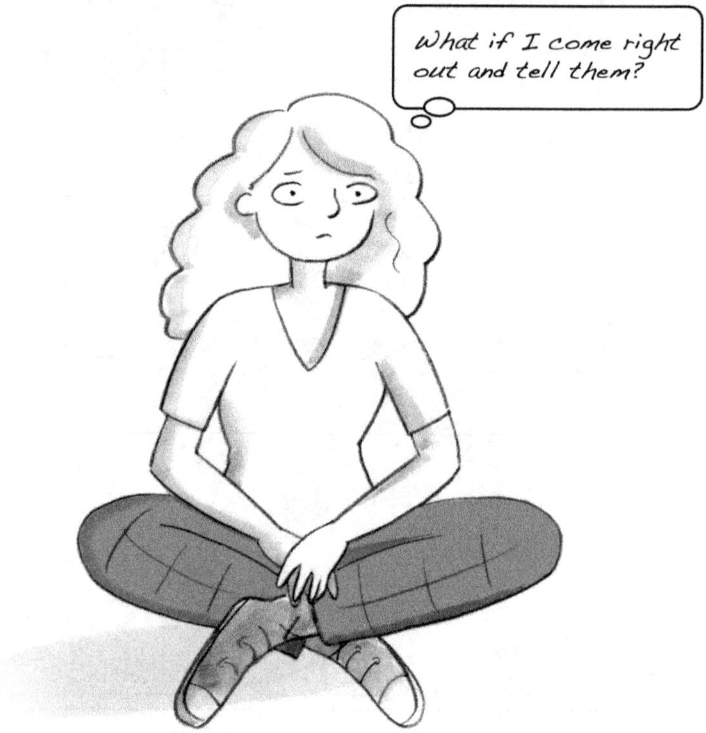
What if I come right out and tell them?

WHEN I'M FREE OF THAT,

I can be truly happy.

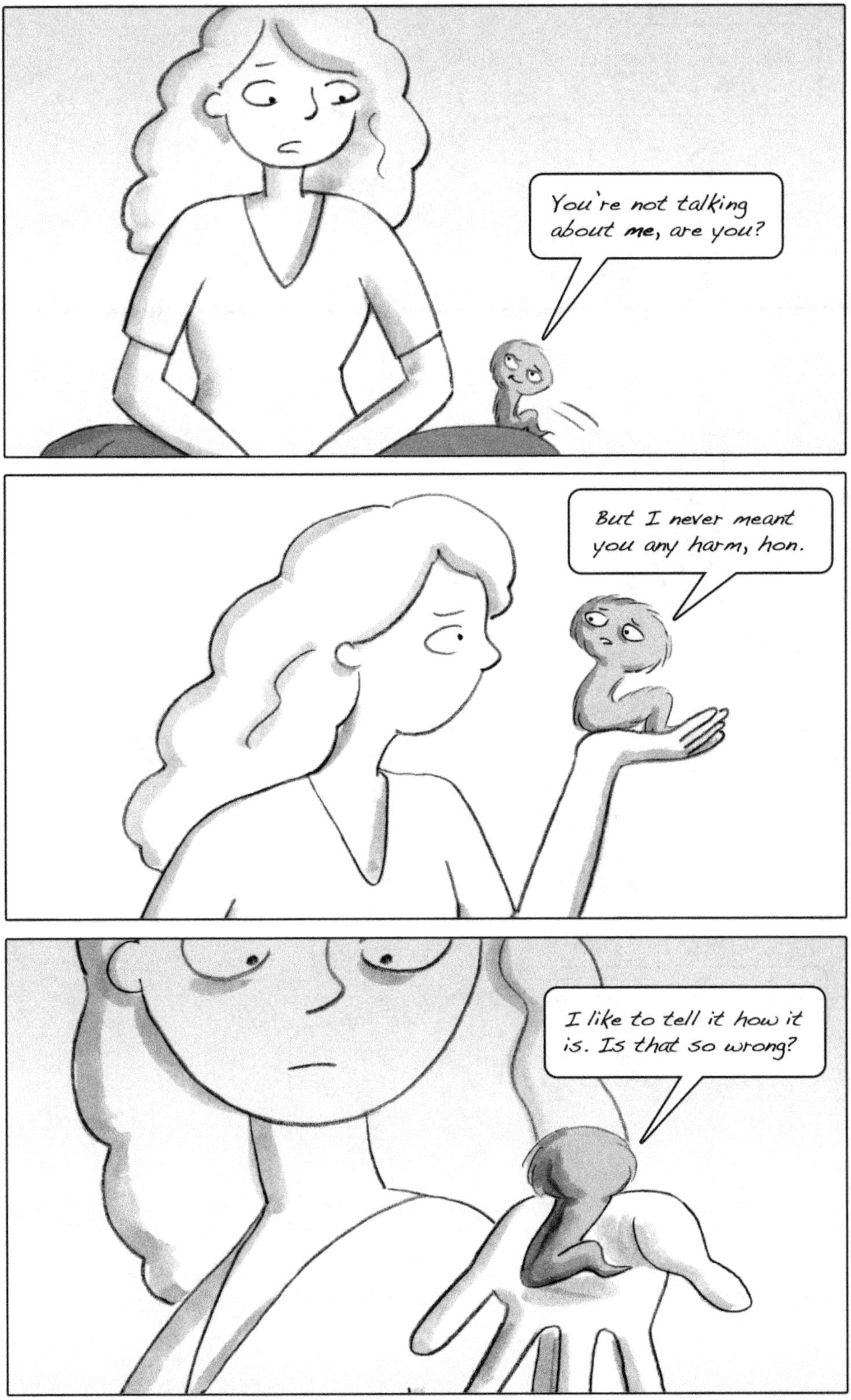
You're not talking about **me**, are you?
But I never meant you any harm, hon.
I like to tell it how it is. Is that so wrong?

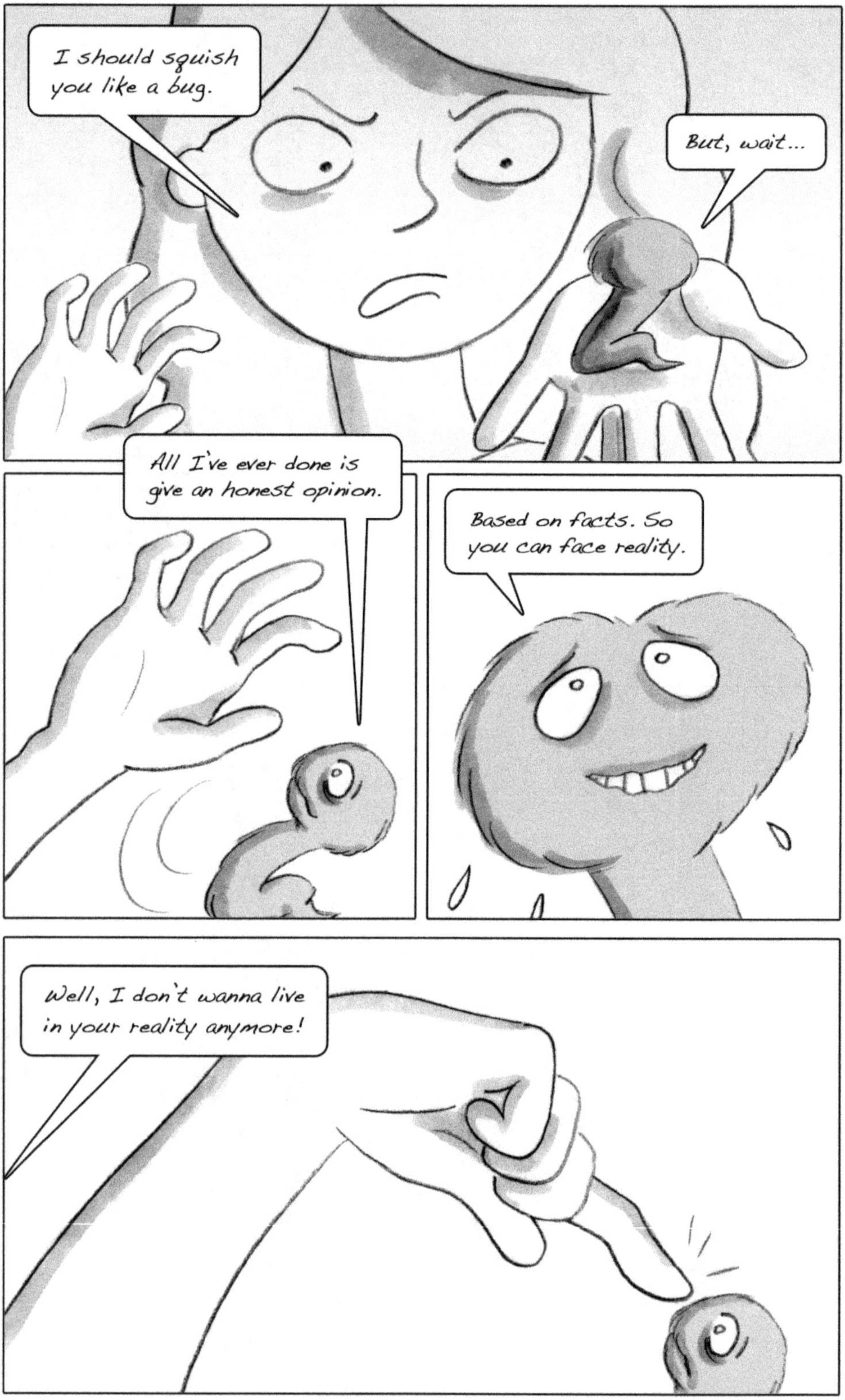
I should squish you like a bug.
But, wait...
All I've ever done is give an honest opinion.
Based on facts. So you can face reality.
Well, I don't wanna live in your reality anymore!

You're nothing but a stupid...
LITTLE...
NO-GOOD...
LIAR!

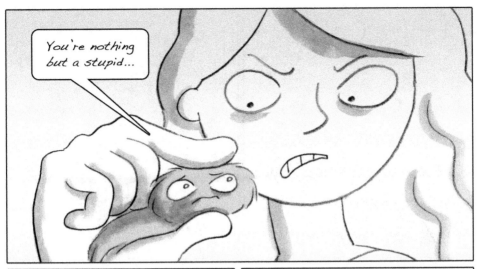

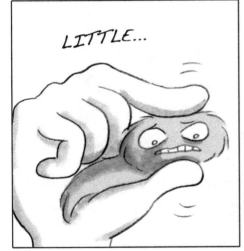

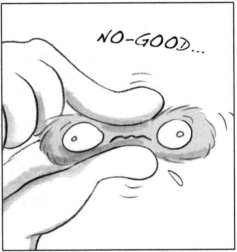

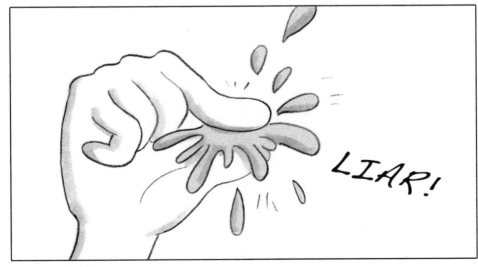

Could it be that simple?
Gone... forever?

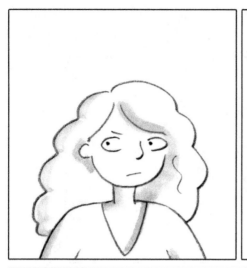

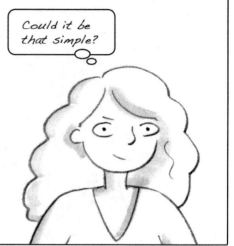

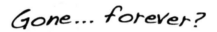

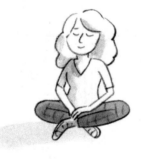

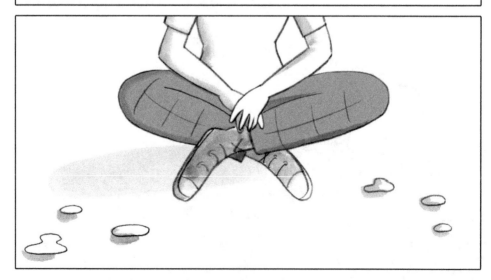

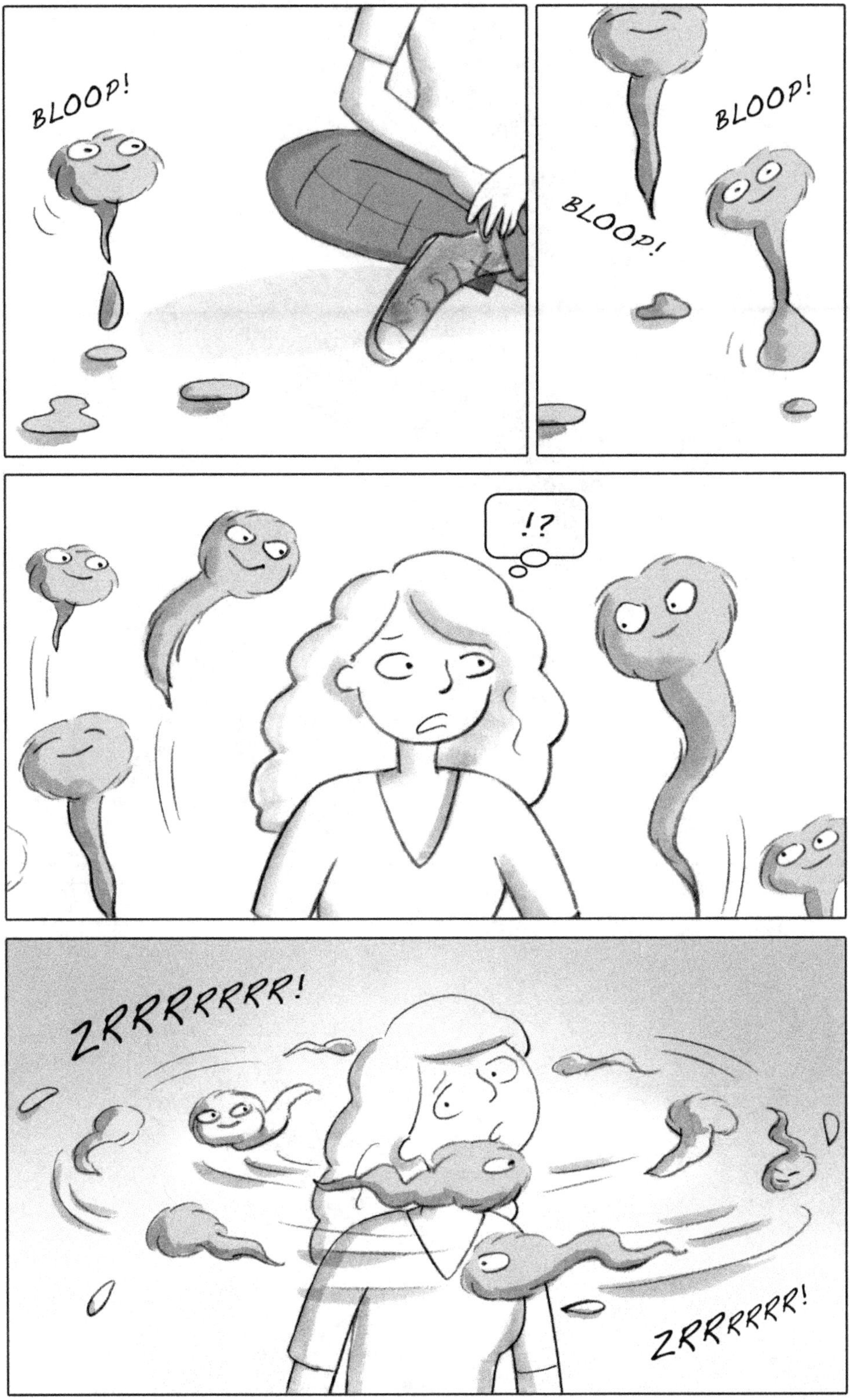
BLOOP!
BLOOP!
BLOOP!
!?
ZRRRRRRR!
ZRRRRRR!

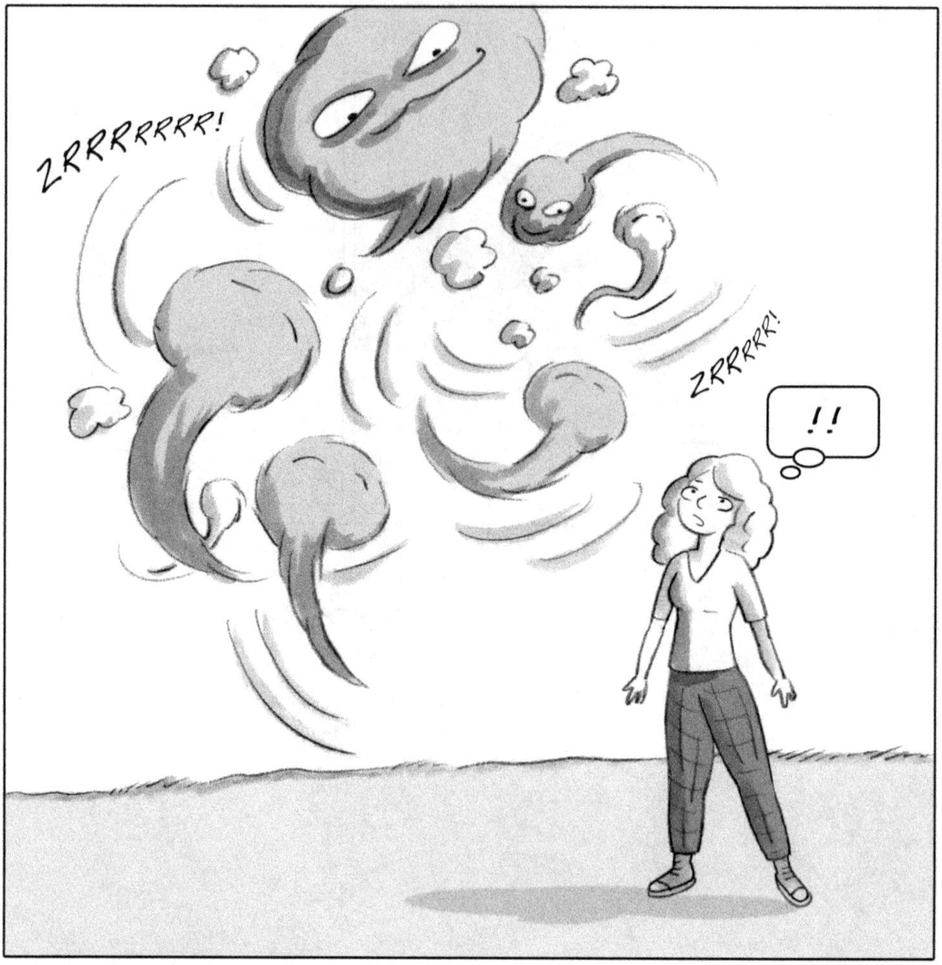
ZRRRRRRR!
ZRRRRR!
!!

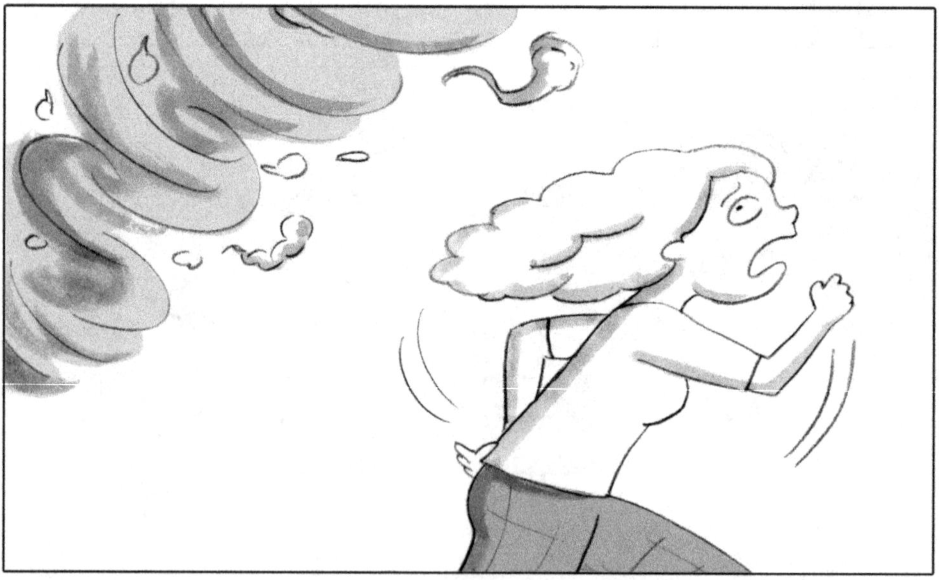

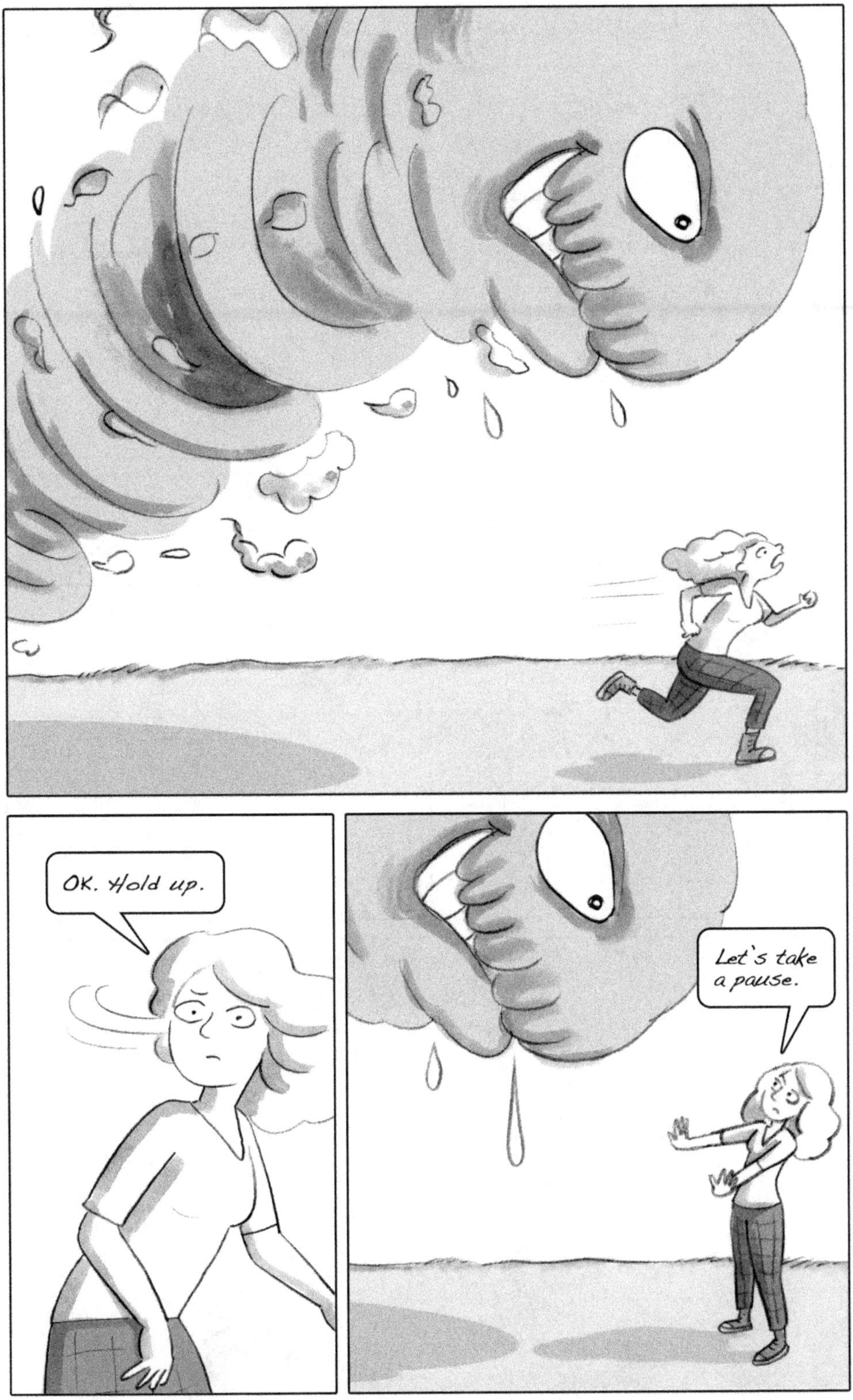
OK. Hold up.
Let's take a pause.

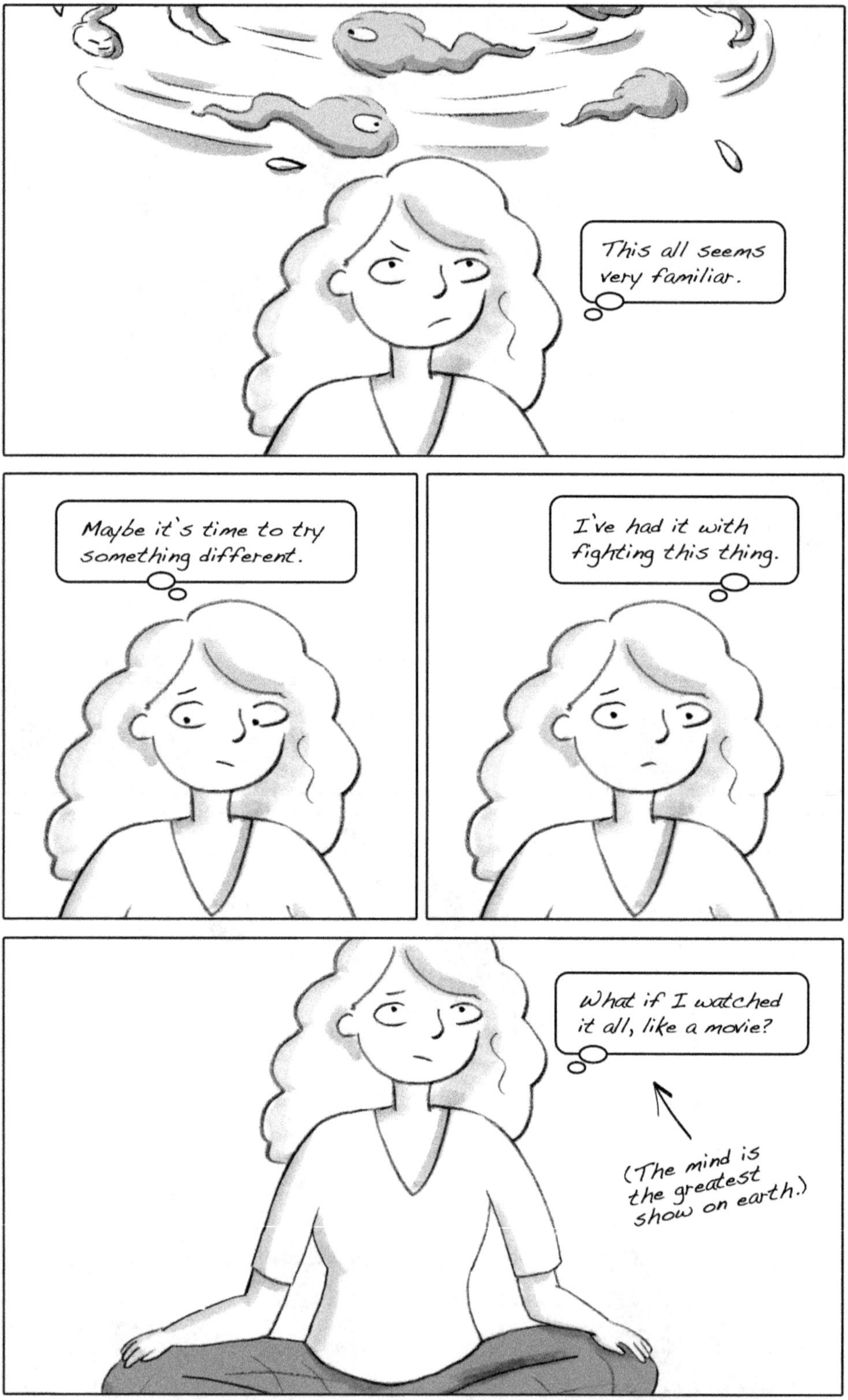
This all seems very familiar.
Maybe it's time to try something different.
I've had it with fighting this thing.
What if I watched it all, like a movie?
(The mind is the greatest show on earth.)

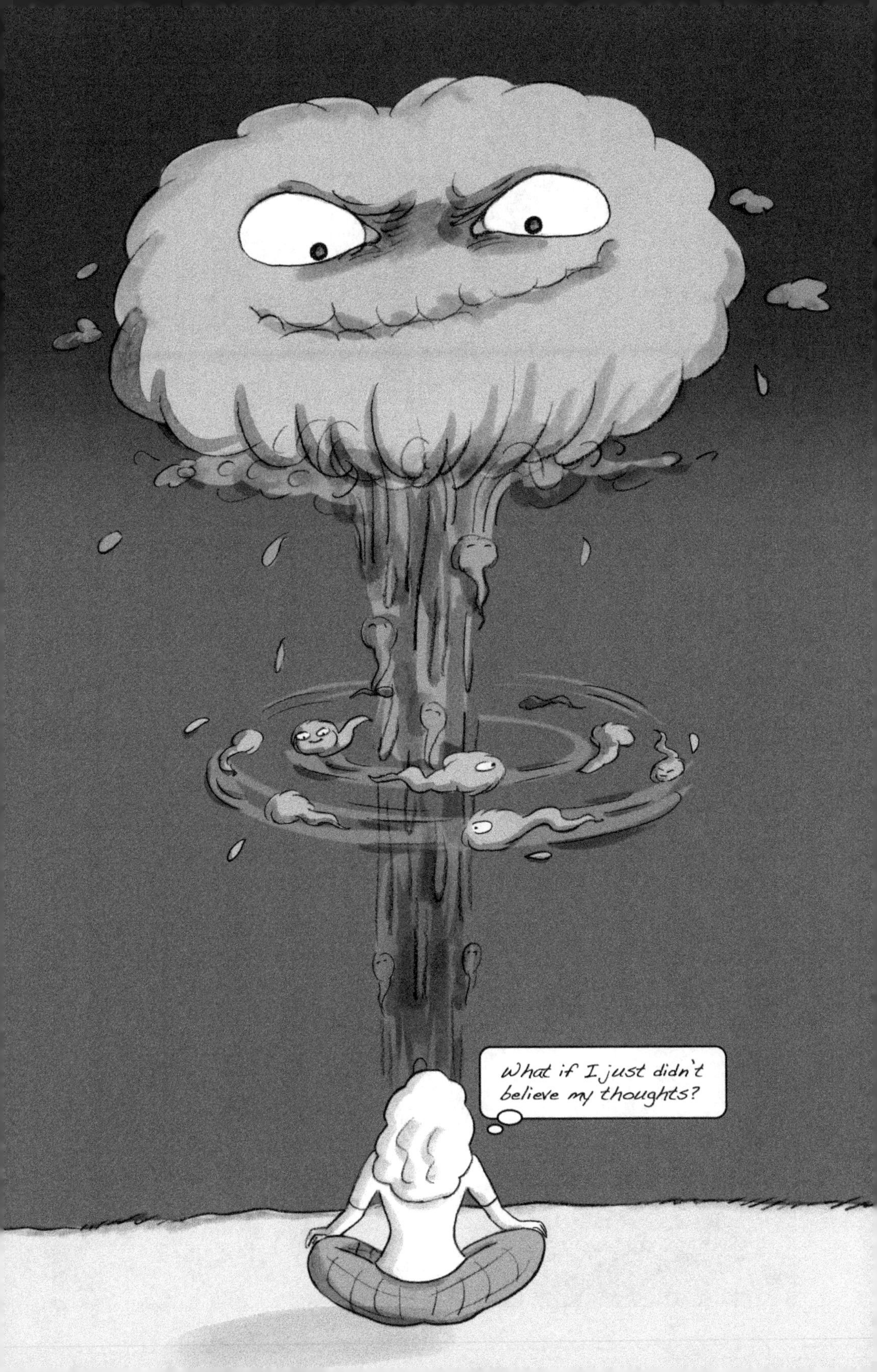
What if I just didn't believe my thoughts?

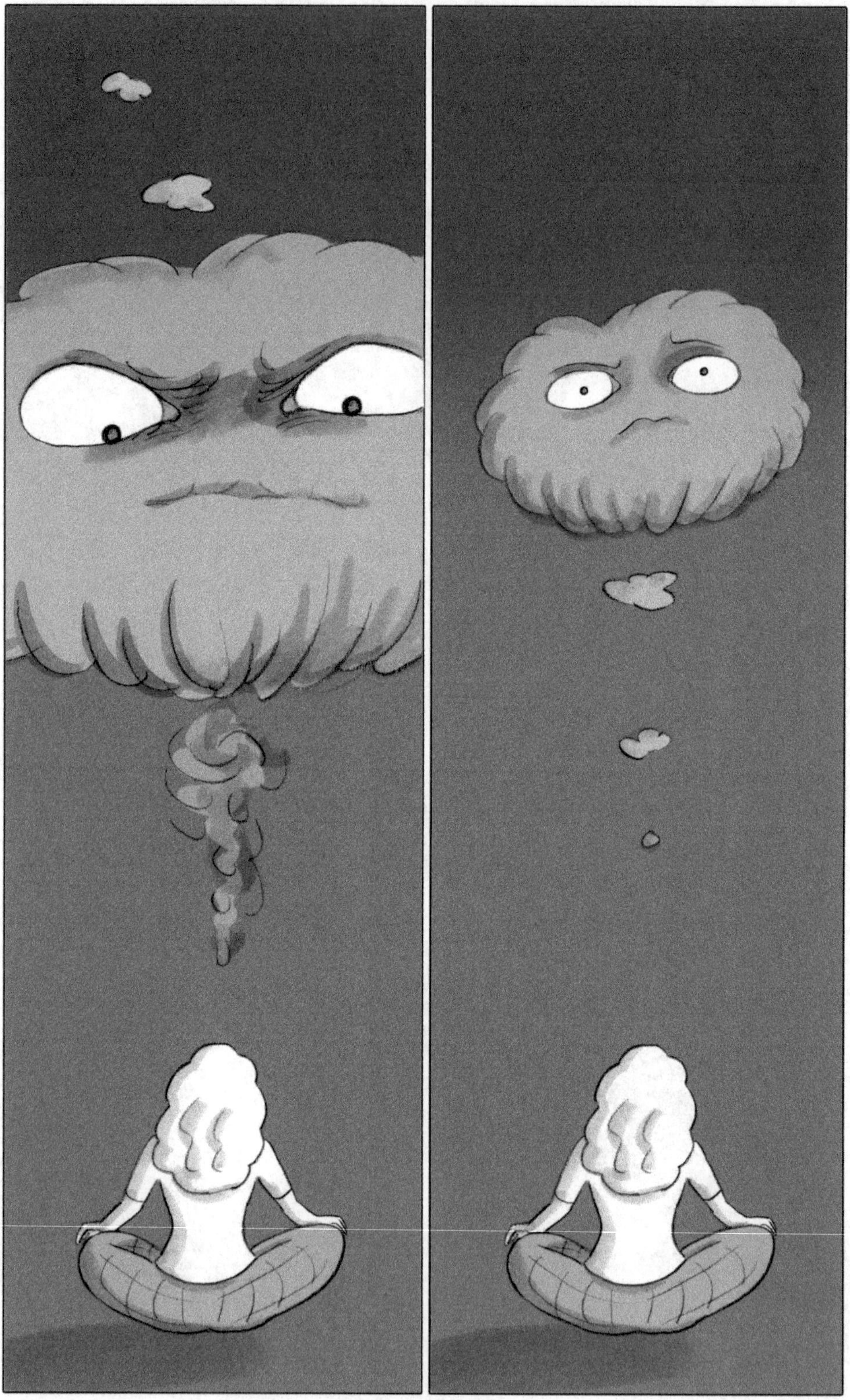

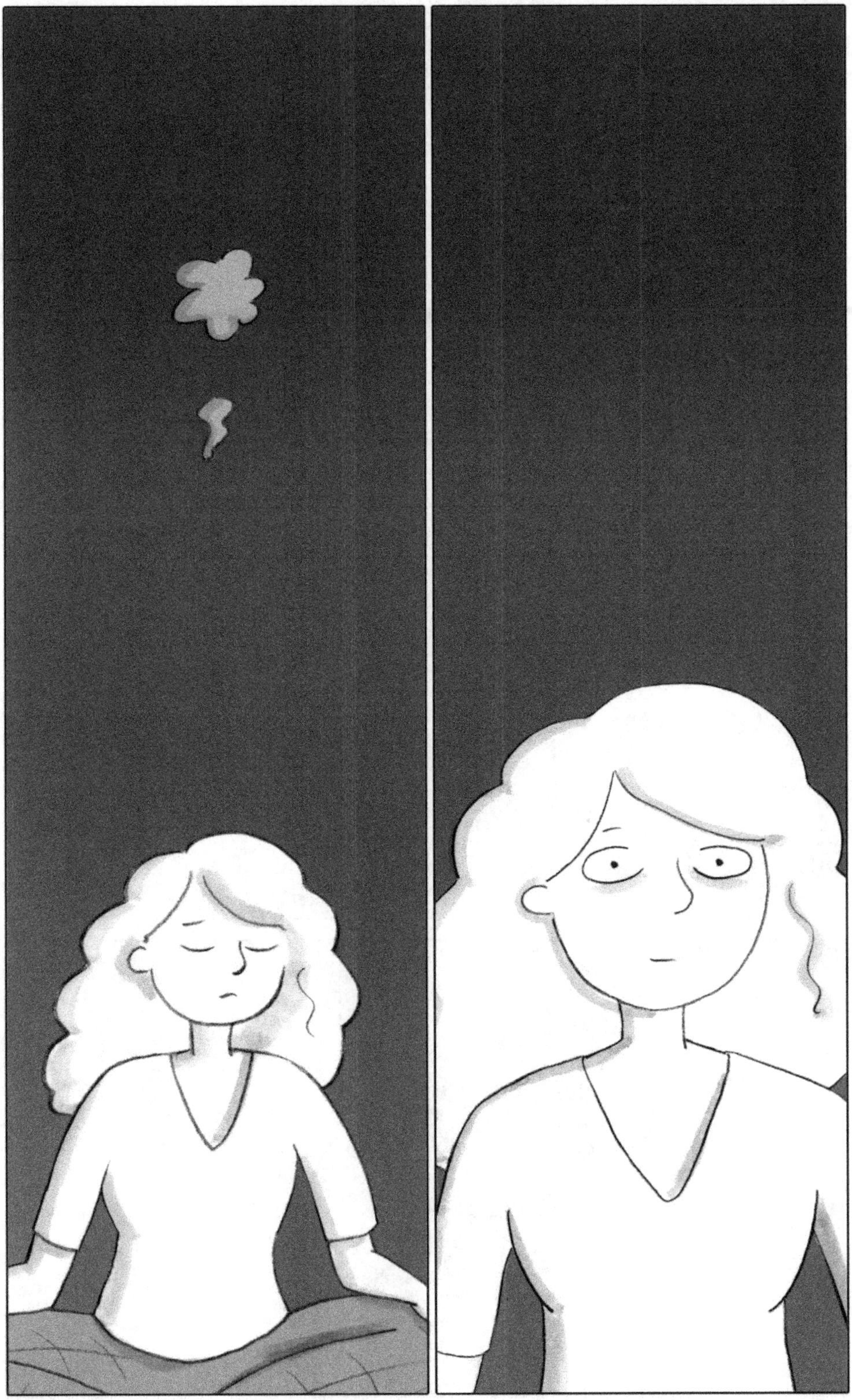

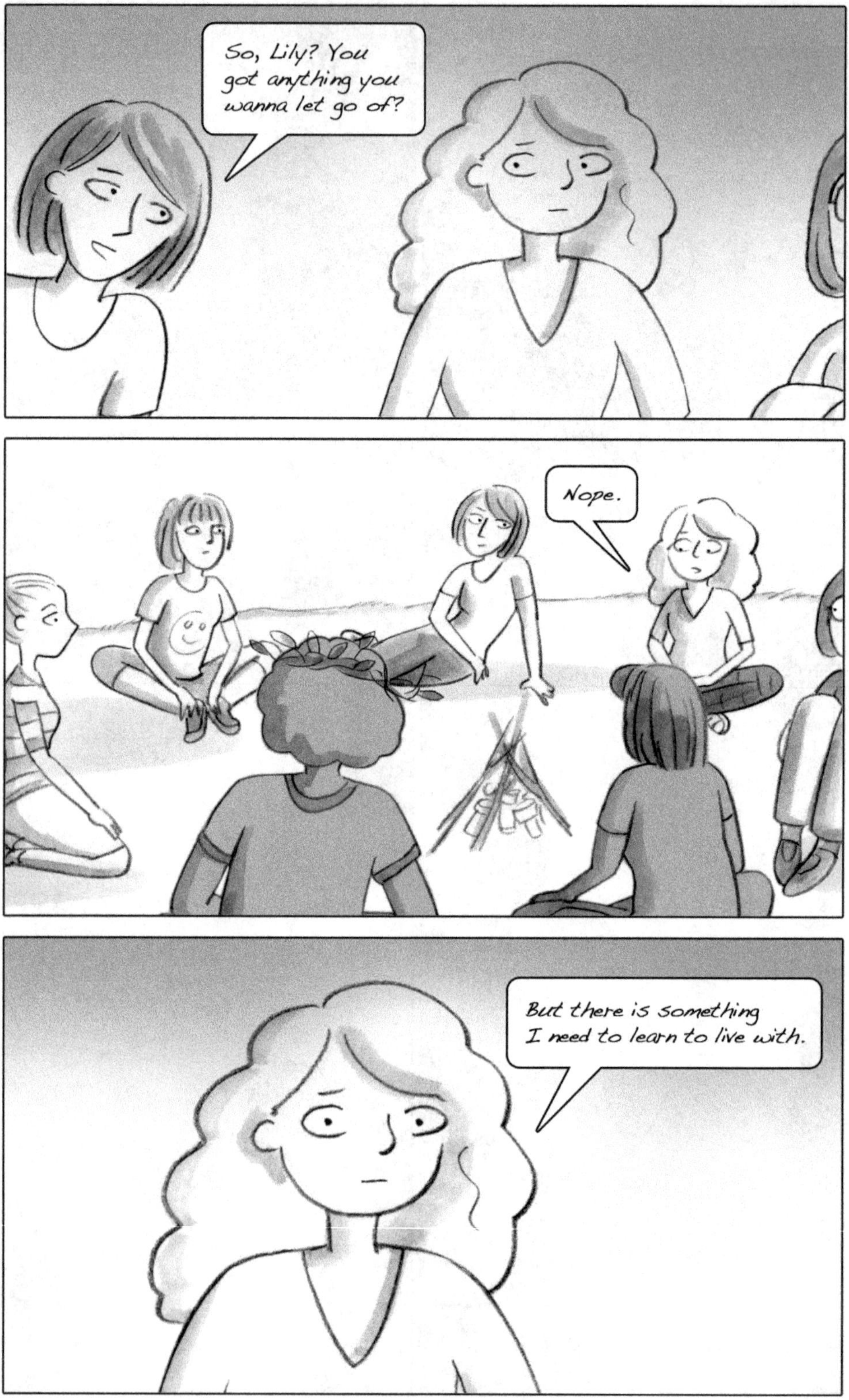
So, Lily? You got anything you wanna let go of?
Nope.
But there is something I need to learn to live with.

Your presence, your being,
is the greatest gift you have. You
don't need to try to be
"somebody".

ANANTA KRANTI

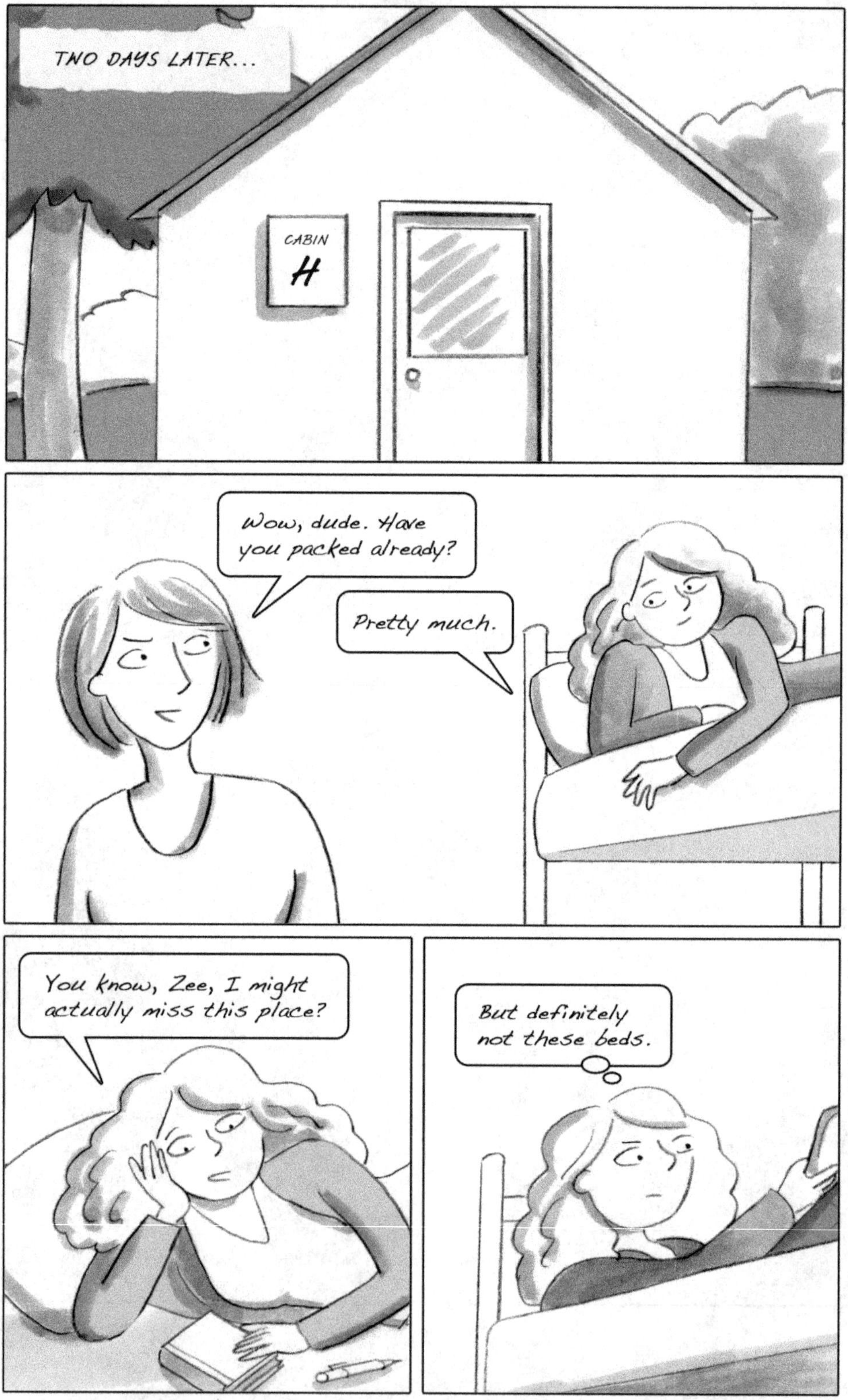
TWO DAYS LATER...
CABIN H
Wow, dude. Have you packed already?
Pretty much.
You know, Zee, I might actually miss this place?
But definitely not these beds.

OUR LAST DAY

It's been quite a week, dear diary. OK, I didn't become the world's greatest kayaker (minor fiasco yesterday when I flipped upside down and turtle thought life jacket was food). Nor did I rappel down a cliff in record time (got stuck on thorny bush halfway down and forgot to note genus while dangling there).

But I did spill my guts about the demon. And it turns out I'm not the only one with crazy thoughts. Booker feels like a misfit, Wriggly's not smart enough, Zeta has to be cool all the time... And the Lynx Girl, well, that was the biggest surprise of all. She always feels lonely and doesn't even think she's pretty, never mind gorgeous! So, even supermodels can't get a break.

Anyway, we all made a pact to see the best in each other AND let each other know when that voice is really bugging us.

Maybe there was magic in that moon after all.

> Can you take my bag out to the bus? I'll meet you over there.

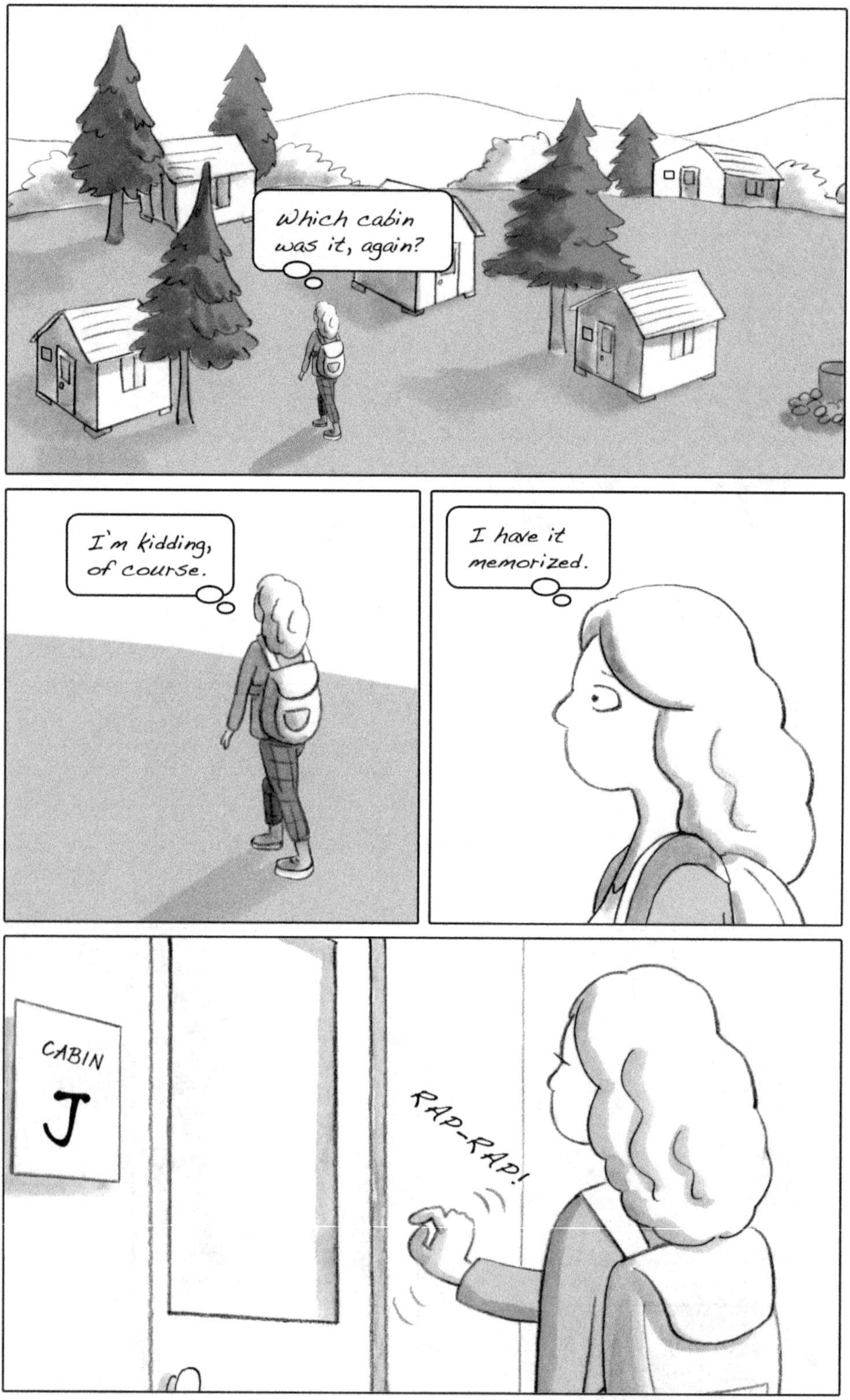
Which cabin was it, again?
I'm kidding, of course.
I have it memorized.
CABIN J
RAP-RAP!

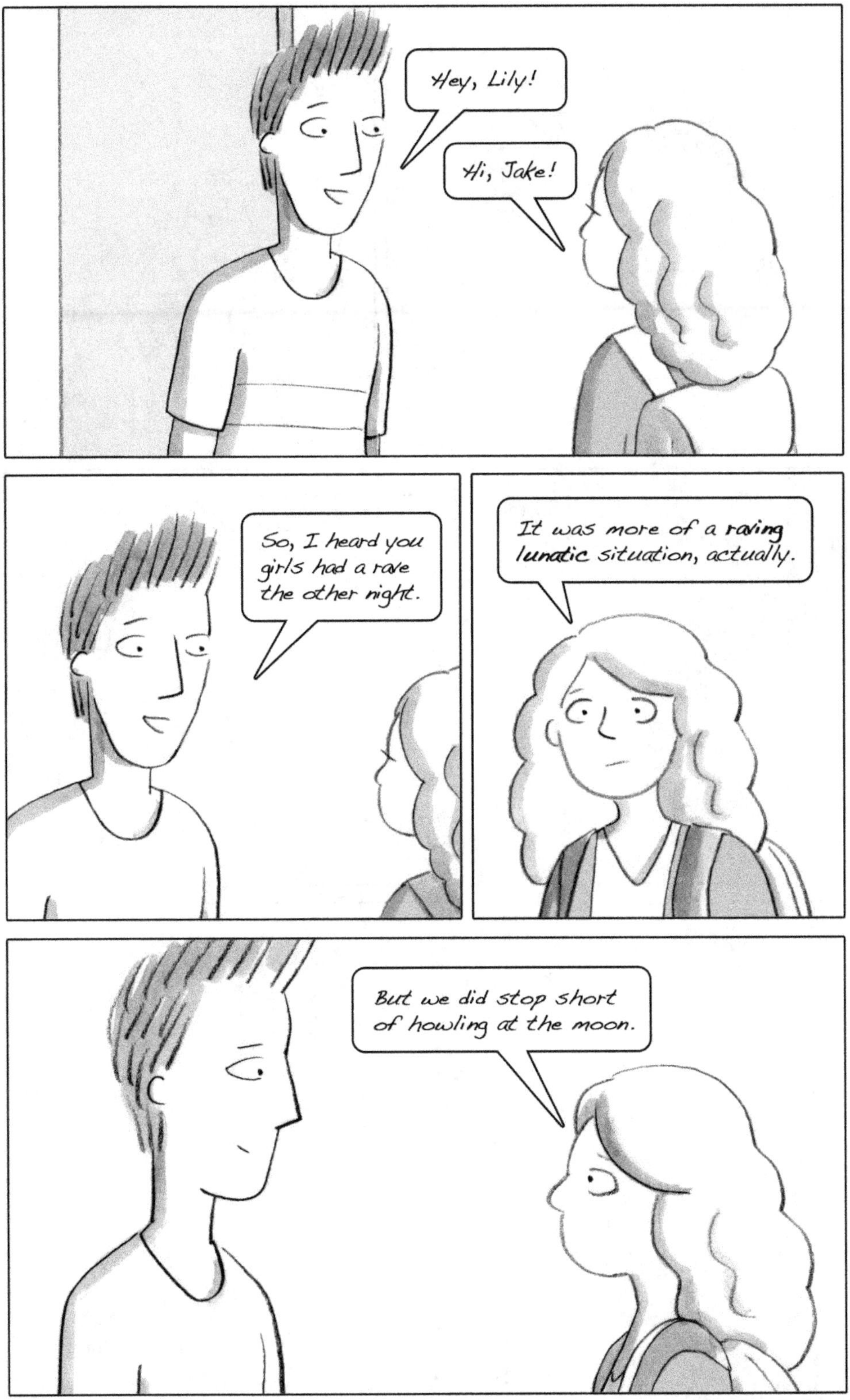
Hey, Lily!
Hi, Jake!
So, I heard you girls had a rave the other night.
It was more of a **raving lunatic** situation, actually.
But we did stop short of howling at the moon.

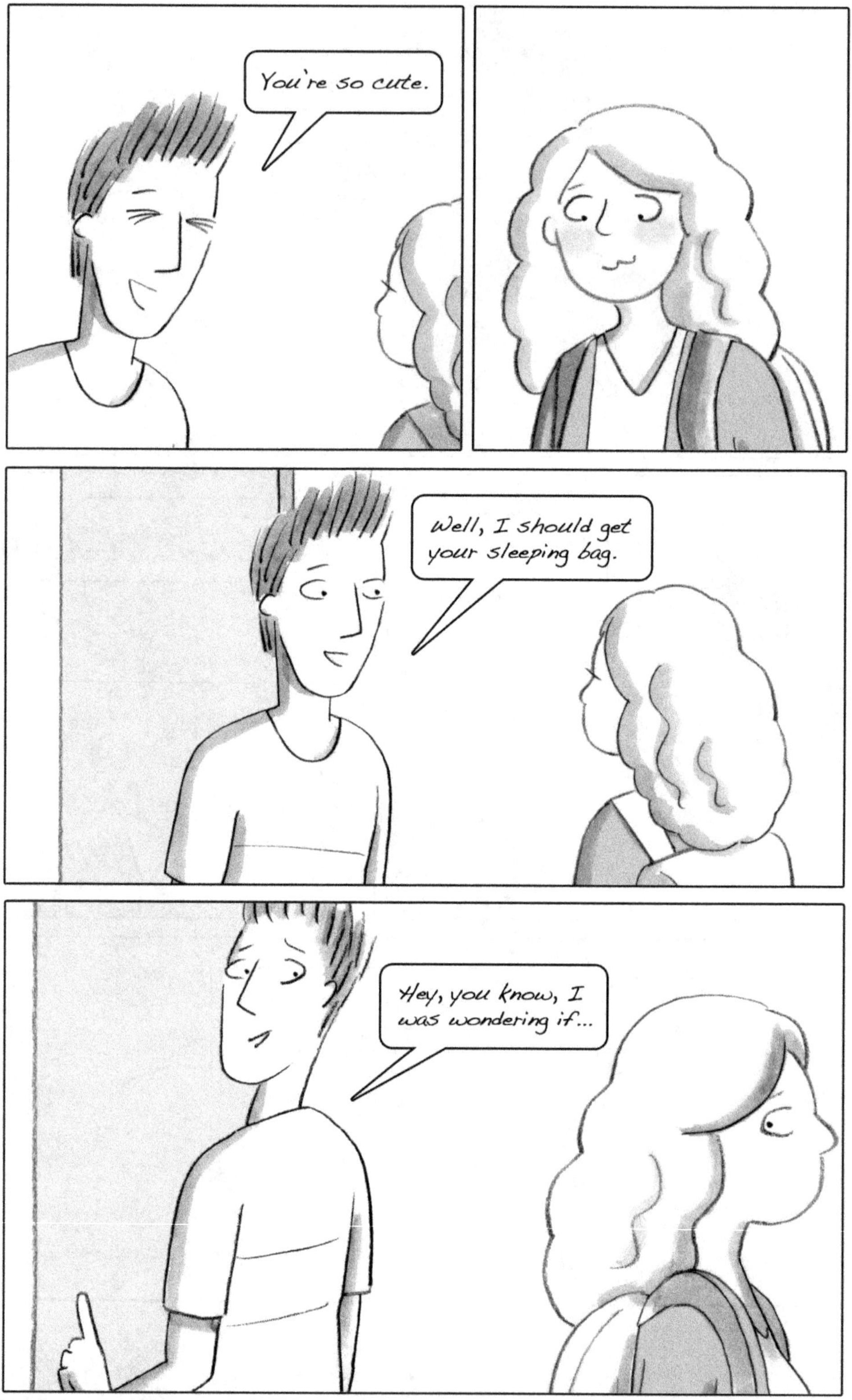
You're so cute.
Well, I should get your sleeping bag.
Hey, you know, I was wondering if...

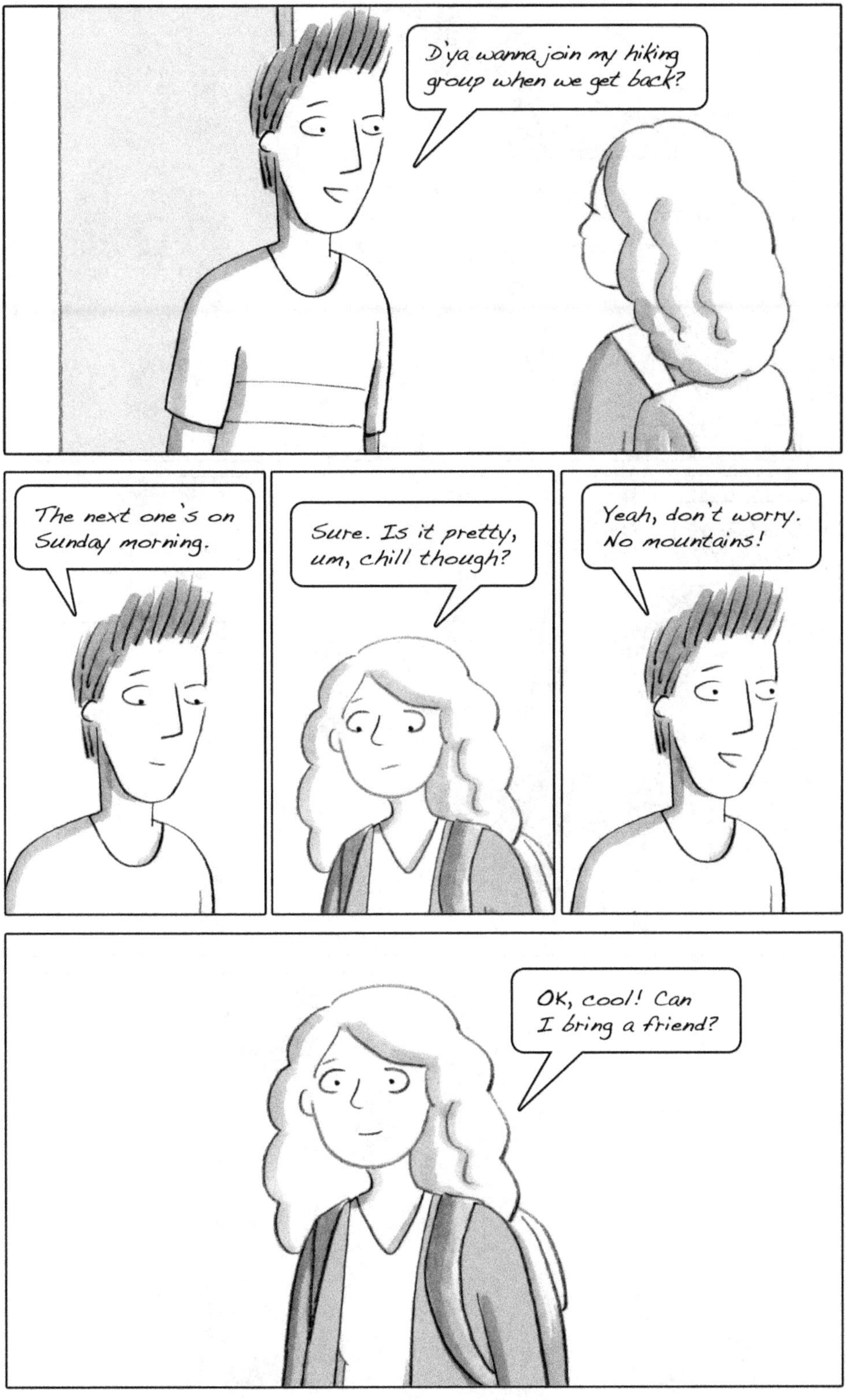
D'ya wanna join my hiking group when we get back?
The next one's on Sunday morning.
Sure. Is it pretty, um, chill though?
Yeah, don't worry. No mountains!
OK, cool! Can I bring a friend?

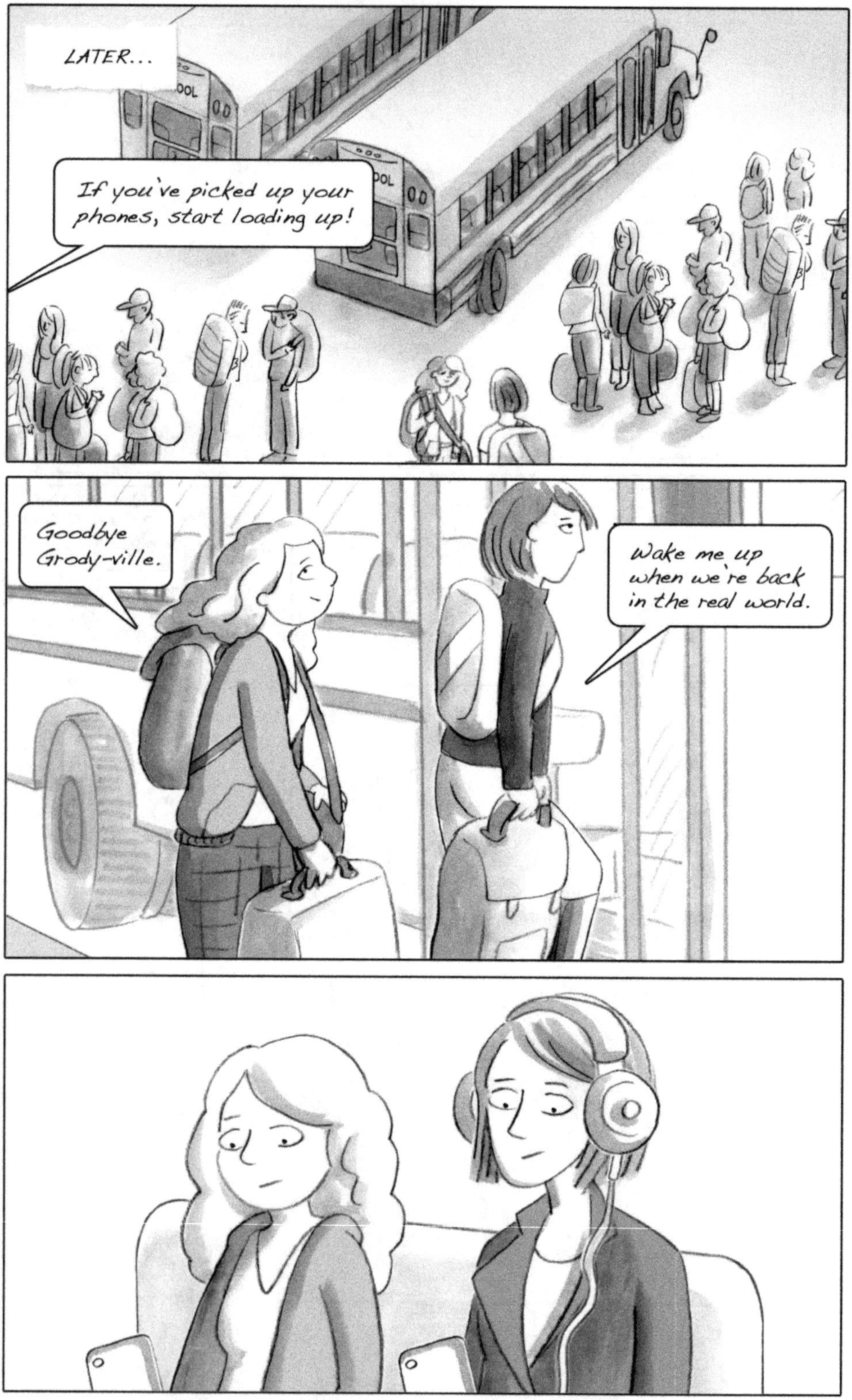
LATER...
If you've picked up your phones, start loading up!
Goodbye Grody-ville.
Wake me up when we're back in the real world.

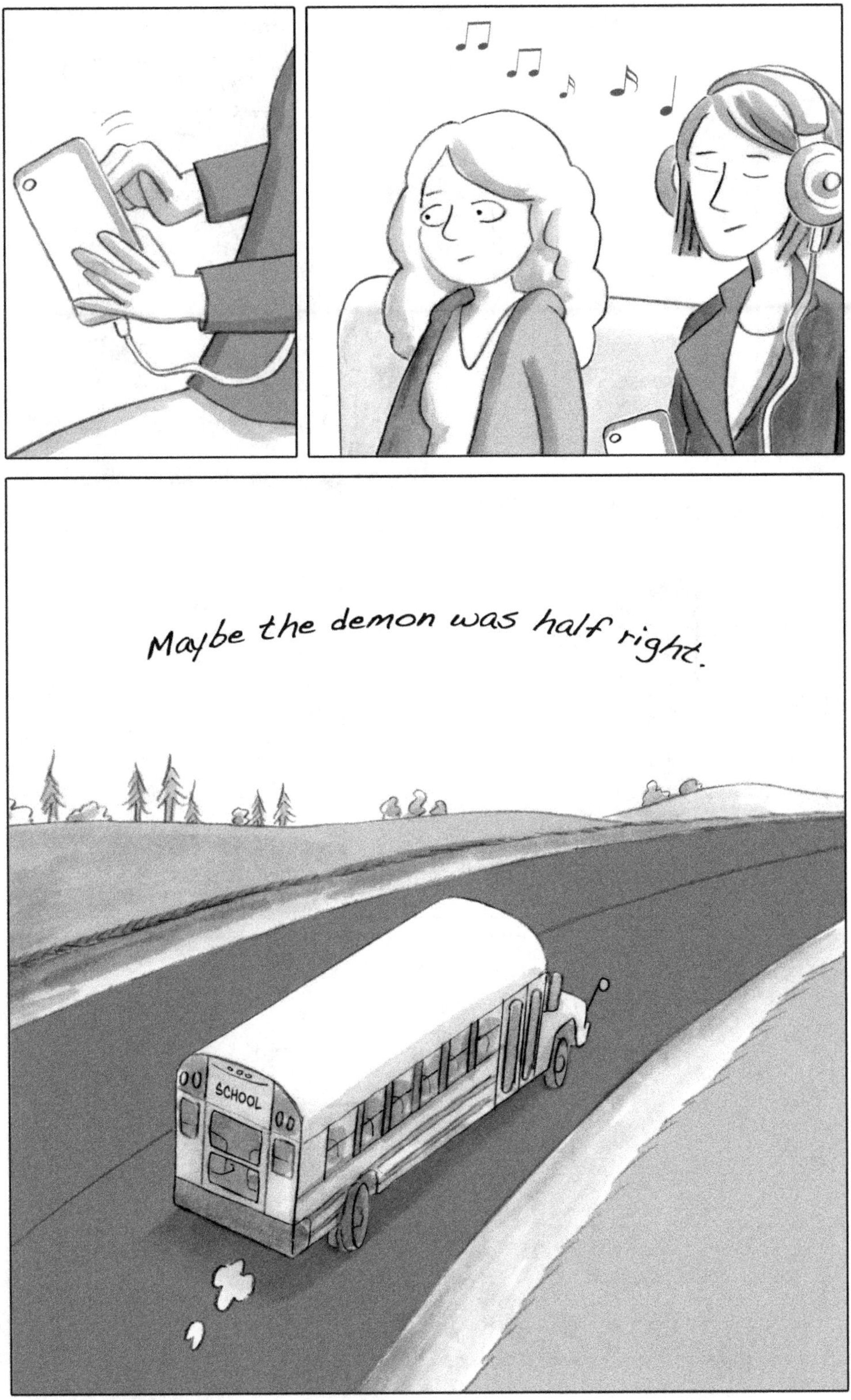
Maybe the demon was half right.
SCHOOL

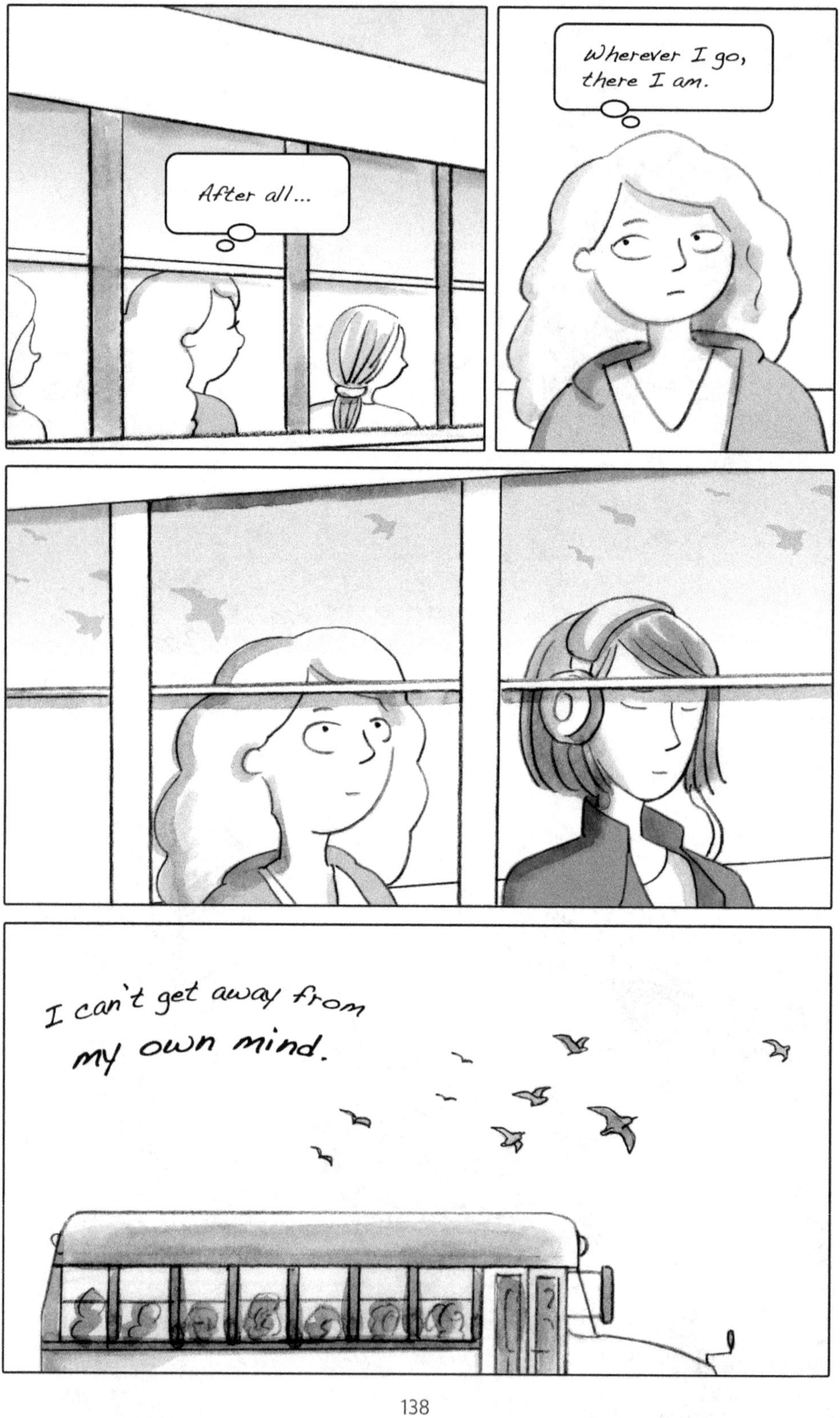
After all...
Wherever I go, there I am.
I can't get away from my own mind.

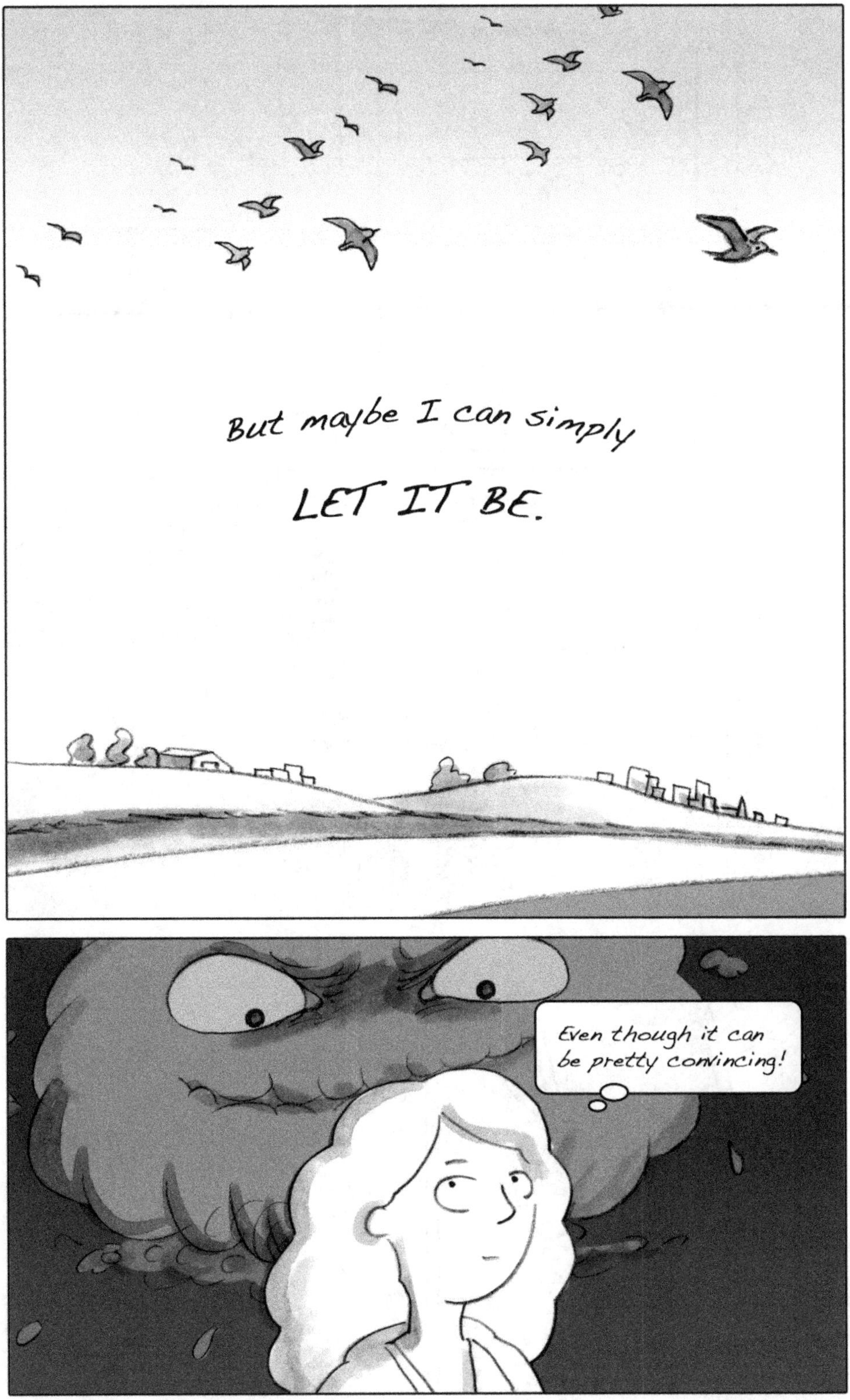
But maybe I can simply
LET IT BE.
Even though it can be pretty convincing!

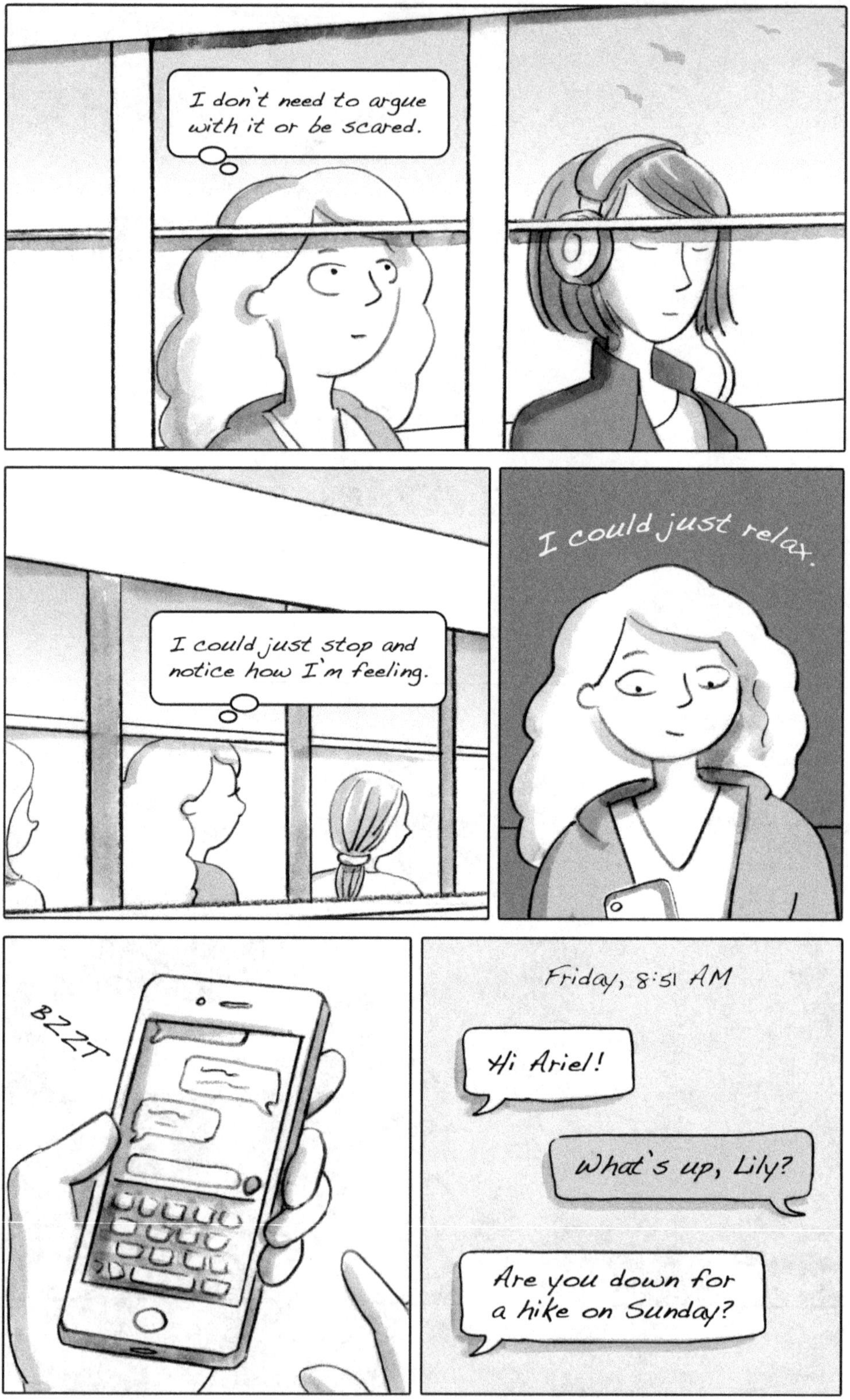
I don't need to argue with it or be scared.
I could just stop and notice how I'm feeling.
I could just relax.
BZZT
Friday, 8:51 AM
Hi Ariel!
What's up, Lily?
Are you down for a hike on Sunday?

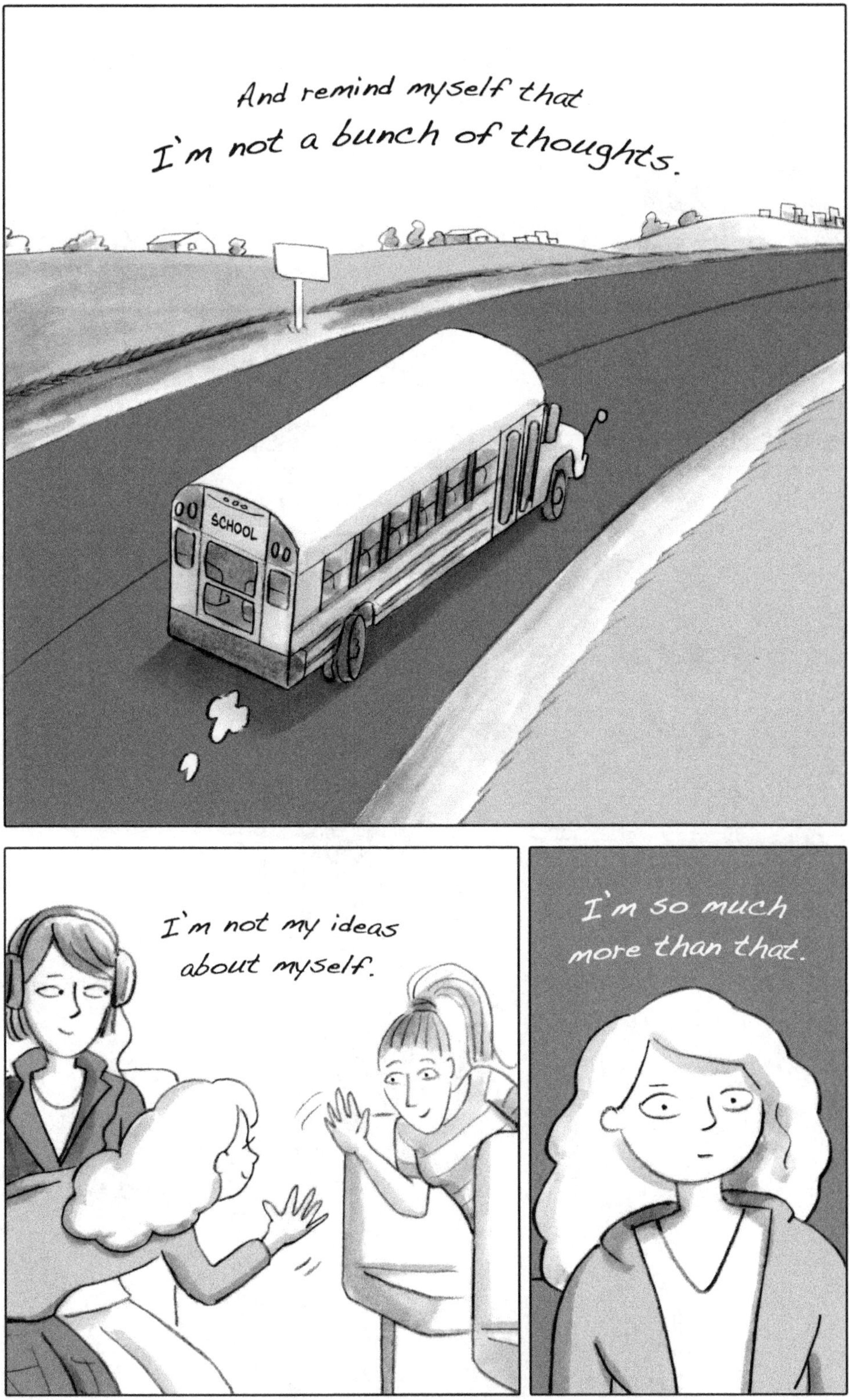
And remind myself that
I'm not a bunch of thoughts.
SCHOOL
I'm not my ideas about myself.
I'm so much more than that.

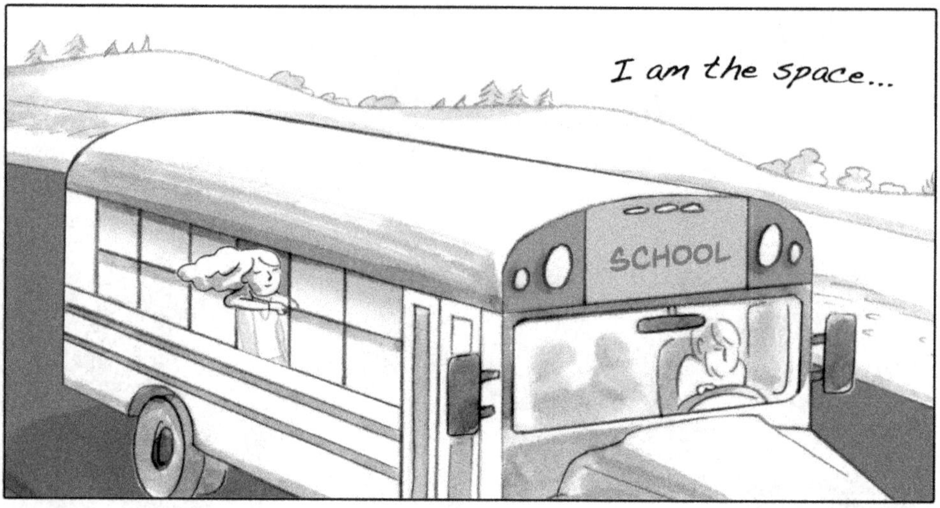
I am the space...
SCHOOL

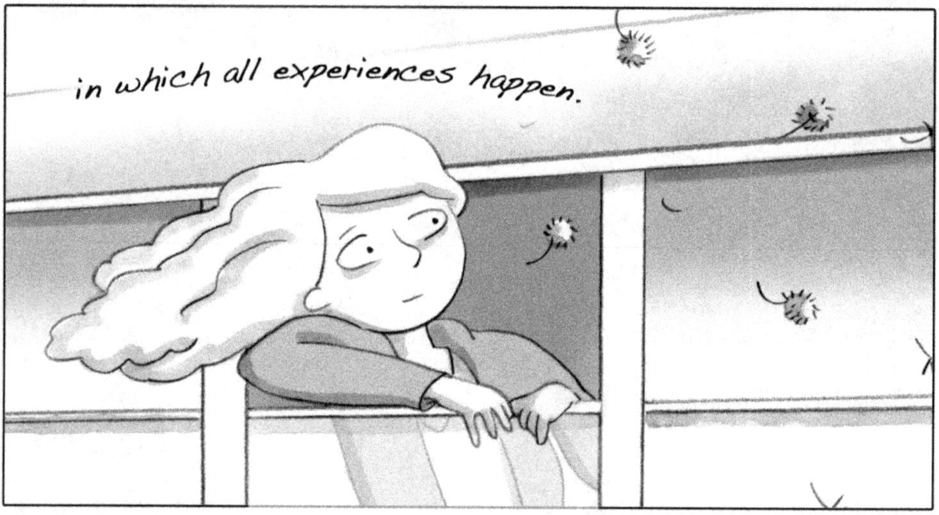
in which all experiences happen.

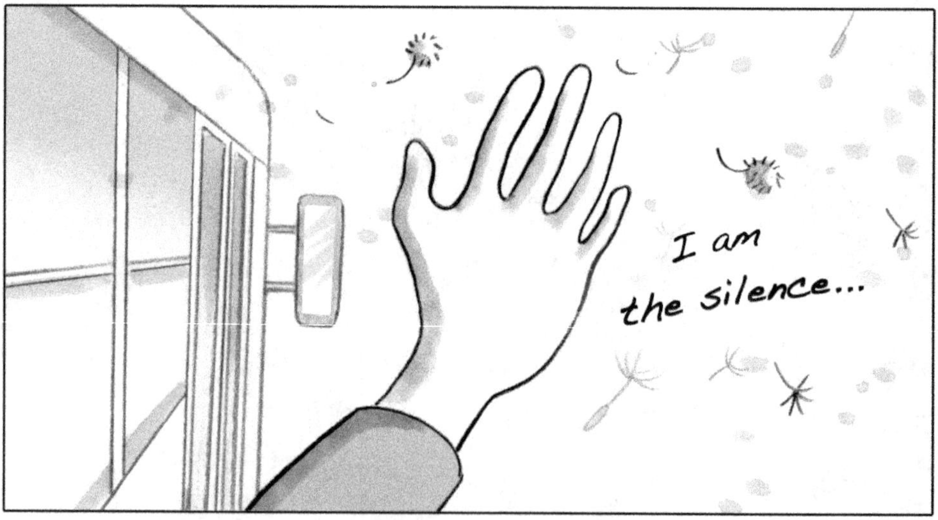
I am
the silence...

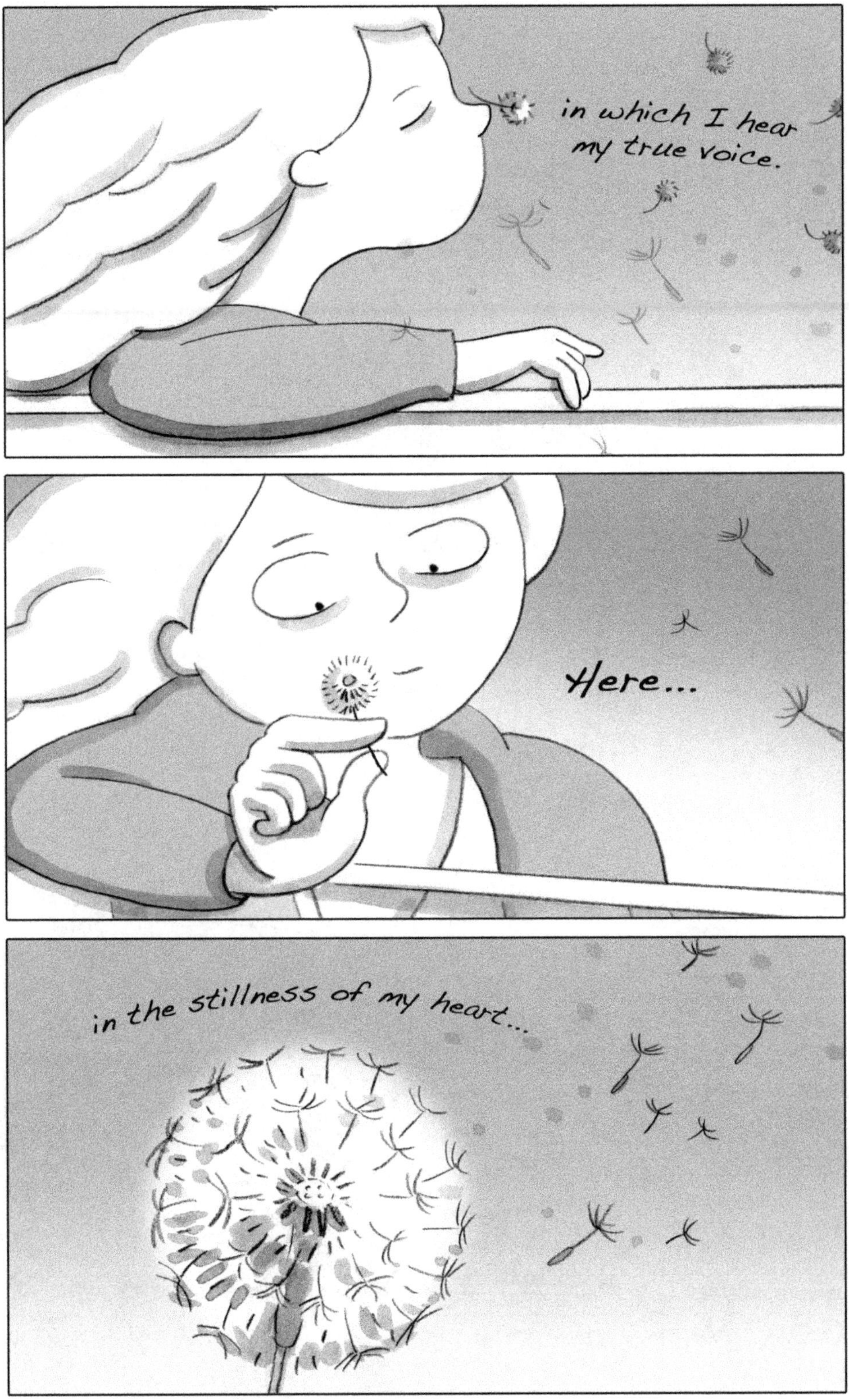
in which I hear my true voice.
Here...
in the stillness of my heart...

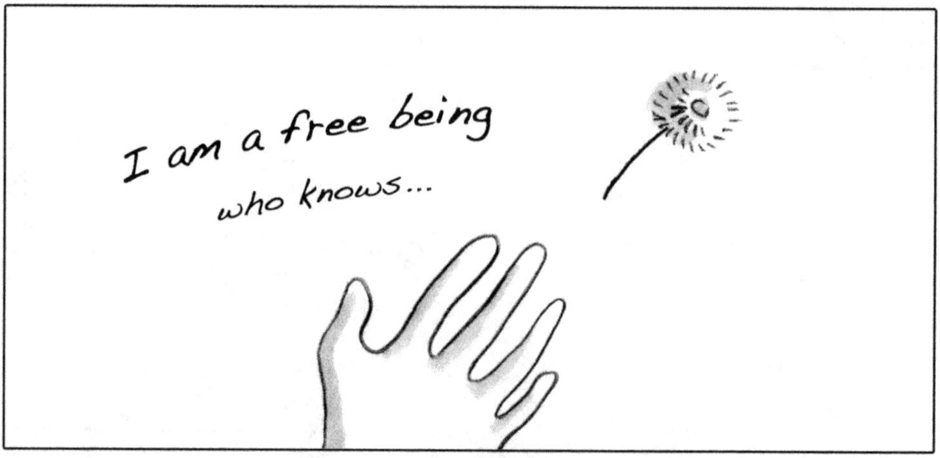
I am a free being
who knows...

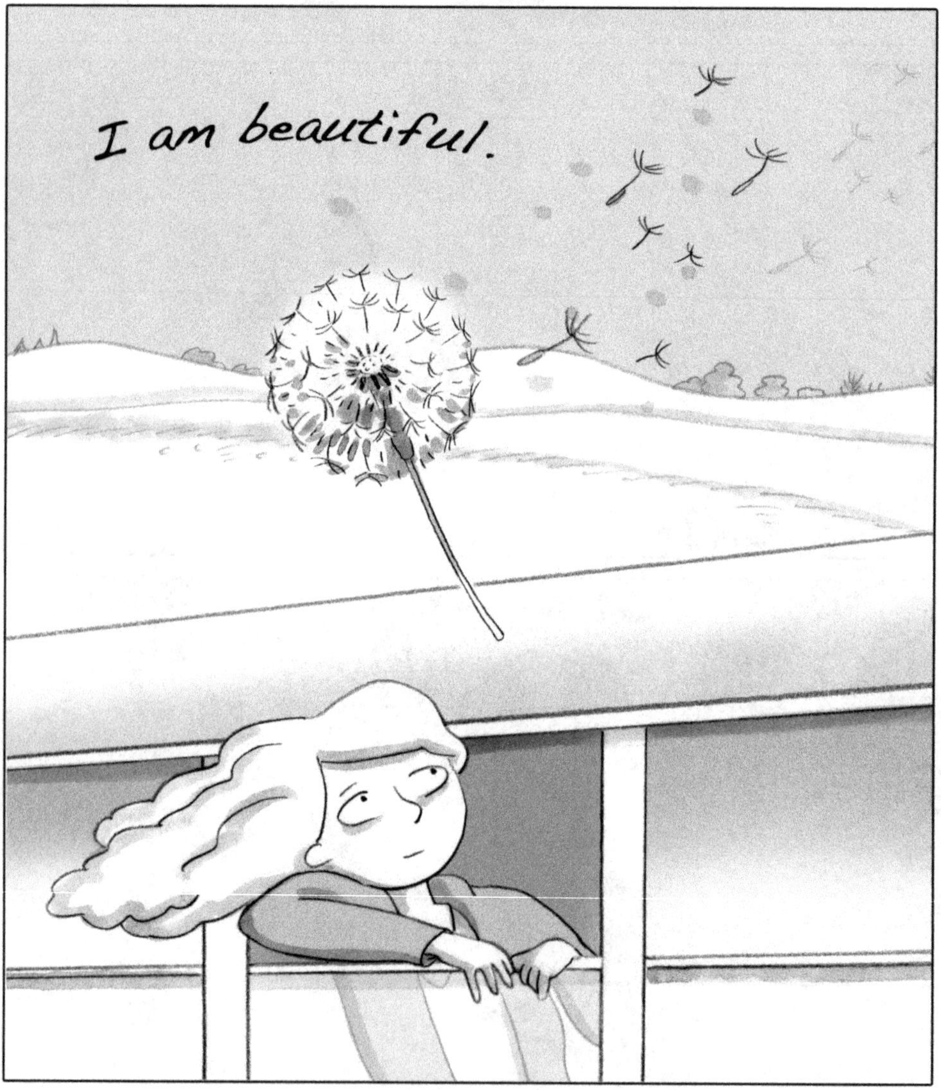
I am beautiful.

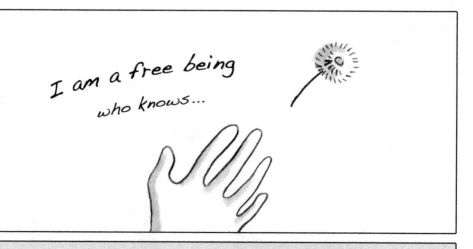

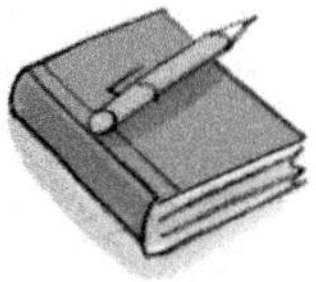

About the author

Marie D'Abreo is a writer, artist and graphic designer. She grew up in Worthing, England, and later went on to get her Bachelor of Fine Arts at the Minneapolis College of Art and Design. She presently resides in San Francisco, California.

Aside from this little number, she's the creator of a few more graphic novels - **Beautiful: a girl's trip through the looking glass**, **Lost in Guyville** and **Sky Orb**.

Say hello by visiting www.mariedabreo.com or any of the usual social media platforms.